Bedtime with Buster

Bedtime with Buster: Conversations With A Handsome Hound

Copyright © 2020
Brooks Eason

ISBN: 978-1-952474-60-6

Illustrations and Cover art by Robert Fugate

The *Portrait of Buster and Mollie* by Denise Monts Flint is used by permission.

Pup-Peroni® brand is owned by the J.M. Smucker Company

All rights reserved. No part of this book may be reproduced, stored in a retrieval system, or transmitted in any form or by any means—electronic, mechanical, photocopy, recording, or otherwise—without the prior written permission of the publisher. The only exception is brief quotations for review purposes.

Published by WordCrafts Press
Cody, Wyoming 82414
www.wordcrafts.net

Bedtime with Buster

Conversations With A Handsome Hound

BROOKS EASON

WordCrafts Press

Contents

Prologue

Carrie and I were a combined 100 years old when we met and 102 on our wedding day. No human children have been born to the marriage, and none will be. We have, instead, the fur children. Carrie and I were matched on eHarmony on May 8, 2010, and met for lunch nine days later. I proposed to her in September, and we got married at our home in Ridgeland, Mississippi, on New Year's Day, 1/1/11. I haven't forgotten our anniversary yet.

My father fell and broke his foot eight months later, two months before his 90th birthday. Carrie drove the three hours north to Tupelo, retrieved him from the home where I grew up, and we began searching for an assisted living facility. But Carrie, who's the world's best wife, daughter-in-law, stepmother, step-grandmother, and mother of fur children, soon decided that Daddy belonged with us.

Daddy's transition from living alone to living with us was smooth except at mealtime. Carrie doesn't eat beef, pork, or chicken, and Daddy ate mostly beef, pork, and chicken. When she presented him with an arugula salad with a homemade vinaigrette on one of his first evenings with us, he poked at it suspiciously and asked if she'd picked it out of the yard. She began cooking two meals every night, one for us and one for him.

Carrie and I both had full-time jobs, and we decided Daddy needed a companion during the day while we were at work. We were temporarily without a dog, so we planned a trip to an animal shelter in Jackson called Community Animal Rescue and Adoption, CARA for short. Our goal was to find a dog that was grown, small, calm, gentle, and housebroken. We walked among the pens, wanting to adopt them all, and picked four that might fit the bill. The staff brought them one a time to the get-acquainted room to audition. My favorite based on looks alone was a male terrier, but he circled the room, marked it thoroughly as his territory, and disqualified himself. Carrie's pick was a cocker spaniel named Mollie. Carrie had two cockers before I met her and loved them both. Photos of them adorn our living room and her office. I deny Carrie nothing, so we brought Mollie home with us.

And when we did, Mollie hit the mother lode. Carrie immediately bought a plush dog bed, which she placed in the master bedroom alongside ours. Even that wasn't good enough on stormy nights. When it thundered and Mollie got nervous, Carrie lifted her up and put her in bed with us. I disapproved, but I deny Carrie nothing.

Carrie also bought Mollie the finest dog food and fanciest gourmet treats, which Daddy supplemented with a generous supply of human food. At the end of every meal, he saved his last few bites for her. He would lean over and hold his plate a few inches off the floor while she licked it clean. I disapproved of that as well, but how do you tell your 90-year-old father not to feed the dog? Daddy also shared his nightly ice cream with Mollie. She was living large and getting larger.

Daddy and Mollie spent their days watching reruns of *Law and Order* and *NCIS* and entertaining each other with a tennis ball. From his recliner, he tossed and she chased. She learned to drop into a slide on our slick hardwood floors before slamming into the far wall. The game lasted until Mollie grew tired and declined to return the ball.

Daddy insisted that Mollie was a male, said "good boy" when she retrieved the tennis ball, and invariably used masculine pronouns to refer to her. More than once, Carrie held her belly up to show Daddy that he was wrong, but he was either unconvinced or forgot because Mollie was always a boy to him.

In the spring of 2013, Daddy's health began to fail. He died at home on the first of July, two days before my 56th birthday and four months before his 92nd. He outlived my mother and all three of his younger sisters. Sweet Chris, his sitter for the last six months of his life, told us that being with him when he passed away was a blessing on her soul.

Taking care of the wonderful father who raised me was an honor and a privilege, and Carrie and I still miss him, but his death changed Mollie's life more than it changed ours. No more food from the table and no more ice cream. No more spending her days in the living room lounging in her favorite chair. With nobody at home during the day, Mollie couldn't stay inside. When we put her in the backyard before leaving for work a few days after Daddy's funeral, she looked forlorn. It was July, the hottest month of the year, and Mollie was used to air conditioning. We tried to soften the blow when we were home by taking on Daddy's role in tennis ball fetch. Later, when the weather turned cold, Carrie bought an electric blanket to put on the couch on our patio. I disapproved yet again and reminded Carrie that Mollie was a dog. "Shhh," Carrie said, "she'll hear you."

We had adopted Mollie because Daddy needed a companion, and now we wondered if Mollie needed one. We had not yet decided when we went to the local PETCO one Saturday looking for a pet door so Mollie could go in and out of the house while we were gone. But when we walked in, our plans changed. A different shelter, the Belzoni Animal Rescue Kennel, BARK for short, was having an adoption day. And there stood Buster, a handsome hound, much more my style than a cocker. He needed a home and was ready to be claimed. We brought him home, introduced him to Mollie, and they became fast friends in no time. Like her, he was calm and gentle. I wonder if Daddy would have thought he was a girl.

We soon learned two things about Buster: He had heartworms, and he was calm because he had heartworms. The treatment was a success, but when the heartworms were gone, so was the calm. We knew Buster was not a purebred, though we assumed he was all dog. But after he took the cure, we decided he was half-dog and half-Tasmanian devil, the one on Bugs Bunny.

Going for walks is Buster's reason to live. The French would say it's his raison d'être. Mollie likes walks too, but it's Buster who's a nut about it. Every morning he watches me anxiously while I eat breakfast, then follows me to the bedroom in anticipation. If I get into the shower, he returns to the living room, head down, dejected. But if I put on shorts and a tee shirt, it's game on. He rushes out, shares the good news with Mollie, and they return together. As I don socks and walking shoes, the histrionics escalate. He jumps up on me and becomes more vocal, whimpering like a baby. By the time I get the leashes and he knows it's a sure thing, he's singing a canine aria and spinning like a whirling dervish. When I open the door, he leaps into the great outdoors, and we're off. When I put on shorts and a tee shirt for any reason other than to take the dogs for a walk, I dress in the garage. Dressing in Buster's presence would be just too cruel.

Not long after we adopted Buster, I was in the kitchen one Saturday having my morning coffee when I overheard a conversation coming from our bedroom. It was Carrie and someone with a high-pitched voice. I was pretty sure no one else was in the house, at least no other person. I tiptoed to the scene to investigate. What I witnessed amazed me. The conversation I observed from the doorway was between Carrie and Mollie, but Carrie was playing both roles. Carrie as Carrie would ask a question, then Carrie as Mollie would answer it, an octave higher. I cleared my throat to announce my presence and asked Carrie what on earth she was doing. I expected embarrassment, but I didn't get it. "Channeling the dog, of course," Carrie as Carrie responded. "Everybody does it." She looked at me like I was the strange one. I assured her that everybody doesn't do it and pronounced that she was crazy. Mollie didn't take sides. I also reminded Carrie that Mollie couldn't understand a word she was saying for either one of them, what with being a dog and all. "Shhh," Carrie said. "She'll hear you."

Well, this was a brand new thing for me. I had never heard of channeling a dog, never seen it, and sure never done it. I was curious, so over the next several weeks I conducted an informal poll of our dog-loving friends and was astonished to learn that channeling is common, at least if my small sample group is any indication. A number of our friends admitted it, some frankly, some sheepishly. Positive responses ranged from "sure, doesn't everybody?" to "yeah, well, I guess maybe I've done that." Our friends may not have called it channeling, but they did it.

And since then, I've done it too. Have I ever! As Carrie will attest, I took to channeling like a duck to water. She often reminds me that I now do exactly what I laughed at her for doing. She says I've come so far.

My channeling is different from Carrie's. She asks the kinds of questions a person would ordinarily ask a dog. Are you hungry? Want a treat? Where's the tennis ball? Need to go potty? Our dogs don't actually use the potty, but still.

The dogs and I, on the other hand, discuss weightier issues. Mollie and Buster whine about the fact that she's been spayed, he's been neutered, they can't start a family, and they have no sex life. Sometimes they confess past sins. One evening Mollie sheepishly admitted that, on the day we adopted her from CARA, she slipped a diuretic into the terrier's water bowl to sabotage his chances. We also do comedy, with me as straight man. The dogs are irreverent and occasionally profane. I wonder where they learned some of the words they use. I use the same high-pitched voice for both of them. It doesn't fit Buster, but I'm no Mel Blanc, and Buster's just had to get over it. (If you don't know who Mel Blanc was, Google him. He did all the Warner Brothers cartoon voices—Bugs Bunny, Foghorn Leghorn, Elmer Fudd, the works. A genius.)

Anyway, most of Carrie's channeling conversations are with Mollie, so in the interest of fairness most of mine are with Buster. But one night, as we sat down for dinner, I channeled someone else. Or, rather, something else. Our robotic vacuum cleaner had finished its route and was headed back to its docking station, but Mollie and Buster blocked its path. To get them to move, I raised my voice to channeling pitch and gave a command: "Out of my way, I'm coming home."

Well, that was too much for Carrie. "Did you just do what I think you did?" I looked out the window and pretended not to hear. "Do you remember when you laughed at me for channeling Mollie?" I shrugged. "And you just channeled *an appliance.*" I hung my head.

Mom and Dad, the fur children, and the vacuum cleaner: We're a happy family, and we all have a say.

On another Saturday morning a year or so after I caught Carrie conversing with our cocker, I found myself in the midst of a deep conversation with Buster about the advantages of having thumbs. Buster's very opinionated, at least for a dog, and he was irate about the hardships caused by having to go through life thumbless. He listed all the things he couldn't do because he had no thumbs. To rub salt into his wound, I looked at him, smiled, and snapped my fingers. Carrie smiled too, quite pleased with herself for converting me into an enthusuastic dog channeler. After reminding me for the umpteenth time that I now do to a far greater degree what I made fun of her for doing to a far lesser degree, she made a suggestion. She said I needed to write down my conversations with Buster and preserve them for posterity. And so I did.

A Great Man

I wish Buster and my daddy could have known each other. A great man who loved dogs and a great dog he would have loved—I would have enjoyed seeing them together. Though their paths never crossed, I found out last night that Buster agrees with me that Daddy was a great man. We disagree, however, about why.

BUSTER: Dad?

DAD: What, Buster?

BUSTER: Mollie says your dad was a great man.

DAD: He was. The finest I've ever known.

BUSTER: Really? What was so great about him?

DAD: Well, for one thing, he always told the truth.

BUSTER: Always? Really?

DAD: Always. I don't think it ever occurred to him not to. And he always did the right thing.

BUSTER: Always means no exceptions. How can you be so sure?

DAD: Because I got to watch him nearly all my life. He died two days before my 56th birthday. He was almost 92.

BUSTER: You said he always did the right thing. What right things did he do?

DAD: I guess the main thing was his work as a Boy Scout leader. He was a leader of Boy Scout Troop 12 in Tupelo for 60 years. He started when he was 25 and kept at it until he was 85.

BUSTER: That's hard to believe. I wonder if anybody else has ever done that.

DAD: Nobody I've ever heard of. He devoted hundreds and

hundreds of hours to the Scouts every single one of those 60 years. And he did it all for free.

BUSTER: For free? Why didn't he get paid?

DAD: Because he always did the right thing. If he spent 500 hours a year working with the Scout troop, and he probably spent more than that, he gave the equivalent of 15 years of his life to the Boy Scouts.

BUSTER: Sounds like he was some kind of hero.

DAD: He was my hero, that's for sure. Other men have told me he was their hero too. You asked if anybody else has been a Boy Scout leader for 60 years. Here's something I'm sure nobody else has done. In 1951, one of the boys in the troop told Daddy they should go camping every month. He agreed and, starting in August of that year, that's what they did. And they haven't missed a single month since.

BUSTER: Did I hear you right? They haven't missed since 1951?

DAD: That's right. They've now gone camping every month for nearly 70 years.

BUSTER: That's amazing. Were you even alive in 1951? Who was president then?

DAD: That was six years before I was born. Harry Truman was president. Troop 12 has gone camping every single month while America has had 13 presidents, from Truman to Trump.

BUSTER: Unbelievable! What else?

DAD: Eagle is the highest rank in Boy Scouts. Four hundred boys in Troop 12 became Eagle Scouts while Daddy was a leader. At his funeral in 2013, the congregation was filled with them.

BUSTER: I wish I could have known him.

DAD: I wish you could have too. He loved dogs. He loved Mollie. Plus he was a wonderful husband and father and grandfather. A wonderful great-grandfather too. He loved my grandchildren. We have a painting of him with them.

BUSTER: I know. It's in the dining room where I like to lie in the sun. Sounds like he was one of a kind.

DAD: He was definitely that. He was the most unselfish person I've ever known. And it wasn't just the Boy Scouts. He served on the

Tupelo City Council and was the interim mayor, he was chairman of the Tupelo Parks and Recreation Commission, and he helped build homes for poor people with Habitat for Humanity. He was always doing things for other people. One year he was named Tupelo's outstanding citizen. He was also active in the First Methodist Church his whole life. Until he was in his mid-80s, he drove the church van to a retirement home to pick up residents and bring them to church. He was older than some of the people he drove.

BUSTER: Was that safe?

DAD: Sure. Daddy was a young man physically until he was very old. He was still camping after he turned 85. On his 90th birthday, a congressman read a resolution honoring him on the floor of the House of Representatives in Washington, and the mayor of Tupelo gave him the key to the city.

BUSTER: Cities have keys?

DAD: Not really. The key doesn't unlock anything. Giving Daddy the key was just a way to honor him.

BUSTER: You ever gotten a key to a city?

DAD: Not a chance. Daddy was the great man, not me. But I'll tell you this; he never channeled a dog.

BUSTER: Then he missed out. But even if your dad didn't channel dogs, it sure sounds like he was a wonderful man. And I'm sure glad I asked you about him. Mollie didn't tell me any of this.

DAD: I thought she told you he was a great man.

BUSTER: She did.

DAD: But if she didn't tell you any of this, what did she say was so great about him?

BUSTER: Ice cream.

DAD: Ice cream?

BUSTER: She said he always shared his ice cream with her, that every night he would hold the bowl a few inches off the floor and let her finish it. What a great man!

DAD: It's true. He did that. I told you he was unselfish.

BUSTER: I wish I could be like that, but I wouldn't share my Pup-Peroni with anybody.

DAD: I'm your dad, right?

BUSTER: Of course.

DAD: That makes my dad your granddad, right?

BUSTER: I guess it does. I'm the grandson of a great man. Cool.

DAD: And you should try to be more like your grandfather, Buster.

BUSTER: We're talking about him, Dad, not me. Mollie said he shared his meat and potatoes with her too.

DAD: Sure did.

BUSTER: Bread?

DAD: He shared everything with her. I tried to get him to stop, but I didn't try very hard. I was his son. It wasn't my place to tell him what to do.

BUSTER: Why'd you try to get him to stop? That's mean.

DAD: Because Mollie got fat.

BUSTER: Still is.

DAD: You're not exactly skin and bones yourself, Buster.

BUSTER: This is not about me, Dad. I just told you that.

DAD: So why are you so interested in the food Daddy shared with Mollie?

BUSTER: Eating nothing but dog food day after day gets old, Dad.

DAD: I see.

BUSTER: It gets real old. How would you like to eat the same thing day after day?

DAD: But Mom gives you Pup-Peroni. She makes you eggs and bacon on the weekend. She gives you cheese.

BUSTER: But not ice cream. I love ice cream, Dad.

DAD: Me too. What's not to love?

BUSTER: And I love meat and potatoes too. And bread. Those Sister Shubert rolls are the bomb. And pasta, that may be my favorite. Fettuccini alfredo, lasagna, spaghetti and meatballs, ravioli, I love it all.

DAD: Buster, I don't think they had fettuccini alfredo on the menu at BARK. How do you know you love it?

BUSTER: Uh-oh.

DAD: Tell the truth, Buster.

BUSTER: Okay, okay, I wasn't supposed to tell, but Mom lets us have a taste sometimes when she's cooking. But just a taste. And I want more than just a taste.

DAD: No, Buster.

BUSTER: Your dad was a great man, true?

DAD: Very true.

BUSTER: And he shared his meals with Mollie, didn't he?

DAD: Yes, Daddy shared his meals with Mollie. I told you that.

BUSTER: And his ice cream? He shared that too, did he not?

DAD: I can't believe I'm being cross-examined by a dog.

BUSTER: You need me to repeat the question?

DAD: No, I remember the question. Yes, he shared his ice cream with Mollie. I told you that too. He was very unselfish.

BUSTER: And a great man.

DAD: Yes, for the umpteenth time, Daddy was a great man, a wonderful man, the best man I've ever known.

BUSTER: You want to be a great man too, don't you, Dad?

DAD: Wow.

BUSTER: Well, you do, don't you?

DAD: And you think the way for me to be a great man is to share my meals with you?

BUSTER: That would be a good start.

DAD: And my ice cream too?

BUSTER: That would be a good finish. He shared his ice cream, and he was a great man. Just sayin'.

DAD: He wasn't a great man because he fed ice cream to a dog, Buster.

BUSTER: That's entirely a matter of perspective, Dad.

DAD: And you're looking at it from a dog's perspective, I suppose.

BUSTER: That's the only perspective I've got, Dad.

DAD: Ice cream's not good for you, Buster. The last thing you need is to add something fattening to your diet.

BUSTER: You told me I should try to be more like my grandfather. Well, you should try to be more like him too.

DAD: You're right, I should, but not by feeding ice cream to you.

BUSTER: C'mon, Dad, have a heart. Mollie says the grandkids called him Big Paul. Whenever you have to make a decision—like what to do with your ice cream, let's say—you should ask yourself, What would Big Paul do?

DAD: Is that right?

BUSTER: It's exactly right. You could even get yourself one of those bracelets. Yours would say WWBPD. And every time you face a decision, you should look at the bracelet, then do exactly what Big Paul would have done. And give me your ice cream.

DAD: Nice try, Buster, but not a chance. Go to sleep.

BUSTER: How about an ice cream sandwich?

DAD: No, Buster.

BUSTER: Can I at least have a Dreamsicle?

DAD: Go to sleep, Buster. You can dream of a Dreamsicle, but you can't have one.

The Miracle Of eHarmony

Scientists have proved that dogs love their people, but those of us who love dogs don't need the scientists. Our proof is our dogs. It's obvious to anyone with eyes to see that Buster loves Carrie and me.

Dogs are also curious. Buster will sniff the same patch of grass for ten minutes to identify all the animals, tame and wild, that have come before. So I was wondering, because dogs are naturally curious and because they love their people, are they curious about the love lives of their people? I don't know about other dogs, but Buster is.

BUSTER: Dad?

DAD: What, Buster?

BUSTER: Tell me the story of how you met Mom.

DAD: Again? Really?

BUSTER: I love that story.

DAD: I love it too. As you know, Mom had been single a long time. I'd been single a year and a half.

BUSTER: But you had girlfriends in the year and a half.

DAD: You want to tell the story, or you want me to tell it?

BUSTER: Sorry. You tell it. I won't interrupt again.

DAD: We'll see. Yes, I had two girlfriends.

BUSTER: But y'all broke up.

DAD: Buster.

BUSTER: Sorry again. Mum's the word.

DAD: Yes, both relationships ended. And right after the end of the second one, I was at Ann Lowrey's house on a Saturday afternoon.

BUSTER: Is she my sister?

DAD: What?

BUSTER: Well, you're Ann Lowrey's dad, and you're my dad. Doesn't that make her my sister?

DAD: Sure, Buster. We'll say she's your sister.

BUSTER: Good. I like her.

DAD: I do too. Anyway, Ann Lowrey told me I needed to stop jumping into relationships so fast, that I needed to play the field.

BUSTER: Good advice. She's smart.

DAD: Very smart. And I agreed with her. But I was 52 years old and didn't know a good way to find women to go out with.

BUSTER: And that's when she said she was signing you up.

DAD: Buster.

BUSTER: Sorry. I love this part.

DAD: Yes, she said she was signing me up. And so I subscribed to eHarmony, and we sat at her computer on a Saturday afternoon and answered the questions and put together my profile.

BUSTER: Dad, I've got a question. You've told me about eHarmony, that it's a dating site for single people to meet each other. But it's just for people, right?

DAD: I've never thought about it, but I'm sure it is.

BUSTER: Then how are single dogs supposed to meet? Is there a dating site for single dogs?

DAD: I've never thought about that either, but I doubt it. I guess there might be a site for the owners of dogs.

BUSTER: Parents, Dad, not owners.

DAD: My apologies. So anyway, there might be a site for the parents of a dog to find the parents of another dog so the two dogs can get together and have puppies. But if there is, I'm sure it would only be for registered purebred dogs.

BUSTER: Hey, it's not my fault my biological parents were not the same breed.

DAD: Nobody's blaming you, Buster. I'm just telling you what I think. And why are you so curious about a dog dating site? What about Mollie?

BUSTER: I love Mollie, Dad, but I never really had a chance to sow my wild oats.

DAD: Maybe you've forgotten, Buster, but as a result of a certain procedure, it's too late for you to sow any oats, wild or otherwise.

BUSTER: But a dog can dream, can't he?

DAD: In your case, that's all he can do. Where was I?

BUSTER: You were about to get to the part where Mom signed up for eHarmony too.

DAD: Buster, you seem to know the story better than I do. You tell it.

BUSTER: Okay then, I will. So Mom's friends bullied her into signing up, and they all got together to write her profile one night. And because they were drinking wine, her profile was funnier and more entertaining than yours.

DAD: Much more.

BUSTER: Don't interrupt, Dad.

DAD: Pot kettle.

BUSTER: What?

DAD: Never mind.

BUSTER: And you and Mom got matched on eHarmony on May 8, 2010. That date should be celebrated like the Fourth of July.

DAD: Like the Fourth of July? Really?

BUSTER: That's what Mollie and I think.

DAD: That's sweet.

BUSTER: Dad, you told me to tell the story, so please quit interrupting.

DAD: You've got the floor, Buster.

BUSTER: Got the floor? I live on the floor. What does that mean?

DAD: It means you can talk. And can you ever. Go ahead with the story.

BUSTER: So you and Mom got matched, you laughed at what she wrote, you looked at her pictures and saw she was a beauty, and you decided you wanted to meet her. So you sent her an email.

DAD: (Nodding, not interrupting)

BUSTER: In her profile, Mom said she saved turtles from the middle of the road, and in your email you claimed you did too. Is that really true, Dad? Or was that just a pick-up line?

DAD: Absolutely true. I saved one just the other day. Plus we were on eHarmony, not in a bar.

BUSTER: But you had romance on your mind, admit it.

DAD: Guilty.

BUSTER: Guilty as sin.

DAD: Guilty of wanting to sin. She was smart, she was funny, she was beautiful. So yes, guilty. Lock me up.

BUSTER: And in her profile she said she was nearly six feet tall in heels and worth the climb. That's kind of racy, don't you think?

DAD: They were drinking, remember.

BUSTER: In your email, you said you wanted to meet her and you'd bring a ladder. But you didn't meet right away. First you emailed each other some more.

DAD: About a thousand times. Lucky we didn't both get fired.

BUSTER: And you talked on the phone.

DAD: For hours.

BUSTER: And then you finally met for lunch. What was that like?

DAD: I was excited. She was nervous. Her best friend's husband came over to speak, and she couldn't remember his name. The place was real loud. I'm kind of deaf, as you know, so I nodded a lot.

BUSTER: What's that? I couldn't quite make out that last part.

DAD: Very funny. A dog who makes fun of his father's lousy hearing might find his supply of treats reduced.

BUSTER: Lighten up, Dad. You tease me too, you know.

DAD: And so I do. Go ahead with the story.

BUSTER: That was on a Monday. Y'all met for drinks on Tuesday, and you kissed her for the first time. Was Mom a good kisser, Dad?

DAD: I couldn't tell. It was just a peck. But I learned later. Mom's a great kisser.

BUSTER: You skipped Wednesday, but then on Thursday she helped you babysit the grandchildren. And you read her that children's book, Amy the Dancing Bear.

DAD: I did. Better than any pick-up line. I read it to her again the night I proposed to her.

BUSTER: Dad, please don't jump ahead in the story that you asked me to tell.

DAD: Well, hurry up then. It's past your bedtime.

BUSTER: Okay, I'll wrap it up. Y'all had your first real date on

Friday, the day after you babysat. After that, the two of you were together all the time even though you lived 100 miles apart. Before long, you both quit eHarmony, which had done its job. Soon you told Mom you loved her, and she said she loved you too. In September, you asked her to marry you, she said yes, and y'all got married on New Year's Day.

DAD: We would have gotten married even sooner, but Paul was studying abroad in Scotland, and we wanted to wait till he got home.

BUSTER: You mean my brother or my brother-in-law?

DAD: What?

BUSTER: You have a son named Paul, and Ann Lowrey's husband is named Paul. So who was in Scotland, my brother or my brother-in-law?

DAD: Your brother.

BUSTER: You think Paul really studied when he was studying abroad?

DAD: I think he went to pubs and studied beer.

BUSTER: Figures. So the beer scholar came home, and y'all got married. Then you adopted Mollie and then me.

DAD: And here we are, Mom and me and the fur children.

BUSTER: It's a beautiful story.

DAD: You told it beautifully, Buster.

BUSTER: Thank you, Dad. I'm sure you realize you outkicked your coverage, don't you? I mean, Mom is some kind of good looking, but you're sort of average.

DAD: Yes, I know I outkicked my coverage. And shouldn't we both be glad that I did?

BUSTER: Thank goodness Mom doesn't have exacting standards. You know what I'm thinking? I'm thinking you and Mom should make a commercial for eHarmony. It could start out with the camera just on you, and you could talk about how you signed up for eHarmony and met Mom and how happy you are. Then Mom would walk into the picture in a cute little outfit that shows off her long legs, look adoringly at you, then look into the camera and smile. She wouldn't say a word, but guys all over America would turn off their TVs, turn on their laptops, and sign up for eHarmony.

DAD: But what about women? eHarmony needs them to sign up too.

BUSTER: Same commercial, but with Mom doing the talking and George Clooney walking into the picture and smiling.

DAD: But Mom's not married to George Clooney.

BUSTER: All's fair in love and marketing, Dad. But even if you insist on being in both commercials, y'all really should do it. It would be your way of thanking them.

DAD: You're right; we should. Without eHarmony, I never would have met Mom, and we never would have adopted you and Mollie. But this story will serve as a commercial for eHarmony, at least if anybody reads it.

BUSTER: Reads it? What are you talking about?

DAD: Nothing. I misspoke.

BUSTER: No, you didn't.

DAD: Yes, I did. Go to sleep, Buster.

BUSTER: Typical. Say something you regret, and when I ask about it, you tell me to go to sleep. I'll ask you again: Reads what?

DAD: Nighty night.

BUSTER: We'll follow up on this. Something fishy's going on.

DAD: Sleep tight.

Like Father, Like Son

I have something in common with Buster that most people don't have in common with their fur children. He and I were both adopted. As some of you know, I wrote a memoir about my adoption story entitled *Fortunate Son*. Although Buster finds things to complain about, he knows in his heart that he's a fortunate son too. Buster's parents love him, and mine loved me, though his parents are more indulgent than mine were.

BUSTER: Dad?

DAD: What, Buster?

BUSTER: I heard Mom tell somebody on the phone today that you were adopted. Were you really?

DAD: Really and truly.

BUSTER: Just like me?

DAD: Just like you.

BUSTER: I didn't know people could be adopted. I thought adoption was only for dogs. Maybe an occasional cat, though I don't know why. Even masochists want pets, I guess. Anyway, I know how I was adopted, but I want to hear how you were adopted.

DAD: Okay, I'll tell you.

BUSTER: Great. Let me curl up at your feet. This is gonna be good, I just know it.

DAD: I always knew I was adopted. My parents told me when I was very young, probably too young to really understand what it meant.

BUSTER: You mean the parents who adopted you?

DAD: Yes. The only parents I ever knew.

BUSTER: I know your dad was a great man, what with the Boy Scouts and sharing his ice cream and all, but what about your mom?

DAD: She was a wonderful mother. She read to me at night. She took me fishing. She was an artist. We have some of her paintings here.

BUSTER: Which ones? I want to see.

DAD: I'll show you. And she could do more than paint. She was very smart, she sang in the church choir, and she could wiggle her ears.

BUSTER: No kidding? I can do all sorts of things with my ears—they're quite expressive, as you've no doubt observed—but I didn't know people could wiggle theirs. I thought adoption and ear wiggling were just for dogs.

DAD: Most people can't wiggle them. I can't. But she could do it, I promise.

BUSTER: So you had a great dad who was a Boy Scout leader and a great mom who could wiggle her ears.

DAD: And great friends too. And a vacant lot beside our house and a creek beside the vacant lot. In the things that really count, I had it all.

BUSTER: And all because your parents adopted you. You sure were lucky.

DAD: Very lucky. I'm grateful every day.

BUSTER: I know your dad's name was Paul. What about your mom?

DAD: Her name was Margaret. She had an identical twin named Marjory.

BUSTER: Margaret and Marjory, the alliterative sisters. So how did Margaret and Paul wind up with you?

DAD: It's a long story. You need to go outside before I start?

BUSTER: I'm good. Go ahead.

DAD: Well, I knew I was adopted from New Orleans, but that's all I knew. I never looked for my birth mother and never would have. Daddy and I found out who she was in 2004. Mama never did. She died in 1999. And I never met my birth mother. She died when she was only 47.

BUSTER: That's sad. So how did you find out who she was?

DAD: First, some background. Ann Lowrey got pregnant in the fall of her sophomore year at Ole Miss.

BUSTER: What's Ann Lowrey and getting pregnant have to do with you and getting adopted?

DAD: Patience, Buster. Ann Lowrey's boyfriend immediately abandoned her, but she's a brave soul and decided she would have and keep her baby. She stayed in school through the spring semester and then came home for the summer. She was due in mid-June.

BUSTER: Due? What's due?

DAD: That's when her baby was supposed to be born. So in early June, before the baby came, Daddy called me one day. He was still living in Tupelo. He'd gotten a message from a woman in New Orleans who said her law firm had been ordered by a court to conduct a nationwide search for Paul Eason, age 46. Well, my first name is Paul, and I was 46 at the time.

BUSTER: I thought your first name was Brooks.

DAD: That's my middle name. My first name is Paul.

BUSTER: Do I have a middle name?

DAD: Mom seems to think your middle name is Bluth. She calls you Buster Bluth.

BUSTER: I've noticed that. Where did I get that name? What's the deal with Bluth?

DAD: It's from a funny TV show. Ask her about it. She's the one who has a bunch of different names for y'all, not me.

BUSTER: No kidding. She has eight or nine different names for Mollie. Poor little dog stays confused.

DAD: So I called the woman in New Orleans, and her first words were, "I can't believe we found you." I asked what this was about. She said an inheritance.

BUSTER: Wow! I knew this was gonna be good.

DAD: I found out the whole story over the next few days. My birth mother's name was Julie Francis. Until my adoption was finalized when I was a year old, my legal name was Scott Francis. Mama and Daddy never knew that, and neither did I.

BUSTER: Did I have another name before y'all adopted me?

DAD: Not at the shelter, you didn't. They said your name was Buster. We thought it suited you, so we didn't change it.

BUSTER: Buster from the beginning.

DAD: Anyway, Julie got pregnant in the fall of her freshman year at Washington University in St. Louis.

BUSTER: Just like Ann Lowrey.

DAD: It was nearly 50 years earlier, but otherwise their situations were just alike. Neither was married, both were in college, and both were teenagers. And I'm sure they felt many of the same emotions. But their experiences were very different. Ann Lowrey got to keep her baby, but not Julie. Eight days after I was born in New Orleans, Julie signed the papers, gave me up for adoption, and never saw me again. Two months after that, Mama and Daddy brought me home to Tupelo. Anyway, Julie's grandfather was a successful businessman and owned lots of oil wells.

BUSTER: What are oil wells?

DAD: That's complicated. What matters to the story is that they're worth a lot of money.

BUSTER: Ah, the inheritance.

DAD: Julie's granddad wanted his children to get the oil wells after he died, then he wanted his grandchildren to get them, and then under some circumstances he wanted his great-grandchildren to get them.

BUSTER: And you're his great-grandson.

DAD: I am. He was still alive when I was born, but I don't know if he knew about me. Julie's little brother didn't even know. He found out she'd had a baby only after she died and they found her will.

BUSTER: He didn't know his own sister had a baby? That's sad.

DAD: Not really. Even though Julie had me, I was never part of her family. I was part of Mama's and Daddy's families. I had grandparents and aunts and uncles and cousins, the whole deal. So when Julie was 40, she was living in Aspen, down the road from Cher.

BUSTER: Of Sonny and Cher?

DAD: That's the one. While Julie was in Aspen, she signed a will that said she'd had a baby boy out of wedlock in New Orleans in July 1957.

BUSTER: So you were adopted just like me, and you were born out of wedlock just like me.

DAD: All dogs are born out of wedlock, Buster. Julie left me only a dollar in her will, but it wasn't clear that she had the right to give away the oil wells that came from her grandfather. Julie died a few years later, alone and much too young. She was married twice and divorced twice and didn't have any other children. Her family had a lot more money than mine did, but I sure wouldn't trade.

BUSTER: I wouldn't trade families either.

DAD: Thank you, Buster. I don't know what effect giving up her only child had on Julie, but it couldn't have been good. Anyway, though it wasn't clear that she had the right to give away the oil wells, the lawyer decided she did.

BUSTER: You can never tell what a lawyer will come up with.

DAD: No kidding. I know one who channels dogs. Julie's little brother, whose name is Sid, wound up with the oil wells. He didn't bother to get the title transferred right away, but years later he decided he needed to. But there was a problem. First there was Julie's grandfather's will, which said he wanted his great-grandchildren to get the wells under some circumstances, and then there was Julie's will, which said he had a great-grandchild, the baby boy born in New Orleans.

BUSTER: You!

DAD: Me. So a lawsuit was filed in Oklahoma, where Julie grew up, to decide who owned the wells. And the judge told the lawyers to go find Julie's son. In the lawsuit, because they didn't know who I was, I was referred to as Baby Boy Francis, although by then I hadn't been a baby in more than 40 years. And while the lawsuit in Oklahoma was still going, another one was filed in New Orleans because the juvenile court wouldn't release the adoption file. The whole thing lasted years because that's what lawsuits do. The one in Louisiana went all the way to the Louisiana Supreme Court.

BUSTER: The Supreme Court—that must be big time.

DAD: In Louisiana, it's the biggest. Finally, in early 2004 the courts in both states ruled. The judge in Oklahoma set a deadline in the summer to find Baby Boy Francis, and the Louisiana Supreme

Court ordered the juvenile court to search its adoption files for Baby Boy Francis.

BUSTER: Did they find you before the deadline?

DAD: Just barely. In the file labeled Paul and Margaret Eason were two birth certificates for the same baby, one with Scott Francis as his name and the other with Paul Brooks Eason. After that, finding me was easy. Daddy still lived at the same address that was listed on the replacement birth certificate, in the same house he and Mama had brought me home to nearly 50 years earlier.

BUSTER: So did you get rich, Dad? Did you? I'm thinking not. Our house is nice and all, but it's hardly palatial. And you and Mom still go to work, and you still mow the yard. Based on what I've seen, the wealthy don't do their own yard work.

DAD: You're right; I didn't get rich. I talked it over with the lawyer in Oklahoma who was appointed to represent Baby Boy Francis before they knew I was Baby Boy Francis. We decided I probably didn't have a strong claim to the oil wells, so I didn't try to get them.

BUSTER: Bummer. All that and you got nothing.

DAD: Not true. I found out who my birth mother was, and I've gotten to know people in her family. They're my family too, after all. And I also got a great story. And if I had gotten rich, who knows how it would have changed my life? I might never have met Mom, and if I hadn't, we never would've adopted you and Mollie.

BUSTER: When you put it that way, I guess I'm glad you didn't get rich. But it sure would be nice if you and Mom could stay home with us all day. And I've always dreamed of having a villa in Tuscany.

DAD: You're an unusual dog, Buster.

BUSTER: You're not so usual yourself, Dad.

DAD: A week or two after they found me, I got a call one day at work. The person on the other end identified himself as Sid Smith. "Uncle Sid," I said. "I guess so," he said. This was before I decided not to try to get the oil wells, and it looked like we would be fighting in court over them, but he was real nice. He asked if I wanted pictures of Julie, and I said absolutely. A few days later, the pictures arrived. There were several of Julie as a little girl, but there was also one of her as an adult. She looked like a younger version of me wearing a wig.

BUSTER: You still have the pictures?

DAD: Of course. I'll show them to you.

BUSTER: Sweet! Paintings by the mom you knew and pictures of the one you didn't. I want to see them all.

DAD: And so you shall. Ann Lowrey's baby was born on June 17, just 16 days before the day I was born 47 years earlier. I found out about Julie a week before she was born, and they were home from the hospital by the time I got the pictures from Uncle Sid. Ann Lowrey looked at the pictures of Julie, then looked at her new daughter asleep in her arms and said, "I'm grateful I live in a time when I can keep my baby."

BUSTER: Was the baby Ada Brooks, Dad?

DAD: Sure was. She's all grown up now, and she looks like Julie too.

BUSTER: I love Ada Brooks. She's always nice to me. I'm glad Ann Lowrey got to keep her.

DAD: Not as glad as I am, Buster. Ada B is beautiful and brilliant, sweet and kind. I used to call her the Grand Prize until Ann Lowrey made me stop.

BUSTER: You're right, Dad. You got a great story, especially the part about Ada Brooks.

DAD: Plus I got a song. A few years ago, I told the story to a friend of mine, Doc Schneider, a lawyer in Atlanta who's also a songwriter. He wrote a song about it, called it "Baby Boy Francis," and had it professionally recorded.

BUSTER: Wow, Dad! There's really a song about you?

DAD: Not just about me, but I'm in it. So are Mama and Daddy, and so is Julie.

BUSTER: Wait a minute. Did you say your songwriter friend is a lawyer named Doc?

DAD: Sure did. I don't know how Doc got to be Doc, but it wasn't from being a doctor. He's a fine lawyer and musician and a great guy, but Doc's no doctor.

BUSTER: Will you play me the song Doc wrote, Dad?

DAD: Sure. You can look at the paintings, see the pictures, and hear the song.

BUSTER: A lawyer named Doc—that's priceless. I have an idea, Dad. You wrote that book about your hiking trips with your buddy. What's his name?

DAD: Bobby Ariatti. The book is *Travels with Bobby*.

BUSTER: Well, I think you should write a book about your adoption story.

DAD: Too late. I already have.

BUSTER: Really? Am I in it?

DAD: You are, but only briefly.

BUSTER: Briefly? I should be a central character. All the events of your past—your birth and adoption, signing up for eHarmony, marrying Mom—led to your one crowning achievement.

DAD: And dare I ask what that was?

BUSTER: Adopting me, of course.

DAD: It's all about you, isn't it, Buster?

BUSTER: It's a sad dog who won't wag his own tail.

DAD: Your tail must stay exhausted. Speaking of which, it's past your bedtime.

BUSTER: I can't believe we were both adopted. Like father, like son. How cool is that?

DAD: Very cool. Goodnight, son.

BUSTER: Sweet dreams, Dad.

Popping The Question

I didn't want Buster to know I was writing this story because I wanted him to be candid and speak freely, but then I slipped up the other night and mentioned people reading it. I avoided explaining it then, but I knew he wouldn't let it go. Buster is persistent. He doesn't forget and, like a dog with a bone, he won't let go. But fortunately he waited long enough to bring it up again for me to come up with a cover story.

BUSTER: Dad?

DAD: What, Buster?

BUSTER: Back to where we were a few nights ago. You slipped up and said something about people reading this story. What were you talking about? What story?

DAD: I meant if I ever wrote the story of how I met Mom, it could be used as a commercial for eHarmony.

BUSTER: Really? I'm not buying it. If that's all you were talking about, why didn't you just say so?

DAD: It's true. I promise.

BUSTER: Okay, I'll drop it for now, but don't think I'm not on to you. Anyway, I want you to expand on something you mentioned when we were talking about eHarmony. Tell me about when you proposed to Mom. I know how y'all met, but I want to hear how you asked her to marry you. Like you, Dad, I'm a hopeless romantic. Though my capacity to act on it is more limited than yours, I'm always thinking about love and the ladies.

DAD: Sorry about the lack of capacity. That's a major bummer.

But since you asked, and since you're a romantic, I'll tell you the story.

BUSTER: I'm all ears. That reminds me of something. Before you start, let me say that you were spot on when you told me that time that Mollie's all ears. I hadn't paid much attention until you mentioned it—Mollie just looks like Mollie—but man she's got some ears on her. When she runs, they look like a couple of beach towels flapping in the breeze. And when she eats and drinks, they're nothing but trouble. She starts out at our water bowl, where she soaks her ears while she's drinking, then moves on to our food bowl, where she dredges her soggy ears through our dog food. Then her ears dry, and she spends the day with Purina particles caked in them. Not a good look. Finally, when she gets thirsty again, the ears go back in the bowl, the particles dissolve, and the water turns brown. When I want a sip, it's like I'm drinking from the Mississippi River.

DAD: You want to hear the story or not?

BUSTER: Yes. Sorry. I distracted myself.

DAD: No worries. I distract myself all the time. So here we go. By the time Mom and I had been dating a few months, I knew I wanted to marry her, and I decided to propose. To make it just right, I wanted it to be a surprise.

BUSTER: Ooh, I love surprises.

DAD: I enlisted two co-conspirators, Ann Lowrey and Mom's friend Bethie.

BUSTER: I know Bethie. She's been here with her kids. I like her.

DAD: Me too. She's very sweet, and she sure loves Mom. She's a devout Catholic and prayed that Mom would find someone. Mom wound up with me, so maybe Bethie should have prayed harder. Anyway, I asked Ann Lowrey and Bethie to help me with the engagement ring. Ann Lowrey's job was to help me find the perfect ring, and Bethie's job was to make sure it was the perfect size.

BUSTER: How'd they do it?

DAD: Ann Lowrey and I shopped for rings together. We took our time and narrowed it down to our five favorites. Then we went through a process of elimination and finally chose just the right one.

BUSTER: What's a process of elimination?

DAD: It's when you have a number of options and go through them one at a time. You eliminate all but one, and that's the winner.

BUSTER: Like when you and Mom adopted Mollie and me?

DAD: That's true of Mollie, but with you we didn't need to eliminate anybody. I spotted you and knew you were the one, just like I knew Mom was the one.

BUSTER: Sweet. You and Mom did an outstanding job picking us, if I say so myself, and you and Ann Lowrey did a great job too. Mom's ring is beautiful.

DAD: Thank you. I agree.

BUSTER: So what did Bethie do? How did she figure out the right size?

DAD: I went on a walk one morning and called her and told her my plan and what I wanted her to do. She was thrilled. She'd been wanting Carrie to find someone for a long time. She said she'd been listening to "January Wedding" and was hoping Carrie and I would get married in January.

BUSTER: I love that song.

DAD: Really? How do you know that song?

BUSTER: C'mon, Dad, everybody knows the Avett Brothers. Plus Mom plays it all the time and, like I said, I'm all ears.

DAD: I guess little pitchers really do have big ears.

BUSTER: Another great song. Sad though.

DAD: You know that one too?

BUSTER: Sure. John Prine. "Sam Stone." A classic.

DAD: I didn't realize you were so into music, Buster.

BUSTER: You love music too, Dad and. like I've heard you say, the acorn doesn't fall far from the tree. Back to Bethie—how did she do it?

DAD: She accepted her assignment with enthusiasm. She met Mom for lunch one day wearing a ring on every finger. She got Mom to put them on her ring finger one at a time to figure out which one fit the best.

BUSTER: Did Mom not figure out what was going on? Seems pretty obvious, at least in hindsight.

DAD: She didn't. She just thought Bethie was being weird.

BUSTER: So you had the perfect ring, and you had the perfect size. The stage was set.

DAD: It was. The ring arrived on a Friday, and Ann Lowrey picked it up. She called and told me it was beautiful, then I met her and got it. She was right.

BUSTER: So how did you pop the question? Did you plan something elaborate? A string quartet maybe? Or a photographer hiding in the bushes to capture the moment? Sorry, I didn't mean to interrupt. I just got a little worked up. Proceed with the story, Dad. This is getting good.

DAD: No apology necessary. There was no quartet and no photographer. I was too excited to wait long enough to plan anything like that, and it's not my style anyway. We had dinner with friends. When Mom went to the ladies' room, I showed them the ring and told them I was going to propose after dinner.

BUSTER: They knew before Mom knew? That doesn't seem right.

DAD: I disagree. It was exactly right.

BUSTER: It's sweet that you think so. Endearing even. Did you propose while y'all were having dessert with your friends? If Mom had said no, that would have been the ultimate buzz kill. You'd have regretted it the rest of your life. Your friends too. Talk about awkward.

DAD: It would have been awkward, but no, I didn't.

BUSTER: Good call. Too risky.

DAD: After Carrie and I got back to my house, I read *Amy the Dancing Bear* to her. It's a beautiful book, the same book I read to her when we babysat for the grandchildren the week we met. You said you like music. *Amy the Dancing Bear* was actually written by a singer, a beautiful woman named Carly Simon.

BUSTER: I don't think I've ever heard of her. Would I know any of her songs?

DAD: Doubtful. She was popular long before you were born.

BUSTER: I know John Prine's songs, Dad. I might know some by the Carly woman.

DAD: Carly Simon. Her most famous song is called "You're So Vain."

BUSTER: Who was it that was so vain? Whoever it was probably thought the song was about him.

DAD: Funny you should say that. There's been a lot of speculation. Carly has hinted, but she's never said for sure.

BUSTER: Back to the book—what's it about?

DAD: About a young bear who keeps convincing her mother to let her stay up so she can keep dancing. I love to dance, and I love the book. I read it to Ann Lowrey and her brothers when they were little. And here's something cool. Long after they were grown, five or six of my friends had baby girls within a couple of months of each other, and I decided to give them all copies of *Amy the Dancing Bear*. It was out of print, but I was able to order used copies on Amazon.

BUSTER: You can buy anything on Amazon. If you've got the money, they've got the goods.

DAD: No kidding. So when the books arrived, I saw that one of them had been signed by Carly Simon. I kept that one. But years later, I gave it to Margo Shipley, who's my birth mother Julie's niece. You've met her. She came here with her husband Reid.

BUSTER: I remember them. They were nice and all, but I can't believe you had a book that was signed by the author and you just gave it away. It might have been worth a fair chunk of change, which could have been converted into an even fairer chunk of Pup-Peroni.

DAD: It wasn't worth a fair chunk of anything, but even if it had been, it was worth more to me to give it to Margo. She had given me something special, a sterling silver fork that was Julie's, so I gave her something special.

BUSTER: You at least should have had it appraised first, but I guess that's spilt milk. Water under the bridge, as they say. Here's something I don't understand. We're talking about a children's book, right? And yet you read it to Mom the night you proposed to her?

DAD: It is, and I did.

BUSTER: I love you, Dad, but you're one weird dude.

DAD: I prefer hopeless romantic to weird dude.

BUSTER: Prefer all you want, but reading a children's book to a woman right before you ask her to marry you is weird. It's bona fide, Grade A, over-the-top weird.

DAD: I was softening her up.

BUSTER: Uber weird.

DAD: Maybe you're right. Mom still shakes her head.

BUSTER: She knows weird when she sees it.

DAD: But it worked, didn't it?

BUSTER: So tell me how you closed the deal, Romeo. Did you sing "Mary Had a Little Lamb"? Or "Baa Baa Black Sheep"?

DAD: There was no singing.

BUSTER: Did you at least get down on one knee?

DAD: No kneeling either.

BUSTER: I guess you thought the bear book was enough.

DAD: Always the critic.

BUSTER: Acorn, tree, once again.

DAD: Don't second guess me. It was a perfect night.

BUSTER: From your perspective maybe, but I'm sure Mom thought it was weird. Any sane person would.

DAD: I think she was pleased, but feel free to ask her.

BUSTER: So you finished the bear book, but you weren't kneeling. What did you say?

DAD: I asked her if she wanted to be with me for the duration.

BUSTER: For the duration? Really? After all the planning, that's the best you could come up with? What does that even mean? Until the rinse cycle ends? The credits roll? The fat lady sings?

DAD: We weren't doing laundry or watching a movie, and we sure weren't at the opera. She knew exactly what it meant. The duration meant the rest of our lives.

BUSTER: More weird. What did she say?

DAD: She said yes.

BUSTER: Since you claim she knew what it meant, I guess you were feeling pretty confident then.

DAD: It's true. I was.

BUSTER: But even assuming she knew, asking a woman if she wants to be with you for the duration hardly qualifies as a marriage proposal. You could have been asking her to shack up with you for the duration. I hope you said more.

DAD: For once, Buster, I did what you think I should have done. I asked her the traditional question, the one a man is supposed to ask: Will you marry me?

BUSTER: Congratulations, for once, on not being weird. Seeing as how y'all are married, I assume she said yes again.

DAD: Very astute.

BUSTER: So then what did you do?

DAD: I pulled out the ring. I had it hidden.

BUSTER: More normal. Good. Then what?

DAD: I put it on her finger.

BUSTER: Did it fit? After that elaborate scheme, I sure hope so.

DAD: It was actually a little too big, but Mom said it was perfect.

BUSTER: That sounds just like her. I hope you realize how lucky you are.

DAD: I do. I'm very fortunate. I married up. No doubt about it.

BUSTER: Not just up, Dad, way up. Mom's out of your league. She's the millionaire runway model, and you're the minimum-wage guy cleaning up after the show.

DAD: Okay, I get your point.

BUSTER: I look at her, I look at you, and I think: Will wonders never cease?

DAD: Enough already. Think what you want, but here's something you should consider. You've got a pretty sweet deal here. You don't want to tell Mom she could have done better and give her any ideas. What if she decides to leave me for a handsome guy who prefers cats? Where will you be then?

BUSTER: I'm just messing with you, Dad. You and Mom are perfect together. She's much better looking than you are, but you excel at channeling.

DAD: I express your thoughts accurately, do I not?

BUSTER: You have a gift, there's no doubt. Sometimes you say what I'm thinking even before I know I'm thinking it. It's uncanny.

DAD: I do my best.

BUSTER: Back to that night. You put the ring on her finger, and she said it was perfect. Then what?

DAD: I kissed her.

BUSTER: Another good call. Was it a long, passionate kiss or one of those quickie you-may-now-kiss-the-bride kisses?

DAD: What do you think?

BUSTER: I'm guessing long and passionate.

DAD: Bingo.

BUSTER: After the kiss, then what?

DAD: So far as you're concerned, nothing.

BUSTER: R-rated stuff?

DAD: Not-for-Buster stuff.

BUSTER: So is that the end of the story?

DAD: It's the end of the story about how Mom and I got engaged, but the rest of our story continued. We got married in January, just like Bethie wanted.

BUSTER: It's a sweet story, Dad. I'm happy you and Mom found each other.

DAD: Thanks. I'm happy we did too. I'm very fortunate.

BUSTER: I've got to say, though, that reading the dancing bear book right before you popped the question is truly the weirdest thing I've ever heard. And who asks a woman if she wants to spend the duration with him? The duration sounds like something grueling, like you were asking her to do the Bataan Death March with you or something. But you know what? The goofy things you did make the story even sweeter. Thank you for telling me.

DAD: You're welcome.

BUSTER: I'm thinking there could be a movie in it, Dad. People love romances. You and I aren't the only hopeless romantics out there, you know. Just think, the story of you and Mom could be the next When Harry Met Sally. *The screenplay could be worth millions, and we could get that villa in Tuscany I've always dreamed of. You need to get to work on it right now.*

DAD: I need to go to bed right now. So do you.

BUSTER: We'll need to find a beautiful actress to play Mom and some weird dude to play you. I'm thinking John Malkovich or maybe Christopher Walken.

DAD: Nighty night, son.

Making A Contribution

Buster leads a life of leisure. Other than when he's on a walk with me, he's almost always reclining on his bed or a couch or a chair. I haven't tried to figure out how many hours a day he sleeps, but I know he's asleep much more than he's awake. Sometimes I wonder if he thinks about doing something exciting and having a more fulfilling life, but on balance he seems pleased with the status quo. He has a very comfortable life. And though he's not a working dog, he definitely makes a contribution.

BUSTER: Dad?

DAD: What, Buster?

BUSTER: What should I be when I grow up?

DAD: You're already grown up, Buster.

BUSTER: I am not! I'm younger than some of your grand children.

DAD: But dogs grow up faster than people do. They say one human year is equal to seven years for a dog. That means you're a middle-aged dog.

BUSTER: Middle-aged? You said "they say" the seven-years business. Who are they? Who put them in charge?

DAD: Good question. Nobody knows who they are, only that they're omniscient and infallible.

BUSTER: Omniwho? Infalliwhat? Dial it back, Dad. I may not be an average dog, but I'm still a dog.

DAD: Sorry. Sometimes I forget. Omniscient means they know everything. Infallible means they're always right. And the reason they say one human year equals seven dog years is that dogs grow up faster than people and don't live as long.

BUSTER: Don't live as long? That's not fair! I protest.

DAD: I didn't make the rules, Buster. Take it up with God.

BUSTER: God? Who is God? Is he omnifallible or whatever it is? How do I take it up with him?

DAD: If you want to take something up with God, just close your eyes and talk.

BUSTER: Really?

DAD: Really. Just close your eyes and talk. There's even a name for it. It's called prayer.

BUSTER: Okay, if you say so, but it sounds weird. I'll look like I'm talking to myself. People will think I've gone straight from middle-aged to senile.

DAD: Try it. You might just like it. But you probably won't have much luck getting God to change the rules about how long dogs live. Those have been the rules for a long time. But maybe God can help you figure out what you should be.

BUSTER: Yeah, back to that. I really want to make something of myself and make a contribution. Also, since I'm now informed that I'm middle-aged, that dogs don't live very long, and that I can't get the rules changed, it's a matter of some urgency. But are you really sure I'm grown up? You're always saying I'm immature.

DAD: You are, but mature and grown up are not the same thing. Take me, for example. I've been a grown man for decades—I'm a grandfather, as you know—but I'm not mature at all. Ask anybody. Maturity is overrated in my book.

BUSTER: I bet you think all the qualities you don't have are overrated. But you're as old as Methuselah, Dad. Are you really immature?

DAD: I channel dogs, Buster.

BUSTER: Well, there's that. So what can I be, Dad? I really want to be somebody, and time's a wastin'. I want a legacy. In the several hours a day that I'm awake, all I do is eat, sleep, pee, poop, bark at strangers, hang out with Mollie, beg Mom for Pup-Peroni, then start the cycle all over again. My life is easy, I'll grant you that, but it's not fulfilling. I want to make a difference, give back, pay it forward. You know, all the clichés.

DAD: Very admirable. Let's see. You could use your keen sense of smell and be a rescue dog. How about that?

BUSTER: A rescue dog? What would I do? A rescue dog—that sounds cool.

DAD: Well, there are actually two kinds of rescue dogs, and you're one of them already. One kind is dogs who get rescued by people, and the other kind is dogs who rescue people. You're the first kind because we adopted you from a shelter. The other kind is dogs that go to sites of disasters—bombings and earthquakes and such—and search for survivors.

BUSTER: What's a bombing? What's an earthquake?

DAD: Bombs are explosives people use to blow up buildings. Earthquakes are when the ground shakes and buildings fall down.

BUSTER: Why would anybody want to blow up a building?

DAD: I don't know, Buster. That's one of the great questions of our age. Some people are filled with hate.

BUSTER: Not me. I'm a lover, not a fighter.

DAD: You wish. You're a lounger, not a fighter.

BUSTER: You said I would search for survivors. Is it possible I might find somebody who didn't survive?

DAD: You might.

BUSTER: Sorry, but I could never risk that. You know how sensitive I am. I'd wind up in therapy for PTSD. What are my other options?

DAD: You could be a seeing-eye dog and help a blind person.

BUSTER: Would I have to help a blind person cross the road?

DAD: Sure. That would be one of the main things.

BUSTER: Roads with cars?

DAD: Sure. Cars are what roads are for.

BUSTER: Dad, let me tell you something I've learned. A dog, like a man, has got to know his limitations, and as you've observed, I pay no attention whatsoever to cars. It would be the oblivious leading the blind. My client and I would get mowed down by an SUV.

DAD: Good point.

BUSTER: You know how it is when we go for a walk. My job is sniffing and marking my territory. I don't even think about looking for cars. That's your job. You're my seeing-eye person.

DAD: But you could learn.

BUSTER: Dad, you just said I was middle-aged. That means I'm on the cusp of old. And you know what they say, those omniwhatever people, that old dogs can't learn. Better scratch seeing-eye dog off the list. What else is there?

DAD: Here's an idea: You could be an emotional support dog.

BUSTER: What's that? I'm all about emotional support. Mollie tells me I'm in touch with my feminine side. What would I do?

DAD: Nothing special really. Just hang out and be supportive and affectionate. Some people have emotional problems. Having a dog can be very calming.

BUSTER: Calming? I don't lack for self-esteem, Dad, but calm's not exactly my strong suit. Exuberant yes, calm no. Come to think of it, Mollie's sort of my emotional support dog. I guess I need a seeing-eye person and an emotional support dog too.

DAD: Don't sell yourself short, Buster. You make Mom and me happy. Mollie too. You're affectionate, and you're very entertaining. You're good for our emotions.

BUSTER: What are you saying, that I'm already an emotional support dog?

DAD: Maybe not officially, but unofficially you definitely are.

BUSTER: Voila! Dad, I've just decided what I'll be. I'll be what I already am—an emotional support dog for you and Mom. And for Mollie too. Let's face it; she needs all the help she can get.

DAD: Great idea, Buster. I think you've found your calling.

BUSTER: Dad, you remember that children's book The Runaway Bunny*?*

DAD: Sure. I read it to my kids a hundred times. But what's that got to do with being an emotional support dog?

BUSTER: If you'll recall, the young bunny has all these grand ideas about what he's going to be—a fish in a trout stream, a rock on a mountain, a sailboat, lots of things.

DAD: And a tightrope walker. A hundred times, like I said.

BUSTER: Anyway, no matter what the bunny says he's going to be, his mother tells him she'll come after him. And at the end of the book, he gives up all his big plans, throws up his paws, and says shucks, I might just as well stay where I am and be your little bunny.

DAD: And she tells him to have a carrot. I know the story well, but what made you think of it?

BUSTER: Well, I think I'm kind of like the runaway bunny. I was thinking I needed to leave home and do something important to make a contribution, but you made me realize that I'm already making a contribution right here. And so I'm thinking I might just as well stay where I am and be your emotional support dog.

DAD: And Mom and Mollie's too. Don't forget them.

BUSTER: I won't, but they're not as needy as you are.

DAD: So says the emotional support dog who needs an emotional support dog. I'm glad you've found your calling. Now it's time for you to go to sleep.

BUSTER: Okay, Dad, but would you sing to me first, please? This talk about my future has me all keyed up, and I'm afraid I'll have a hard time getting any shut-eye. A nice lullaby would sure help. How about "Sweet Baby James"? That's my favorite.

DAD: There is a young cowboy who lives on the range . . . . I can't believe I'm singing to a dog.

BUSTER: Not just any dog, Dad.

DAD: There's no doubt about that. Goodnight, Buster.

BUSTER: Finish the song, Dad, then let me go down in my dreams.

The King And The Hound Dog

Elvis and I both grew up in Tupelo, but he was a generation older and I didn't realize what a big deal he was until he died. Then, the day after his death, two of my enterprising friends bought all the Tupelo newspapers they could lay their hands on, drove to Graceland, sold the papers to grieving Elvis fans, and made more in a day than I made all summer as a bank teller. I wish I'd thought of it first.

Dogs are smart, but how smart? Chaser, a border collie reputed to be the world's smartest dog, learned the names of more than 1,000 different objects. When I read about Chaser, it made we wonder what else a dog can learn. For example, can a dog learn song lyrics? Last night I learned that one dog can.

BUSTER: Dad?

DAD: What, Buster?

BUSTER: Elvis was big time, wasn't he?

DAD: Sure was. He was a superstar, a legend, the king of rock and roll. But his life was cut short. He died when was only 42. It was during the summer when I was in college.

BUSTER: I heard he was from Tupelo. Is that true? Did he really grow up where you grew up?

DAD: He did. My aunt Marjory taught him in the eighth grade.

BUSTER: I'm sure I would have been very fond of Marjory, but as for her famous student, well, that's a whole nother thing. He may be dead, but I've got a bone to pick with your home boy Elvis.

DAD: What's your problem with Elvis? He's been dead more than 40 years. What did he ever do to you?

BUSTER: What did he ever do to me? Let me ask you this: What if somebody famous sang a song about you? And what if millions of people heard it and learned the words and sang along?

DAD: Sounds pretty cool so far. Doc Schneider wrote that song about me, and I thought that was way cool.

BUSTER: We're talking about the king of rock and roll, Dad, not your lawyer friend with the goofy name. And we're not talking about a nice song either. What if this song, this famous song, insulted you and called you names?

DAD: I guess I wouldn't much like it.

BUSTER: And that's not all. What if the song said you were a whiner? That you complained constantly?

DAD: I wouldn't like that either.

BUSTER: And what if this song, this song heard throughout America, said you had no class? And this singer, who was popular throughout the land, made a point of declaring that he wasn't your friend?

DAD: I guess it would bother me. But what on earth does this have to do with you and Elvis?

BUSTER: "Ain't Nothin' But A Hound Dog," *that's what. Elvis may be dead, but his hateful song lives on. I heard it today on Spotify.*

DAD: Spotify?

BUSTER: Sure. I figured out how to play that cool new Sonos speaker you bought. Great sound quality in a small package.

DAD: You're quite a dog, Buster.

BUSTER: I'm quite an angry dog.

DAD: But that song's not about you.

BUSTER: Dad, that song insults all hound dogs, from my forebears who were alive when it was first recorded down through the generations to me. "Ain't nothin' but a hound dog"—the very idea.

DAD: It's not complimentary, I'll grant you that.

BUSTER: And "cryin' all the time"—what's with that?

DAD: You do complain a lot, Buster.

BUSTER: Only when I have a valid complaint, and I've got a compelling complaint today. Here's another insult: "They said you was high-class, but that was just a lie." Do you, like Elvis, believe that hound dogs are low-class?

DAD: Not all of them, that's for sure. Your beginnings may have been humble, but you're anything but humble now.

BUSTER: Then there's this: "You ain't never caught a rabbit, and you ain't no friend of mine." What does that even mean? Is it just a non-sequitur, or must a hound dog catch rabbits to be worthy of friendship? If the hound dog had caught a rabbit, would Elvis have laid off the insults?

DAD: I have no idea. I didn't write the song.

BUSTER: And what's with the deplorable grammar? You was, not you were, and all the ain'ts and double negatives. "You ain't never caught a rabbit"—does that mean the poor hound dog caught a whole warren full of rabbits? "Ain't no friend"—were Elvis and the dog really bosom buddies? I can't believe anybody who wrote or sang that ungrammatical disaster would have the gall to call anybody low-class. Talk about your pot kettle and your glass house.

DAD: There's a point I think you're missing, Buster.

BUSTER: What? Yet another insult? I just heard the song once and, being a low-class hound dog, I couldn't write down the defamatory lyrics.

DAD: No, not another insult. What you're overlooking is that Elvis is insulting a person, not a hound dog.

BUSTER: I know that, Dad. I'm not a dummy. But how is Elvis insulting the person? By likening him to a hound dog, that's how. To a whiny, low-class hound dog who's so worthless he's never even caught a rabbit.

DAD: Have you ever caught a rabbit, Buster?

BUSTER: No, but only because we have a fenced yard. Let me roam, and you'll have rabbits stacked up to the ceiling.

DAD: Let me look something up. It says here that Elvis recorded the song in July 1956, which is exactly a year before I was born. Elvis died in 1977, which is more than 30 years before you were born. I can see that the song offends you, but after all this time, what exactly do you propose that we do about it?

BUSTER: First of all, we'll organize protests to ensure that this despicable song never sullies the airwaves of America again. We'll get the ASPCA involved, and PETA. Surely they don't tolerate hate speech directed at dogs and will join in our quest to get "Hound Dog" banished from the air. And we'll increase the pressure by contacting advertisers.

We'll get them to boycott Spotify and any other streaming service that plays the offensive song.

DAD: The people in those organizations love dogs, no doubt, but I'm not sure they'll take the song as seriously as you do.

BUSTER: That's because they're not dogs, much less hound dogs. You'll have to explain it to them from my perspective.

DAD: I don't know about that. Anything else you have in mind?

BUSTER: File suit for defamation. Not only does Elvis's defamatory song live on, but so does his estate. You'll represent me on a contingency basis, and we'll both get rich.

DAD: I'm afraid the statute of limitations on any defamation claim ran a long time ago.

BUSTER: Not so. Just as the statute of limitations doesn't run on a child's claim as long as he's a child, it doesn't run on a dog's claim as long as he's a dog.

DAD: But dogs can't file suits.

BUSTER: Then you'll have to make new law, establish new precedent. Get creative, Dad. Do some forum-shopping. Find a judge who loves dogs and hates rabbit hunting and rockabilly music.

DAD: No, thanks. I'm not going to spend my time pursuing a defamation claim for a dog based on a song that is not about him and was written more than 50 years before he was born. If you can find some other lawyer willing to tilt at windmills, have at it.

BUSTER: Tilt at windmills? I want a lawyer to sue Elvis's estate, not fool around with windmills.

DAD: Sorry. It's an expression. It means to engage in a hopeless quest.

BUSTER: I see. And when you ask me to find another lawyer, you're asking me to tilt at windmills. Lest you've forgotten, I can't talk.

DAD: Good point. That handicap would also make you an ineffective witness at trial, I'm afraid.

BUSTER: Is there no justice in the world? Must I suffer in silence?

DAD: You never suffer in silence, Buster, and you've gotten yourself all worked up. You're overreacting and overwrought.

BUSTER: Given the gravity of the insult, I'd say I'm underreacting and underwrought.

DAD: Think about this, Buster. The lyrics of "Hound Dog" may not portray dogs in a favorable light, but many songs do.

BUSTER: Like what?

DAD: My favorite is by John Hiatt. It's about his dog, a dog he loved. The title is "My Dog and Me."

BUSTER: That sounds better so far. What's it about?

DAD: Well, it reminds me of you. The song is about John and his dog going for a walk together. The song asks a question at the beginning: How many times can one dog pee?

BUSTER: I know the answer to that one, at least for me. As many times as it takes to mark my territory so the other dogs will know who's boss. What else is in the song?

DAD: They walk all day. She chases some deer and barks at the birds in the trees. She runs up ahead and comes back to tell him the coast is clear. She looks at him like she'd give up her life for him. She's a good dog, just like you.

BUSTER: Thanks, Dad. I'm liking this one so far. Anything else?

DAD: At the end of the song, John sings I've never felt so free, it's just my dog and me, and the two of them fall asleep by the fire.

BUSTER: Pure poetry.

DAD: I love the song.

BUSTER: Please do me a favor, Dad. That Sonos speaker is portable, isn't it?

DAD: It is.

BUSTER: Run go get it real quick, and let's listen to that song together.

DAD: Great idea.

When the song ends, the conversation resumes.

BUSTER: That was beautiful. It's light years better than that ridiculous Hound Dog song.

DAD: I agree. And who listened to it together just now? It was just my dog and me.

BUSTER: I love you, Dad.

DAD: I love you too, Buster. Goodnight.

Separation Anxiety

When a dog's people come home, he has no idea how long they've been gone. At least that's what I've been told, and I believe it. When we come home after a week of vacation, Buster acts just the same as he does when we come home after an hour at the grocery store. Even after all these years, he cries like a baby and jumps up on us. When we walk in the door, it's like he thought we were never coming home again. It seems that a dog as smart as Buster would have figured out by now that we always come home. And maybe he has.

BUSTER: Dad?

DAD: What, Buster?

BUSTER: What is separation anxiety?

DAD: Why are you asking me that?

BUSTER: I heard Mom on the phone telling somebody I have separation anxiety. If I've got it, I should know what it is.

DAD: Fair enough. Separation anxiety is a condition in which being separated from somebody or something makes you very upset and worried, excessively so.

BUSTER: And you think I've got it?

DAD: Sure do. In spades.

BUSTER: Why do you think that? My life is a piece of cake. I may be excitable, but I don't suffer from anxiety. To the contrary, I'm carefree and easygoing, even whimsical. What makes you think I have this so-called condition?

DAD: Because of how you act when we get home.

BUSTER: And how is that?

DAD: You know exactly how, Buster. You go nuts. You whimper and cry and jump up on us. It's like you've been worried sick that we'll never come home again. You do it when we've been gone for less than an hour.

BUSTER: So I'm glad to see you. What's wrong with that?

DAD: Nothing. You just take it to extremes. Mollie doesn't cry like a baby when we walk in the door.

BUSTER: Maybe I'm just more emotional than she is. Maybe my love for you and Mom is stronger. Maybe I'm just a deeper person.

DAD: Dog, Buster. You're a dog.

BUSTER: Whatever. So what am I supposed to do, act like a cat or something?

DAD: How would you know how a cat acts? We don't have a cat.

BUSTER: I came from a shelter, Dad. There are cats in shelters. Duh.

DAD: But the name of your shelter was BARK, remember?

BUSTER: That's just because BARK is a cute acronym. The place was crawling with cats, I assure you. And I can understand why. Why would anybody want to keep a cat? If I got stuck with one, I'd dump it at a shelter in a New York minute. And that's obviously what the people in Belzoni did. There were so many cats at BARK they should have changed the name of the place to MEOW.

DAD: Okay, so you're familiar with cats. Tell me how they act.

BUSTER: You know good and well how cats act, Dad. You've been a cat owner.

DAD: I thought people with pets were parents, not owners. At least that's what you say.

BUSTER: Not when the pets are cats, Dad. Cats are the worst, the lowest, the scum of the earth.

DAD: What's so awful about cats?

BUSTER: To start with, they're insolent and aloof. They're ungrateful. They think they're better than everybody else. Better than people and better than dogs. They won't look you in the eye. They won't give you the time of day.

DAD: I guess you have been around cats.

BUSTER: Have I ever. And I know how they are. Arrogant, condescending, supercilious.

DAD: Impressive.

BUSTER: Impressive? There's nothing impressive about cats.

DAD: Not cats, Buster. Your vocabulary.

BUSTER: Some dogs learn tricks, Dad. I learn words. And you know I'm right. Do you really want me to act like a cat? Not greet you at the door? Not wag my tail? Not even look up from the stupid ball of yarn I'm batting with my stupid paw?

DAD: That's not what I'm saying, Buster. Maybe you could shoot for something halfway between a cat and how you act now. You act like a Tasmanian Devil.

BUSTER: A Tasmanian Devil? What on earth is that?

DAD: It's an animal that lives on Tasmania, an island south of Australia. But I'm not talking about the real thing. I'm talking about the character on Bugs Bunny.

BUSTER: Ooh, I love me some Bugs.

DAD: Really? How on earth do you know about Bugs?

BUSTER: You and Mom are gone all day, Dad.

DAD: Interesting. Anyway, the cartoon Tasmanian Devil is wild and crazy and spins in circles so fast you can barely see him. Maybe you could achieve a happy medium. Don't act like a cat, but don't act like a Tasmanian Devil either.

BUSTER: I've got a confession to make, Dad.

DAD: Uh-oh. What is it now?

BUSTER: Will you promise to keep this between us guys?

DAD: Sure.

BUSTER: And not tell Mom?

DAD: I won't tell Mom.

BUSTER: Okay then. I hate to admit it but, well, the whole thing's an act.

DAD: The whole what?

BUSTER: The whimpering, the crying, the jumping up on y'all. The whole shooting match.

DAD: You're kidding.

BUSTER: Why would I kid about it? That would be like confessing to a crime I didn't commit.

DAD: But why do you do it? Why did you ever start doing it?

BUSTER: Well, one day right after y'all adopted me, I was asleep when Mom came home. And I was right in the middle of the wildest, most exciting dream.

DAD: About what?

BUSTER: That's not important. Let's just say you would have been excited too. Anyway, Mom startled me, and I was so worked up from my dream that, before I knew it, I'd done the whole whimper, spin, jump up on Mom thing.

DAD: Is that right?

BUSTER: The whole shebang. But here's the thing: Mom was thrilled. She was more excited than I was about my dream. She told me she loved me, got me two Pup-Peronis instead of the usual one, scratched me behind the ears, and let me lick her nose.

DAD: I don't know why she lets you and Mollie do that.

BUSTER: Don't ask me; it's pretty disgusting. But she likes it, so we do it. Anyway, the way I acted made Mom happy, so I decided to do it every time one of you walks in the door. And when y'all come in together, I go extra nuts. I do it for y'all, Dad, not for me.

DAD: Sure you don't do it for the Pup-Peroni?

BUSTER: That's harsh, Dad. I'm not some mercenary. I love you and Mom, you know that.

DAD: And you love Pup-Peroni too. I'll tell you what. Let's modify your little act if you don't mind. You can go berserk when Mom comes home, but when I'm the one, give it a rest.

BUSTER: You know why Mom likes it and you don't?

DAD: No, why?

BUSTER: Because she's a dog and you're a cat.

DAD: We're people, Buster. Human beings.

BUSTER: Don't be so literal, Dad. I mean she's like a dog and you're like a cat.

DAD: That's pretty harsh after what you just said about cats.

BUSTER: You know it's true, Dad. Mom is friendlier and more outgoing than you are. More affectionate, more enthusiastic. Let's face it, she's more likeable. It's not a criticism, it's just a fact.

DAD: I can't disagree, but I've never thought about the whole dog/cat thing.

BUSTER: Well, think about it. You're—what's the right word for it? Taciturn. That's it. We can always tell how Mom's feeling and whether she's in a good mood, which she almost always is by the way. But not you. Sometimes you're downright inscrutable.

DAD: Is that right?

BUSTER: Sometimes you make me think of that line from that old John Prine song about Lydia hiding her thoughts like a cat.

DAD: I hope I don't make you think of the next line.

BUSTER: You mean behind her small eyes, sunk deep in her fat? That line?

DAD: That's the one.

BUSTER: Not really, but you could definitely stand to lose some weight, and you have to admit that your eyes are downright beady in comparison to my big, brown, dewy eyes. Doe-eyed I think is the term.

DAD: Everybody knows you're handsome, Buster. Don't brag.

BUSTER: As I've said before, it's a sad dog who won't wag his own tail. And you know I'm right about the whole Mom/Dad, dog/cat thing.

DAD: I don't know that I like it, but it's pretty perceptive. Where'd you come up with it?

BUSTER: I'm a dog, Dad. And in my capacity as a dog, it's natural for me to consider whether people are like dogs. Plus I spend a lot of time with you and Mom. I may not watch y'all like a hawk, but I watch y'all like a dog. And, to quote the late, great Yogi Berra, you can observe a lot by just watching.

DAD: I loved Yogi.

BUSTER: Yogi was the best. If you don't want me to, Dad, I won't jump up on you anymore.

DAD: Thank you.

BUSTER: At least if you won't tell Mom I'm a fraud. It would break her heart.

DAD: I won't. I promise.

BUSTER: And it might cost me some Pup-Peroni.

DAD: We can't have that.

BUSTER: Don't get me wrong. I really do miss y'all when you're gone. I even miss you. Just not as much as I let on.

DAD: Thank you for your candor, Buster. Now go to sleep.

TAILS OF THE SEA

A Dog Of Letters

I was thinking again yesterday about that brilliant border collie named Chaser and wondering what else a dog might be able to learn. If Chasher could learn the names of more than 1,000 objects, surely a dog could learn the names of 26 letters and the sounds they make. And who knows? A dog might even be able to learn the sound that a combination of letters makes. There's a word for such a combination; it's called a word. So how big of a leap would it really be from learning 1,000 objects to learning how to read? It doesn't seem like a huge leap to me, but what do I know?

BUSTER: Dad?

DAD: What, Buster?

BUSTER: How do you pronounce an upside down e?

DAD: What?

BUSTER: You heard me. How do you pronounce an upside down e?

DAD: Buster, that's got to be the weirdest question a dog has ever asked.

BUSTER: Just answer the question, Dad. Either you know or you don't.

DAD: You tell me how you came up with the question, and I'll tell you the answer.

BUSTER: Okay then, we'll see if you know. You know how we have lots of free time during the day?

DAD: I'm well aware. The only sign of any activity is when you've been digging in the backyard.

BUSTER: I'm chasing moles, okay? And one of these days, I'm going to catch one.

DAD: Hopefully before we have to resod the backyard.

BUSTER: You should be glad that I have a new hobby to take my mind off the fiendish, elusive moles.

DAD: I'm delighted. So what's this new hobby?

BUSTER: Learning to read.

DAD: What?

BUSTER: Hard to believe, isn't it? I'm teaching myself to read. I'm autodogdactic.

DAD: Autodogdactic?

BUSTER: A person who teaches himself how to do something is autodidactic. I learned that Friday. Since I'm a dog, I figure I'm autodogdactic because I'm teaching myself to read.

DAD: Fascinating. Tell me more.

BUSTER: Well, I was bored one day, Mollie was asleep, and I was looking for something to do. You know how I'm always looking to better myself, so when I spotted the dictionary on the bookshelf, I pulled it down and opened it.

DAD: Buster, you're a dog. You can't read.

BUSTER: Make that couldn't. At first it was all Greek to me, I'll admit. But even a dog, with enough time on his paws, can teach himself to read. I'm not saying Mollie could do it—it took her a week to learn how to use the pet door—but I can and I am. So how do you pronounce an upside down e? Quit stalling.

DAD: I'm not stalling. An upside down e is a pronunciation symbol for a sound sort of like a short u.

BUSTER: Hold on, Dad. I've had time on my paws, but not that much time.

DAD: It sounds like *uh*. As in the sound of the vowel in the first word in "The dogs have gotten into the Pup-Peroni again." Or in "Believe it or not, Buster can read."

BUSTER: Is there a name for it? The upside down e?

DAD: There is, but I've forgotten. Let me look it up. Here it is. It's called a schwa.

BUSTER: Schwa? That sounds like something you would say when you've been overserved. "Bring me more brandy and some Schwiss schwocolate."

DAD: You've come a long way, Buster. How far have you gotten in the dictionary?

BUSTER: I'm just in the Cs. I was going to stop yesterday at corn, but I kept going to cornucopia. What a cool word. An abundant supply of something good. Like a barrel of bacon. That's alliteration. I learned that one last Thursday.

DAD: I wondered about that when you said Mama and Marjory were alliterative sisters. So what do you plan to do with your new skill?

BUSTER: Get rich for one thing. You blew your chance on the oil wells, but I'm not going to blow mine. I'm going to be the Jeff Bezos of hounds.

DAD: And just how are you going to do that?

BUSTER: Think about it, Dad. A dog who can talk has got to be worth millions, and a dog who can read has got to be worth millions. Just imagine how much a dog who can talk and read is worth.

DAD: So who's going to pay you the big bucks?

BUSTER: I've got lots of ideas. Talk shows. Vegas. Atlantic City. Branson when I get old. I can have a television show for children. Kids would hang on every word with a dog reading to them.

DAD: It's got potential.

BUSTER: Rich people would pay me big bucks to channel their dogs.

DAD: Just because you can read and talk doesn't mean you can channel other dogs, Buster.

BUSTER: So I'll fake it. There's no way they'll know. You say you're channeling me, but who's to say you're not just making it up? I know you're not, but that's because I'm the one being channeled. Somebody else might think you're making it all up.

DAD: Nobody could make up the things you say, Buster.

BUSTER: Pot kettle. I haven't gotten to the Ps, but I figured out what pot kettle means.

DAD: Any other ideas for how you'll capitalize on your amazing new skill?

BUSTER: I have one, but I'll have to do it before I become world famous.

DAD: World famous, huh?

BUSTER: I'll be the first ever dog who can talk and read, Dad. Think about it. I might get to be universe famous. But anyway, before I become famous, I want to do something for my country.

DAD: Is that right?

BUSTER: Dogs can be patriotic too, Dad. Unlike cats, dogs are very loyal, to their parents and their country. I get tears in my eyes whenever I hear Kate Smith sing "God Bless America" or see Old Glory flapping in the breeze like Mollie's ears.

DAD: Touching. So what are you going to do for your country?

BUSTER: Join the CIA. Become a spy.

DAD: You think you're qualified?

BUSTER: I might need a little training, but imagine the possibilities. I could act like a hungry stray and get a Russian diplomat to take me in. I could listen to top-secret discussions and provide reports. I could read classified documents. I've even thought of a code name for the operation: Spydo.

DAD: You really think you could get away with it?

BUSTER: Nobody's gonna suspect a dog, Dad. If somebody comes in while I'm reading documents, I'll just start chewing on them or hike my leg and fire away. And you really think some underling is going to tell his boss he suspects a dog of reading classified documents? He'd be in Siberia by sundown.

DAD: But if you're living at the embassy, how are you going to report on what you find?

BUSTER: I've already thought of that, Dad. I'll dig a tunnel.

DAD: Now there's a skill you already have.

BUSTER: I'll sneak out, tell my contact what I've learned, then sneak back in.

DAD: I admire your patriotism, but the plan's not foolproof. If they suspect you, they have ways of making you talk.

BUSTER: You really think they're gonna waterboard a dog because he won't talk?

DAD: Good point, but it would still be risky. And you know what they do to spies, Buster.

BUSTER: I do know, and it's scary. But I'm willing to risk it all for my country, to lay down my life if I have to. Though if worse comes to worst, I'll wish I were a cat.

DAD: But you hate cats. Why a cat?

BUSTER: Nine lives, Dad. Dogs, like people, have but one.

DAD: I admire your patriotism, Buster, but I'm afraid there's a flaw in your plan.

BUSTER: I don't think so. I've studied all the angles.

DAD: Think about it, Buster. I can channel you, but you can't actually talk.

BUSTER: Oops.

DAD: Oops is right. And because you can't talk, you can't appear on talk shows or read to children. And you can't report what you've found from your spying.

BUSTER: C'mon, Dad, there's got to be some workaround. There's got to be a solution. My heart is set.

DAD: I don't know what it would be.

BUSTER: I know what we'll do: We'll combine my reading and your channeling. When I come out of the tunnel, you can channel me and tell my contact what I've learned.

DAD: Let's play this out. I tell a member of the intelligence community not only that my dog can read but that I can channel his thoughts. The agent, amazingly enough, says okay and files a classified report about what I've told him. Then, when the brass reads it and questions him about his sources and methods, he says a reading dog and a channeling man.

BUSTER: Sure. What's wrong with that?

DAD: I'll tell you what's wrong with that. If I told that story to the CIA, I'd be the one in Siberia by sundown. Or at least I'd get locked away in the funny farm.

BUSTER: C'mon, Dad. Surely there's got to be a solution. If I can't capitalize on learning to read, I might as well go back to digging for moles.

DAD: Don't do that. I'll tell you what: You lay off the moles, keep reading the dictionary, and I'll try to think of something. You try to think of something too.

BUSTER: I will. I sure hope one of us has an epiphany.

DAD: Epiphany? I thought you were just in the Cs.

BUSTER: I heard Mom tell a friend that she'd had an epiphany about how to get you to pull your weight around here. I didn't know what an epiphany was, so I skipped ahead and looked it up.

DAD: So what was this epiphany Mom had?

BUSTER: You better get it straight from the horse's mouth, but I'll give you a hint. You like it when Mom's affectionate, don't you?

DAD: I see. I do my most creative thinking in the morning. I suggest we both sleep on it and see what we come up with.

BUSTER: Good idea. Right now I'm too upset to think straight. I was sure I'd found a way to punch my ticket to fame and fortune.

DAD: Here's something that will make you feel better: Even if we don't think of a way for you to capitalize on your new skill, you'll be the first dog who gets to experience the joy of reading. I love to read—millions of people do—and you will too. You can even read my books about my hiking trips with Bobby and about my adoption and Julie and Ada Brooks.

BUSTER: I want to monetize my skill, Dad, not waste my time on your silly books.

DAD: You think they're silly? Just wait till you read this one.

BUSTER: This what?

DAD: Nothing. Never mind.

BUSTER: I won't never mind. And I won't never mind on achieving my goal either. I want to be a spy. I want to be Spydo. Then I want to go public and see my picture on the front page of the New York Times. *Above the fold. And I want that villa in Tuscany I've always dreamed of.*

DAD: Get a good night's sleep, and maybe you'll think of something.

BUSTER: But I'm too distraught to sleep.

DAD: I've got an idea to help you doze off.

BUSTER: What's that?

DAD: Read the dictionary.

BUSTER: Very funny, Dad, very funny. You're a regular Jerry Seinfeld.

DAD: Go to sleep, Buster.

My Kingdom For A Thumb

One afternoon last week, Buster and I were playing fetch with a tennis ball. As he was chasing after the ball, I wondered, do dogs realize that we have thumbs and they don't? And if they had thumbs, how would it change their lives? If Buster had thumbs, would he still pick up the tennis ball in his mouth and bring it back? Or would he grab it with a paw and throw it back? Would we play catch instead of fetch?

BUSTER: Dad?

DAD: What, Buster?

BUSTER: I was thinking about human versus canine physiology today, and I've got some questions. You have two legs and two arms, right?

DAD: Right.

BUSTER: But I've got four legs and no arms. And you've got two feet and two hands, but I've got four feet and no hands.

DAD: Also true.

BUSTER: So why don't I have arms and hands? What gives?

DAD: I think it's because people walk upright and dogs don't. If dogs walked upright, their front legs might be called arms and their front paws might be called hands. Some primates walk upright, and they have arms and hands.

BUSTER: Primates? What are primates?

DAD: Actually people are primates, but that's not what I was talking about. Lots of animals are primates too. Chimpanzees, gorillas, orangutans, many more.

BUSTER: I read about chimpanzees in the Cs, but I've never heard of those other animals.

DAD: They have some things in common with you and some things in common with me. They have hair covering most of their bodies like you do.

BUSTER: No bald spot like you, huh?

DAD: But they walk upright like I do.

BUSTER: What do they look like? I want to see them.

DAD: They have lots of them at the zoo. I wish we could take you.

BUSTER: What's the zoo? Why can't you take me?

DAD: A zoo is a place where they have all sorts of animals. Many of them are not native to America.

BUSTER: If they're not native to America, what are they doing here?

DAD: They were brought from other countries so people here could see them.

BUSTER: Taken away from their homes?

DAD: Afraid so.

BUSTER: That's awful. I hope nobody ever takes me away from my home.

DAD: No worries. There's not much demand for mixed-breed hounds in zoos.

BUSTER: Thank goodness, I guess. So at the zoo, do you just walk around with all the animals?

DAD: No, usually they're in cages or behind fences.

BUSTER: Cages? They're not just taken away from their homes, but they're locked up in cages? How emasculating. I'm in the Es now.

DAD: Interesting. Well, the cages are big. Not like a kennel at the vet.

BUSTER: Don't mention the vet. You know how I hate the vet. The people there smile and act all friendly when you drop me and Mollie off, but as soon as you walk out the door, away go the smiles and out come the needles.

DAD: The needles are to give you medicine, Buster. We take you to the vet to keep you healthy.

BUSTER: I said don't talk about it. Why do the animals have to be in cages and behind fences?

DAD: Wouldn't be safe otherwise. Some animals would try to eat others. Some might try to eat people.

BUSTER: If you take me to the zoo and some animal gets out of his cage, I'll protect you.

DAD: Buster, there are animals at the zoo that would eat a little dog like you.

BUSTER: Little? I'm not little. I'm big. And ferocious.

DAD: Ferocious when it comes to Pup-Peroni. Ever heard of a Siberian tiger?

BUSTER: What's that?

DAD: Or a Bengal tiger? Or a lion or a jaguar?

BUSTER: I've heard of a jaguar. My favorite is the '66 E Type.

DAD: Not the car, the cat. All the animals I mentioned—the tigers, the lion, the jaguar—are big cats. They are much bigger than you are, and they eat animals your size.

BUSTER: I don't believe you.

DAD: Buster, I don't lie to you.

BUSTER: Sure you do. And now you've lied to me by saying you don't lie to me. I'm bigger than cats. I should know. I was stuck with a whole herd of unherdable cats at BARK, and I was bigger than all of them.

DAD: But you're not bigger than all kinds of cats. Cats come in all different sizes just like dogs do. You remember that Chihuahua that lived across the street, the one that yapped non-stop.

BUSTER: How could I forget? He never shut up.

DAD: Well, that Chihuahua was a dog.

BUSTER: Really? I thought he was maybe a guinea pig or something.

DAD: A dog, I promise. And you know that huge dog we see sometimes on the walking trail?

BUSTER: You mean the Rottweiler that crazy Mollie acts like she wants to fight?

DAD: That's the one. The Rottweiler is much bigger than the Chihuahua, and the cats at the zoo are much bigger than the cats at BARK.

BUSTER: I'm having a hard time picturing a cat that's bigger than I am. Just how big are these big cats?

DAD: The biggest of all is the Siberian tiger. One can weigh more than 600 pounds. That's more than ten times as much as you weigh. And one of them could eat you for a snack.

BUSTER: I don't think so.

DAD: And why not?

BUSTER: Because I'm very fast. I'm the Secretariat of hounds.

DAD: And the Jeff Bezos as well. But I don't think you're faster than a tiger.

BUSTER: But I won't have to be. If a tiger starts chasing us, I won't have to outrun him. I'll just have to outrun you, which will be a piece of cake. I won't be the one getting eaten.

DAD: And all this time, I thought you were man's best friend.

BUSTER: Being man's best friend doesn't include volunteering to get eaten by a Siberian tiger, Dad. I love you, but don't you think that's a bridge too far?

DAD: I guess I know where I stand.

BUSTER: Yep, between me and the tiger. Listen, we've got to go to the zoo so I can see these big cats and all the other animals. The gorilla and that orange thing.

DAD: Orangutan.

BUSTER: Whatever.

DAD: I'll find out if you can go, but don't get your hopes up. The people who run the zoo probably won't let you. Dogs are natural prey of some zoo animals and natural predators of others.

BUSTER: As for being a predator, tell them I lead a life of leisure and my predatory instincts disappeared long ago. I'm a danger only to Pup-Peroni or a bowl of Rocky Road. And as for being prey, if some big animal escapes from his cage and chases me, I'll get in the car and lock the doors. I'll be safe from the big animals, and the little animals will be safe from me. Even if they have a general no-dog rule, surely they'll make an exception.

DAD: I'll point out that you're totally harmless, but I still think it's a long shot.

BUSTER: Well, there's no harm in asking. Let's get back to the primate thing. If I'm not a primate, what am I?

DAD: Dogs are members of an order called carnivores. So are bears and wolves and cats, big and small.

BUSTER: Are you telling me I'm more closely related to a cat than to my own father?

DAD: Afraid so.

BUSTER: I don't accept that. What makes primates different from carnivores? Just walking upright and having hands instead of feet? That's not much.

DAD: For one thing, primates' brains are more advanced than carnivores'.

BUSTER: What? I resent that. I've never met one of those orange things, but I'll pit my brain against one of theirs any day.

DAD: Orangutan.

BUSTER: Whatever.

DAD: You'd be more convincing about your brain if you'd quit calling them orange things. I hate to break it to you, Buster, but it's a scientific fact that primates' brains are more advanced than dogs' brains.

BUSTER: All dogs, Dad? You're not saying all primates are smarter than all dogs, are you?

DAD: I didn't say that.

BUSTER: And you're not saying all primates are smarter than I am, are you?

DAD: I'm not saying that either.

BUSTER: And scientists haven't studied my brain, have they?

DAD: No, but they should.

BUSTER: And since scientists haven't studied me, there's no evidence that primates are smarter than I am, is there?

DAD: I guess not. And you're not an average dog.

BUSTER: Thank you for acknowledging the obvious. You got anything else on the primate versus carnivore issue? Anything else primates supposedly have that I don't?

DAD: One more. Thumbs.

BUSTER: Thumbs? What are thumbs?

DAD: Look at my hand. You see the short finger on the end that sticks out by itself? That's my thumb. And see how it folds into the middle of my hand. It's called an opposable thumb. It's what allows me to grab things. Most primates have thumbs. Dogs don't.

BUSTER: Wow. I never noticed that. I bet having a thumb comes in handy. Handy—get it?

DAD: You have no idea how handy. I use my thumbs from the time I wake up in the morning until I go to sleep at night. From putting on my robe to holding the book I read in bed. And I use them for everything in between. Driving, writing, eating, you name it.

BUSTER: But if thumbs are so great, why don't I have them?

DAD: That's another God question. Ask him.

BUSTER: I will ask because I'd like to hear God try to defend my lack of thumbs. It looks to me like yet another example of how dogs are always getting shafted. We don't live as long as people do, we're supposedly not as smart as some orange whatchamacallits, some huge cat on steroids could eat us, and we don't have thumbs.

DAD: Once again, take it up with God. But I don't think life is so hard for you. Not many dogs get bacon and eggs.

BUSTER: This isn't about breakfast food, Dad, this is about thumbs. And the fact that dogs have been wrongfully deprived of them.

DAD: But you don't need thumbs, Buster. You don't grab things. You don't use utensils; you eat straight from your bowl. You don't drive a car, and you don't brush your teeth.

BUSTER: And just why is it that I do none of those things, Dad? Because I don't have thumbs, *that's why. If I did, I just might eat with a knife and fork like you and Mom. And I might enjoy a nice glass of Cabernet too.*

DAD: I'd love to see that. The dog who reads, talks, eats with utensils, and enjoys fine wine.

BUSTER: I can't actually talk, remember?

DAD: You can't eat with a knife and fork either because you don't have thumbs.

BUSTER: It's a travesty. You know why you think I don't need thumbs, Dad?

DAD: No, but I'm sure you do.

BUSTER: Because I don't have thumbs, *that's why. You say I don't need thumbs because I eat out of a bowl. I say I eat out of a bowl because I don't have thumbs.*

DAD: Interesting. I've never thought of it like that.

BUSTER: Just think of all I could do if I had thumbs, Dad. I could work the TV remote, open the top of the Pup-Peroni jar, and fetch a tennis ball with my paws instead of my mouth.

DAD: But you love fetching a tennis ball with your mouth.

BUSTER: Have you ever put a tennis ball in your mouth, Dad? And gotten that yucky yellow fuzz stuck to your tongue? I'm guessing not.

DAD: You're guessing right.

BUSTER: If I had thumbs, I not only could fetch the tennis ball with my paw, I could throw it and you could chase it. And while you're running after it, you could channel me and say, "Fetch, old man."

DAD: Not gonna happen, Buster. You're never gonna have thumbs. Get over it. And we'll never know if you're the way you are because you don't have thumbs or if you don't have thumbs because you're the way you are. It's a question with no answer, sort of like which came first, the chicken or the egg?

BUSTER: The chicken came first, Dad. Duh.

DAD: But don't all chickens come from eggs? If the chicken came first, where did it come from?

BUSTER: But if the egg came first, who laid it? A thumbless chicken, that's who.

DAD: A thumbless chicken that hatched from an egg. The point is, there's no way to know which came first. Just like the question about you and thumbs. But the fact is, through the many thousands of years there have been dogs in the world, they have not evolved to have thumbs.

BUSTER: Evolved? What's evolved?

DAD: You exhaust me, Buster.

BUSTER: Don't blame me, Dad. You brought it up. And don't blame me for being curious. You're just as curious as I am. You look up stuff on your stupid iPhone all day long.

DAD: With my thumbs.

BUSTER: Very funny. I've just learned that I'm missing a crucial body part, and all you can do is make jokes.

DAD: It's not a tragedy that you don't have thumbs, Buster. You've never had them. No dog has ever had them.

BUSTER: I don't know what evolved means, but I demand to know why dogs don't have thumbs.

DAD: Talk to God about it. In fact, talk to him about it right now. It's past your bedtime.

BUSTER: You expect me to be able to sleep after this? I don't know why you tell me these things. Now I'll get mad whenever I look down at my thumbless paws. It's not fair, Dad.

DAD: Life's not fair, Buster. Goodnight.

Sniffing The World

Buster and Mollie are pacifists by nature. Neither of them has ever bitten a person or another dog. There's not an aggressive bone in their bodies, except when they're on leashes. Then, for some reason, they're transformed into vicious attack dogs. We pass another dog on the trail, and they growl and strain, wanting to get at him.

I've seen other dogs act the same way. If they met alone in a park, they would go through the sniffing routine and become friends. But when they're on leashes, they act like sworn enemies. So what's the deal? Maybe when they're on a leash, I wondered, their instinct is to defend the person holding it. Or maybe it's something else. Last night I found out.

BUSTER: Dad?

DAD: What, Buster?

BUSTER: Why can't we go for a walk every day?

DAD: Lots of reasons. Sometimes I need to get to work early, sometimes it rains, and sometimes it's too hot, especially for somebody who's covered in fur from head to tail.

BUSTER: C'mon, Dad. The work will still be there, and getting a little damp doesn't bother a robust dog like me. As for hot days, we can take rest breaks in the shade, and you can make sure we hydrate.

DAD: Hydrate. Interesting.

BUSTER: Or you can set the alarm and we'll go before dawn. No telling the fauna we'll see if we go then. I'm in the Fs now.

DAD: You can forget about going before dawn. I'm not a farmer, and I'm not getting up before the sun does. I take you whenever I can, Buster, but I can't take you every day.

BUSTER: Have a heart, Dad. You know how I love our walks. You see how excited I get when we're about to go for one.

DAD: You do make a spectacle of yourself.

BUSTER: It's only natural, Dad.

DAD: Natural? I don't think it's natural for a dog to squeal like a pig or spin like a whirling dervish.

BUSTER: What's a whirling dervish?

DAD: It's a member of some religion—I'm not sure which one —but I know that one of the things they do is spin in circles.

BUSTER: Like a Tasmanian Devil?

DAD: And like you. And speaking of you, I thought the squealing and spinning were all just an act.

BUSTER: It is when you and Mom walk in the door, but not when I realize we're about to go for a walk. Then it's the real deal, I assure you. When I see you put on your shorts and walking shoes, I go a little bit crazy. And when you get the leashes, well, you see what happens.

DAD: So I guess going for a walk makes you happier than seeing Mom and me.

BUSTER: Don't play the victim, Dad. Going for walks and seeing y'all both make me happy. But you come home every day. I'm glad to see you, sure, but it's no surprise. Your arrival time may vary, but you always arrive. But walks are different. I never know when I'll get to go for one. I get my hopes up every morning. Sometimes they're dashed, but when they're not, it's game on.

DAD: So you would be calm if we went for a walk every day, is that what you're saying?

BUSTER: I can't make any promises, Dad, though I sure would try if we could go every day. And I should start acting calmer now that I'm getting on up in years.

DAD: On up in years? Really?

BUSTER: I'm sure you remember when you told me that I'm already grown. And that dogs don't live as long as people do. Well, I'm even older now, I'm aging seven times as fast as you are, and I've been doing some soul-searching. I've been forced to come to grips with the fact that

I will shuffle off this mortal coil in the not-too-distant future. I need to prepare to meet my maker, get my affairs in order.

DAD: Exactly what affairs do you have, Buster?

BUSTER: It's just an expression, Dad. Back to why I go bonkers. It's not just that a walk is a special treat—lagniappe, let's call it—but it's the only opportunity Mollie and I have to get out and about and see things.

DAD: Why do you need to get out and about? We have a nice house, you have your own beds, and we have a backyard that's your own personal restroom.

BUSTER: I'm a dog, Dad. I don't have a personal anything. And it may be nice here, but without walks, every day's the same. Wake up, go outside, use my so-called personal restroom, come in, have a snack, take a nap, lather, rinse, repeat. Same sights, same smells, same everything.

DAD: A lot of dogs would love to swap places with you, Buster.

BUSTER: I know that. I came from a shelter filled with filthy felines, remember? I'm just trying to get you to understand why I get so excited. I think of walks as my chance to see the world.

DAD: The world? Really?

BUSTER: At least a little corner of it. Think about it, Dad. On the walking trail, we see all kinds of people, white and black, old and young, fat and skinny. Some are walking, some running, some riding bikes. Some even ride those goofy recumbent bikes. By the way, here's an amusing aside. It always tickles me when a biker approaches us from behind and yells out, "passing on your left," or words to that effect. Do those bikers in their ridiculous shorts really think dogs know left from right? I know, but I daresay I'm the exception to the rule.

DAD: You're the exception to every rule, Buster.

BUSTER: Where was I? Oh, yeah, I was about to talk about the aromas. You probably don't realize this, but on every walk I encounter new and different smells I've never smelled before. Delectable smells. Mysterious smells. Smells are a big deal to all dogs, Dad, and they're a huge deal to me. I'm a hound after all. I was born to sniff.

DAD: I hadn't thought about the smells.

BUSTER: No surprise there. You couldn't smell a dead skunk if someone whopped you upside the head with it. In addition to the people, we get to see and smell all kinds of dogs. All shapes and colors, all fragrances and sizes. I didn't know dogs got to be as big as some of the ones we see.

DAD: That reminds me of something I've been meaning to ask you. Mollie is a little dog, and you're medium-sized.

BUSTER: I'm big, Dad. I've told you that. I'm in the top 40 percent, if not the top quartile.

DAD: In terms of vocabulary, no doubt, but in terms of size, you're not half as big as the German shepherds and the Rottweiler we see on the trail.

BUSTER: I can't argue with that. The shepherds are huge, and that Rottweiler's enormous. I'd like to throw a saddle on that bad boy and take him for a spin. So what's your question?

DAD: Well, I've never seen you or Mollie bite a person or an animal or get in any kind of fight. Mollie's the gentlest dog I've ever known. But when we see other dogs on the trail, both of you act like attack dogs, straining at your leashes. And it doesn't matter if the dogs are twice as big as you are and four times as big as she is. So my question is this: What on earth are you thinking?

BUSTER: It's like this, Dad. As you said, we act *like attack dogs, but that doesn't mean we* are *attack dogs. I could be tough if I wanted to, but not Mollie. She's a complete wimp, and she knows it. The way Mom treats her like a baby is embarrassing.*

DAD: She doesn't look very embarrassed when she sits in Mom's lap and gets a belly rub.

BUSTER: But she is embarrassed, I promise. I know her better than anybody does. She knows she's a wimp, and she's self-conscious about it. Acting like she wants to attack another dog, especially a big dog, is her chance to act tough.

DAD: But she tries to attack dogs that are big enough to chew her up and spit her out, and you're right there with her, straining at your leash too.

BUSTER: I'm her wing man, Dad. What can I say?

DAD: I don't get it. Yesterday morning y'all tried to attack that huge pair of German shepherds. Do you have a death wish?

BUSTER: Dad, do you really think we're stupid enough to get into a fight with two dogs that big? Two dogs that could eat us alive?

DAD: You don't want me to answer that, Buster.

BUSTER: Then I'll answer it. We're not. Even Mollie, who is the product of many generations of in-breeding, bless her heart, has more sense than to fight a dog four times her size.

DAD: But y'all were doing everything you could to attack them. Both of you. It was all I could do to hold you back.

BUSTER: Pretty convincing, huh? But we weren't really trying to attack them. The leashes are the essential prop in our little act. With you holding them, we can act tough without having to be tough. It's a nice reward with no risk. And Mollie acts tougher than I do because she's not as tough as I am.

DAD: Mollie's not as tough as anybody.

BUSTER: Agreed. That old expression—a dog's bark is worse than his bite—fits Mollie to a T. She barks her fool head off, but it takes all she's got to chew up a chunk of dry Purina.

DAD: Okay, I get it, but as a favor to me, can you just knock it off? It's embarrassing when my very own fur children act like attack dogs. It makes me look like I can't control you, it makes you look mean and, when you try to attack those German shepherds, it makes you look stupid too.

BUSTER: I've told Mollie it's ridiculous, but she won't listen to reason.

DAD: Well, tell her this: Tell her if she doesn't stop, I'll leave y'all at home. I can go for walks by myself, you know.

BUSTER: I could tell her that, but she'd know you were bluffing. She knows you love us too much to leave us cooped up in the house while you go off traipsing through the woods. But I have thought of one thing that might work.

DAD: What's that?

BUSTER: Next time she goes into attack mode and she's straining at her leash, drop it.

DAD: Drop it?

BUSTER: Drop the leash. You'll need to be careful and break up the fight pretty quick so she won't get hurt bad, but there might not even be a fight. When she realizes you're not holding her back, she might just hold herself back. She might hide behind you, quivering. It's funny: Being restrained is what gives her the liberty to act tough.

DAD: You really think it might work? Mom would kill me if Mollie got hurt because I let go of the leash and let her get into a fight.

BUSTER: You can't tell Mom the truth, you dummy. If Mollie gets hurt, tell Mom the other guy dropped his dog's leash.

DAD: I'll consider it, but it seems risky.

BUSTER: Life is filled with risks, Dad, and if you want to break Mollie of a bad habit, you have to be willing to take this one. But pick out the right dog so she won't get chewed to pieces right before my very eyes. Talk about your guilt and your PTSD. I would be an emotional wreck.

DAD: I'll think about it.

BUSTER: But if you're not sure you can keep Mollie from getting mangled, don't try it. In addition to the emotional trauma I would suffer, I can't imagine what it would be like to live without her by my side. Having to follow the very same routine day after day after day is hard enough even when you have a trusted companion to follow it with you. I don't want to go through this vale of tears alone.

DAD: But if something happened to Mollie, you would still have Mom and me.

BUSTER: But would y'all stay home all day and keep me company? If I had to spend all day by myself, I might develop real separation anxiety, not the faux kind, and it might be exacerbated by the PTSD. Exacerbate means to make something bad even worse, by the way.

DAD: I know what it means. No, we wouldn't be able to stay home all day, but I'll be careful if I go with your drop-the-leash scheme.

BUSTER: Thank you. Since it was my idea, I could never forgive myself if something happened to Mollie. Forgive you either.

DAD: I'll be careful and, if it works, I'll take y'all for walks as often as I can so the two of you can see the world.

BUSTER: And sniff it. I want to sniff it all, Dad. I want to smell everything there is to smell.

DAD: You need your rest if you're going to be ready for a walk in the morning. Maybe we'll take a different route so you can see and smell a different part of the world.

BUSTER: Sweet! You better get some rest too, Dad.

DAD: I will, but first I need to talk to Mom and see what she says. I couldn't lie to her about the great horned owl that tried to attack Mollie down by the lake, and I don't think I can lie to her about the drop-the-leash plan.

BUSTER: Sometimes I wonder about you, Dad. You're like a lot of people, a fancy education with letters after your name but not a lick of common sense. And now you've gone from dumb to dumber.

DAD: How so?

BUSTER: You know what happened when you told Mom about the owl? Mom made you hire some stupid guy to move the stupid fence to keep us hemmed in next to the house. And who was the victim? I was, as usual. I lost countless sniffing opportunities because you told Mom about the stupid bird. You tell her about my plan, and she'll put the kibosh on it for sure.

DAD: You may be right.

BUSTER: I am right. And what do you think she'll do if you say you got the idea from me?

DAD: I don't know. What?

BUSTER: Have you committed, that's what. Just the other day, I heard Mom tell one of her friends she was afraid you were losing your marbles.

DAD: Did not.

BUSTER: Did too. And who can blame her? You said you'd wind up in the funny farm if you told the CIA you could channel me.

DAD: But Mom knows I channel you.

BUSTER: She used to think you were just joking, but now she's decided you believe you really do channel me. At least that's what she told her friend.

DAD: But I really do channel you.

BUSTER: I know that, and you know that, but we have no way to prove it. And if you tell Mom that it was my idea to let Mollie fight another dog, that might just be the last straw. She might just summon an Uber and get the driver to take you straight to the nuthouse.

DAD: You think?

BUSTER: I know. You need to do one of two things: Lie to Mom, deny dropping the leash, and break Mollie of a bad habit. Or drop the idea, not the leash, and Mollie will keep imdoganating a deadly Doberman.

DAD: Imdoganating?

BUSTER: Sure. You can't very well impersonate a dog.

DAD: Interesting. Maybe you're right about not telling Mom. What do you think I should do?

BUSTER: Easy call. Lie to Mom and teach Mollie a lesson. It's the only way to get her to knock it off.

DAD: You're not much of a role model, Buster. Goodnight.

Call Of The Wild

Choosing between a life of comfort and a life of adventure has been a dilemma through the ages. There are many issues to consider: three healthy but boring meals a day versus living off the land; a soft bed versus sleeping under the stars; reliable health care versus no more trips to the doctor; central heat versus a campfire; a ceiling fan versus a cool lake breeze. Since the nation's founding, Americans have struggled to decide between a life of ease and a life of exhilaration. And so it is with Buster.

BUSTER: Dad?

DAD: What, Buster?

BUSTER: What are those brown animals we see when we're on the walking trail?

DAD: You mean other dogs?

BUSTER: I know what dogs look like, Dad. After all, I am a dog. I mean the animals with the long legs and the huge ears. The ones that stick their tails straight up when they go bounding through the woods.

DAD: Those are white-tailed deer. Why are you interested in deer?

BUSTER: I want to bring one home to live with us.

DAD: Why?

BUSTER: Because they're beautiful, that's why. They're easy on the eye.

DAD: They're certainly attractive.

BUSTER: They're more than attractive. They're gorgeous. If they weren't a different species, I'd ask one out.

DAD: But no matter how gorgeous they are, you can't bring one home.

BUSTER: Why not?

DAD: Because they're wild animals.

BUSTER: Are not. I've watched them. They stand there in the woods, perfectly still, not moving a muscle. They're the picture of serenity, the polar opposite of wild.

DAD: I'm not saying they *act* wild. I'm saying they *are* wild.

BUSTER: Act, are—what's the diff? If they can't live with us because they're wild animals, how do I get to live with us? We've both seen how wild I can act. You know how I get when we're about to go for a walk. I'm wilder than the Kardashians. I've never seen a deer act nearly as wild as I do. Deer are calm, and having one live with us would have a calming influence on me.

DAD: Maybe so, but I'm not talking wild versus calm. I'm talking wild versus domesticated.

BUSTER: Domesticated? What's domesticated? I don't remember that in the Ds.

DAD: Domesticated animals are animals that live with people as pets or on farms.

BUSTER: We don't live on a farm, Dad, so are you saying you think I'm a pet? If so, think again. I'm your son, not your pet. Are we clear on that?

DAD: Sorry. Forget I said pet. Let's just say living with people then. As father and son or as farm animals.

BUSTER: Or father and daughter. Don't forget Mollie.

DAD: Or mother and daughter. Don't forget Mom.

BUSTER: Forget Mom? Are you kidding? She's the purveyor of Pup-Peroni, the baker of bacon, and the enabler of eggs.

DAD: Enabler of eggs?

BUSTER: Sure. She enables us to eat eggs. Plus I'm all about alliteration. So domesticated animals live with people and wild animals don't?

DAD: That's right.

BUSTER: And deer are wild animals because they don't live with people?

DAD: You've never seen a person walking in the woods with a deer, have you?

BUSTER: Come to think of it, I haven't.

DAD: And you've never seen a deer on a leash either.

BUSTER: I've definitely never seen that. I would remember a deer on a leash.

DAD: The reason you haven't seen it is that deer are wild animals. They don't live with people, and one can't live with us.

BUSTER: But why? Why are deer wild but dogs domesticated? We both have four legs. We're both covered in fur.

DAD: That's another God question, Buster.

BUSTER: C'mon, Dad, you're bound to have some idea.

DAD: Well, I don't know the whole story, but I know some of it. Over many thousands of years, some animals came to live with people, and some didn't. Dogs, who descended from wolves, are some that did. Deer didn't.

BUSTER: Whoa, whoa, whoa, did I hear you right? Did you just say that dogs descended from wolves? My ancestors were wolves?

DAD: That's right. If you go back far enough.

BUSTER: Well, that's got to be the coolest thing I've ever heard. Buster the hound, great-grandson of a wolf.

DAD: I should've told you before now.

BUSTER: Wait a minute. What about Mollie? Are you saying her ancestors were wolves too?

DAD: That's the way I understand it.

BUSTER: You expect me to believe that? That the wimpy little cocker spaniel is related to wolves? That the lap dog who loves belly rubs and is afraid of her shadow is related to predators who roam the tundra and hunt caribou?

DAD: I know it's hard to believe, but from what I've read, all dogs are descendants of wolves.

BUSTER: Bummer. It would be way cooler if I descended from wolves and Mollie descended from possums or something.

DAD: Sorry. You asked, so I told you.

BUSTER: Listen, please don't let Mollie know her ancestors were wolves. You think she likes to act tough on our walks now. Just imagine how she'll act if she finds out her great-grandfather was a timber wolf.

DAD: I won't tell her. Scout's honor.

BUSTER: Here's a question, Dad: Which is better, wild or domesticated? What would you rather be?

DAD: That's hard to say, Buster. There are some good things about both. It depends on the animal.

BUSTER: How so? Seems like it should be one size fits all.

DAD: Well, for instance, think about a red-tailed hawk, a wild animal, and a chicken, a domesticated animal. I'd much rather be a hawk than a chicken. Hawks live in nature. They can fly wherever they want. Chickens live in crowded chicken coops. They are raised to lay eggs for people to eat, and sometimes dogs, and to get eaten themselves.

BUSTER: Eaten themselves? Who eats chickens?

DAD: People do.

BUSTER: That's disgusting. What about the feathers? Talk about your bad mouth feel.

DAD: The feathers get removed first. And people eat lots of animals, Buster.

BUSTER: Not dogs, surely. Please tell me people don't eat dogs, Dad.

DAD: Actually in some places they do.

BUSTER: You said in some places. At least tell me this isn't one of those places.

DAD: It's not. You're safe here. Nobody is going to eat you.

BUSTER: Well, if anybody tries, I hope you'll have my back.

DAD: Of course I will. I wouldn't let anyone eat my own son.

BUSTER: So being a wild hawk is better than being a domesticated chicken. That seems obvious enough. But is it ever better to be domesticated than wild?

DAD: Sure. Consider a cat and a mouse. A cat gets to lie around all day sleeping. All its food is provided in a nice bowl. It never has to lift a paw.

BUSTER: Watch it, Dad. You're getting a little close to home there.

DAD: But a mouse has to find all its own food. And it has to be on constant watch so it won't get eaten by a cat or a hawk or some other animal.

BUSTER: I thought you said a cat's food is provided in a bowl.

DAD: All the food a cat needs is. I think cats eat mice just for fun, and for snacks.

BUSTER: That's just wrong. Poor little mice. What did they ever do to anybody other than make those annoying squeaky noises?

DAD: I hate to tell you this, Buster, but dogs have been known to eat cats.

BUSTER: I've got no problem with that.

DAD: That seems like a double standard to me.

BUSTER: Dad, removing a cat from the gene pool should be viewed as a public service.

DAD: I like cats.

BUSTER: Only weird people like cats.

DAD: I channel dogs, Buster.

BUSTER: Touché. Let's get back to the issue at paw. Here's what I really want to know: Is it better to be a dog or a deer?

DAD: That's hard to say. There are some things I would like about being a deer.

BUSTER: Like what?

DAD: Well, as you said yourself, they're beautiful.

BUSTER: I never said they were better looking than I am.

DAD: But they're better looking than most dogs, don't you think?

BUSTER: Granted. What else?

DAD: Freedom. Deer can go where they want to go, roam the woods, see new sights.

BUSTER: And smell new smells?

DAD: I guess so. And deer never have to live in shelters, and they never get neutered. They can mate and have baby deer called fawns.

BUSTER: That settles it. I would rather be a deer. I'd love to have a baby Buster to carry on my name.

DAD: Not so fast. Let's think about the things that you have that deer don't.

BUSTER: Like what?

DAD: First of all, we provide all your food. Deer have to find their own.

BUSTER: That means they get to eat what they want, doesn't it?

DAD: They do, at least if they can find it.

BUSTER: I wouldn't mind getting my own food if I could eat what I wanted. We'll put food in the deer column.

DAD: Well, deer don't get bacon and cheese, I promise you that. And they sure don't get Pup-Peroni.

BUSTER: You didn't tell me that. So deer can eat what they want, but selections are limited. We'll call food a draw. What else?

DAD: Well, if you're sick or need a shot, we take you to the vet. Deer get no medical care.

BUSTER: And you think that's a plus for dogs? Wrong, wrong, a thousand times wrong. I'd rather be sick, sore, and lame then go to the vet. We'll put that down as a big plus for deer. You better come up with something big because deer are in the lead, and the lead is growing.

DAD: Okay, how about this one? Deer have to stay outside, no matter how hot, no matter how cold, even if it's raining.

BUSTER: Even if it's raining? Are you saying they don't even have a screened porch?

DAD: No porch.

BUSTER: Do they at least get to sleep inside?

DAD: No. They never get to come inside. For wild animals, there is no inside.

BUSTER: So no bed with a foam mattress like mine, I'm guessing.

DAD: You're guessing right. Maybe a bed of pine needles.

BUSTER: Ouch, prickly. No air conditioning either, I guess.

DAD: And no heat.

BUSTER: Ceiling fans?

DAD: None.

BUSTER: I guess I'll put getting to come inside in the dog column. I love me some AC. And getting up on the couch when you're gone.

DAD: Getting up on the what?

BUSTER: Nothing, Dad. I misspoke.

DAD: Yeah, right. Even though you misspoke and you don't get up on the couch, your life is much easier and more comfortable than a deer's life. On balance, don't you think it's better to be a dog?

BUSTER: But you forget how tough I am, Dad. Unlike Mollie, I don't just act tough. Plus I love adventure. I've still got deer in the lead. If you don't have anything else, I'm voting for deer.

DAD: I do have something else.

BUSTER: What?

DAD: Deer season.

BUSTER: Deer season? I thought winter, spring, summer, and fall were all the seasons. I've never heard of a season called deer. Tell me about this so-called deer season.

DAD: It's when people get to shoot deer.

BUSTER: Do what?

DAD: You heard me. It's a set time in the fall and winter when it's legal for people to shoot deer.

BUSTER: You mean with a gun?

DAD: Or a bow and arrow.

BUSTER: Why would anybody want to shoot a deer?

DAD: People do it for sport. Also for meat. Deer are one of the animals people eat. The meat is called venison. People love it.

BUSTER: But deer are beautiful, Dad. How could anybody shoot a deer?

DAD: I'm with you, buddy. You don't see me hunting deer.

BUSTER: If people want to shoot an animal and eat it, why not a possum? They're some kind of ugly. Ever had one bare its teeth at you?

DAD: Deer are more attractive than possums. Nobody could argue with that, other than maybe a possum. But I don't think beauty should be the test of whether an animal gets eaten.

BUSTER: I do. Then I'd be in the clear.

DAD: You know, Buster, a little humility would make you a better dog. You should try it.

BUSTER: I've tried, Dad, really I have. But when I walk past a mirror, it's all I can do not to lick the glass.

DAD: If Carly Simon hadn't written "You're So Vain" before you were born, I would think she wrote it about you.

BUSTER: I hear songs that I think are about me all the time.

DAD: Of course you do. Anyway, deer season is something you need to consider.

BUSTER: I think I'd be safe.

DAD: And why is that?

BUSTER: Again, Dad, my looks. Nobody is going to shoot an animal that looks like me.

DAD: But if you were a deer, you wouldn't look like you.

BUSTER: Fair point.

DAD: And even if you did, I don't think the best-looking deer get a pass during deer season. People want to shoot handsome bucks—they're male deer—so they can mount their heads on the wall.

BUSTER: People are barbaric. So deer season is a downside, but it's not all bad. It's dangerous, but it's bound to be exhilarating, what with dodging bullets and arrows and all.

DAD: Exhilarating until one hits you.

BUSTER: But even if my looks wouldn't protect me, I still think I'd be okay.

DAD: Why is that?

BUSTER: Speed, Dad, blazing speed. I'm as fast as the wind. You've seen me run. Here one second, there the next. I move faster than Scotty beamed people up.

DAD: You're not as fast as a bullet, Buster. You're not even as fast as a deer.

BUSTER: But just imagine how fast I'd be if I were a deer. With my natural athleticism and legs that long, I'd be nothing but a blur.

DAD: Buster Eason, deer sprinter.

BUSTER: So I think I'd be safe. Faster than a speeding bullet, more powerful than a locomotive.

DAD: Super Buster.

BUSTER: Super Buster, descendant of the titans of the tundra. But there might still be some slight risk. I shouldn't be overconfident.

DAD: Overconfident? You?

BUSTER: Acorn doesn't fall far, Dad.

DAD: So what's it going to be, Super Buster? Dog or deer?

BUSTER: I can't decide, Dad. I love the life I have, I really do. But I've always been drawn to the great outdoors. I want to test my mettle in the wilderness. Call it the call of the wild.

DAD: I think somebody else has already called it that, but whatever. Dog or deer? Make up your mind. Fish or cut bait.

BUSTER: Fish or cut bait? I thought we were talking about dog or deer.

DAD: Never mind. Just decide.

BUSTER: Help me out here. Is there anything else I should know?

DAD: Well, there's one more thing. You need to keep in mind that wild animals don't have human parents.

BUSTER: You mean you wouldn't be my dad?

DAD: No man would.

BUSTER: I wouldn't have anybody to take me for walks?

DAD: You'd have to go by yourself.

BUSTER: Or scratch me behind my ears?

DAD: That either.

BUSTER: Or rub my belly?

DAD: No more rubbing.

BUSTER: What about our talks, Dad? Would there at least be someone to channel me? To express my innermost thoughts and feelings?

DAD: I'm afraid not, Buster. No more channeling.

BUSTER: But I've got a lot to say, Dad. Important things. It's not fair.

DAD: But life's not fair. I've told you that. Life is all about trade-offs. If you answer the call of the wild, there are some things you'll have to give up.

BUSTER: Lots of things, it sounds like to me.

DAD: Well, there's having someone to channel you. And Mollie and Mom and me. And bacon and cheese and Pup-Peroni and a bed with a foam mattress and a screened porch to get out of the rain. And air conditioning when you come inside and that couch you don't get up on. And not getting shot at, don't forget that.

BUSTER: Boy, when you put it like that, I really do have it good, don't I?

DAD: So do I, but don't forget the adventure and exhilaration of being a deer. Don't forget the call of the wild.

BUSTER: That call's getting weaker and weaker. A minute ago, it was loud and clear, but now I can barely hear it.

DAD: Is that right?

BUSTER: There's this expression, Dad. You may have heard it. The grass is always greener on the other side. And what that means is . . . .

DAD: I know what it means, Buster.

BUSTER: There's also a line from a song I heard—that you don't know what you've got till it's gone.

DAD: Joni Mitchell. "Yellow Taxi."

BUSTER: What?

DAD: That's the songwriter and the song. And it's not about you.

BUSTER: I like the song—paved paradise is great alliteration—but I disagree with one thing. I don't think you actually have to lose something to appreciate having it. I think it's enough just to understand what it would be like without it.

DAD: I hear you. We should all count our blessings.

BUSTER: I'm thinking of the runaway bunny again, Dad, and I'm thinking I might just as well stay where I am and be your Super Buster.

DAD: Good. I would miss you if you left home and became a deer.

BUSTER: I'm not leaving. I'm staying here, and I'm staying a dog.

DAD: I'm very relieved.

BUSTER: Me too. I was really torn there for a minute. I was thinking, on the one paw dog, on the other paw deer. You sure we can't bring one home to live with us?

DAD: I'm sure. Go to sleep, Buster.

Night Noizz

I'm told that I snore, and I believe it. Carrie is not the only one who's told me. My camping buddies complain about it too, though some of them are throwing stones from a very loud glass house when they do.

Snoring is not an attractive trait, but it's a common one among men of a certain age. And though I'm surprised to find that I'm as old as I am, there's no denying either my age or the noise I make at night. But I'm not the only in our family who snores. Misery loves company, and it pleases me that there's someone else to share the blame.

BUSTER: Dad?

DAD: What, Buster?

BUSTER: Your snoring has become intolerable.

DAD: Sorry, Buster, but I can't help it.

BUSTER: But it's awful. Sometimes I think there's a freight train coming through the bedroom.

DAD: I said I'm sorry. But I'm not the only one. You snore too, you know.

BUSTER: What? I deny it.

DAD: It's true, I promise.

BUSTER: But I've never heard me snore.

DAD: That's because you're asleep. I've never heard me snore either.

BUSTER: You're making it up. You think the best defense is a good offense, but I can see through your tricks.

DAD: Want me to record you and play it back the next morning?

BUSTER: How would I know I was the one doing the snoring? You could record somebody else and falsely claim I'm the guilty party. For that matter, you could record yourself.

DAD: I'll video you too.

BUSTER: I really snore? I thought only people snored.

DAD: Before you came along, I thought so too.

BUSTER: Well, if I do snore, I'm not as loud as you.

DAD: How could you possibly know how loud you snore? You're asleep.

BUSTER: Two reasons: First, if I snored as loud as you do, I would wake myself up. We both know that I have far better hearing than the other party to this conversation. And second, Mom has never had to abandon her own bedroom and sleep somewhere else to escape my snoring. You can't say that about yourself.

DAD: Again, Buster, how do you know? If Mom leaves, how do you know you're not the one sawing logs?

BUSTER: Sawing logs? I thought we were talking about snoring.

DAD: Sawing logs is an expression for snoring because snoring sounds kind of like someone sawing a log. Back to my question: How do you know it's not your snoring that makes Mom leave the room?

BUSTER: Because your snoring is so loud it wakes me up even when I'm across the room under my dog bed with my paws over my ears. When you're the one who's sawing logs, it sounds like it's with a chainsaw. And when I'm lying there wondering if you'll ever knock it off so I can get some sleep, Mom gets out of bed, looks at you, shakes her head, and walks out the door.

DAD: Ouch. She really does that?

BUSTER: You find her in the guest room in the morning, don't you? The poor woman is a refugee from night noise. Mom loves you, and she deserves better. You know how she needs her sleep.

DAD: But I can't help it. If I could, I would. But just because I'm guilty some of the time doesn't mean I'm guilty all of the time.

BUSTER: Sure you are.

DAD: How do you know? How could you possibly know?

BUSTER: Here's how. As both of us are prone to forget, I'm a dog.

Not an average dog, granted, but still a dog. And Mom wouldn't leave her own husband and her own bed in her own bedroom and go sleep by herself because I was snoring. She'd wake me up and make me go sleep in the guest room.

DAD: I'm not so sure. You know how she spoils you and Mollie.

BUSTER: Mollie more than me and you most of all. What's more rotten than rotten? Whatever it is, that's how spoiled you are.

DAD: Well, she's very good to you and me, and it would be better if neither of us snored.

BUSTER: Especially you. But how can we stop? You've already said at least twice that you can't help it. And assuming for the sake of argument that I snore too, which I don't concede, I don't know how I could help it either.

DAD: If I lost some weight, I think I might not snore as much. That might help you too. Neither of us is obese, but we could both stand to lose a few pounds.

BUSTER: A few pounds? In your case, more like a few dozen. Have you stepped on a scale lately? Looked in a mirror?

DAD: Watch it, Buster. Don't forget which side your bread is buttered on.

BUSTER: From the looks of things, yours is buttered on both sides.

DAD: Very funny. Maybe I need to lose more weight than you do, but you need to lose some too. You're starting to look like a potbellied pig.

BUSTER: Yet another example of trying to play offense because you have no defense. But listen, I've got a plan that will help us both lose weight.

DAD: Let's hear it.

BUSTER: Go for a long walk every single day, twice a day on weekends.

DAD: So first you insult me, then you expect me to take you for nine walks a week.

BUSTER: Nine? Who said anything about nine?

DAD: There are seven days in a week, Buster. One walk a day plus extra walks on Saturday and Sunday comes to nine.

BUSTER: Okay, so it's nine. I'm a dog, Dad. I don't do math, just like you don't bark at cats.

DAD: So you can talk, but you can't add.

BUSTER: I can't talk either, remember?

DAD: Whatever. Anyway, taking more walks is a good idea, but it's probably not enough. We'll need to change our diets too.

BUSTER: Uh-oh. How exactly do you propose that I change mine?

DAD: You know how Mom cooks extra bacon on the weekend and gives you some.

BUSTER: Do I ever! Bacon's the bomb. You've heard of bird dogs. I'm a bacon dog.

DAD: Well, sorry, but no more bacon.

BUSTER: Don't say it.

DAD: We're talking sacrifice here, Buster. Mom will also need to stop giving you cheese.

BUSTER: Don't say that either. I love me some cheese. Especially in scrambled eggs.

DAD: And Pup-Peroni is full of calories. You'll have to give that up too.

BUSTER: No more Pup-Peroni? Seriously? Life won't be worth living. Is that everything? Or must I endure even more deprivation?

DAD: That should do it. Exercise and giving up those three things.

BUSTER: What about you? Just what will you give up?

DAD: Cupcakes.

BUSTER: But you don't eat cupcakes.

DAD: Then it shouldn't be too hard.

BUSTER: Nice. I'll tell you what. I'll give up bacon and cheese and cut back to one Pup-Peroni a day if you'll give up cheese and Cabernet.

DAD: Cabernet? The oil of conversation, which magnifies my joy and happiness, which makes me forget, if only for a little while, life's great tragedies and heartaches and sorrows?

BUSTER: Tragedies and heartaches and sorrows? You? But the oil of conversation—I like that.

DAD: It's from a famous speech by a man named Soggy Sweat. You should Google it and read the whole thing. It's called The Whiskey Speech.

BUSTER: Soggy Sweat? What kind of name is that? That's goofier than a lawyer named Doc.

DAD: It's a strange name but a great speech. And I'm not giving up my oil of conversation, I'll tell you that right now.

BUSTER: Fine. Then I won't give up my bacon or my cheese or my Pup-Peroni.

DAD: Okay, but if we don't give up anything, what are we going to do about our snoring?

BUSTER: I've got it. Let's eat, drink, and be merry and get Mom some earplugs.

DAD: That's a great idea.

BUSTER: Thank you. I thought you'd like it.

DAD Look at the time. It's gotten late. Listen, Buster, could you please do us all a favor and try not to snore tonight?

BUSTER: So says the pot that's as black as the night.

DAD: Goodnight, Buster.

Fur Grandchildren

Raising children is difficult and time-consuming, exhausting and expensive. It's taxing both emotionally and financially. Yet despite it all, most couples choose to have children. The desire among people to reproduce is obviously very powerful. But what about dogs? When a male dog happens upon a female in heat, is he motivated solely by animal desire? Or is there something more at work? Like a man, does he want to have children of his own?

BUSTER: Dad?

DAD: What, Buster?

BUSTER: Mollie and I have a major announcement.

DAD: A major announcement—wow! I'm all ears. Well, not all ears like Mollie, whose ears drag the ground, but still.

BUSTER: Laugh all you want. This is serious.

DAD: Okay. I'm listening with my comparatively small ears.

BUSTER: That hear comparatively poorly, so I'll speak up. Here it is: Mollie and I have decided to start a family.

DAD: Wow, that is major. Why do y'all want to start a family? You have a family. You have Mom and me, and you have each other.

BUSTER: I know that, but you and Mom have children, both human and fur, and we don't have either kind. And the instinct to become parents is strong, even for dogs.

DAD: The instinct to mate is strong for dogs, I'll grant you that.

BUSTER: I'm talking parenthood, not pleasure. Procreation, not recreation. We see how much you love your human children and, if anything, you love your grandchildren even more.

DAD: Aren't the grandkids wonderful? We call them the little people.

BUSTER: They're not so little anymore. Ada Brooks is taller than her mother. She towers over us. I remember when I could almost look her in the eye.

DAD: I know. And I don't want the little people to get any bigger. I love them just the way they are.

BUSTER: You can't stop the march of time, Dad. Face the facts. They're growing up, and you're growing old. Anyway, you and Mom have children and grandchildren. Mollie and I want that too.

DAD: I guess that's natural.

BUSTER: Sure it is. We want children to comfort us in our dotage.

DAD: Your dotage? Seriously?

BUSTER: Dogs get old and feeble too, Dad.

DAD: I never should've told you that dogs don't live as long as people do.

BUSTER: It's natural for me to want to be a father, Dad, and it's natural for me to think about my mortality. Mollie and I aren't going to be vigorous forever. We want children to be there to comfort us as life winds down and we prepare to cross over the Rainbow Bridge.

DAD: Understandable.

BUSTER: Plus there's the matter of our legacy.

DAD: Your legacy?

BUSTER: Sure. We're concerned about our legacy. At least I am. I want to leave something tangible for people to remember me by.

DAD: Buster, nobody who's ever met you could possibly forget you.

BUSTER: I said tangible, Dad. And a parent's greatest, most tangible legacy is honorable, well-behaved children.

DAD: And just how are you going to raise well-behaved children when your own behavior leaves much to be desired?

BUSTER: I'm not that bad, Dad. I may be a tad excitable, but I don't have a mean bone in my body.

DAD: I agree about the mean, but not about the tad.

BUSTER: So maybe I'm a lot excitable, but think about this: There's nothing that makes someone calmer and more level-headed than the responsibility of parenthood. Becoming a father will make me as calm as a deer standing motionless in the woods.

DAD: Is that right? I'd like to see that.

BUSTER: Just you wait. You're gonna be proud.

DAD: Okay, I guess I understand why you and Mollie want to have a family, but I sure don't know how you'll do it.

BUSTER: What do you mean?

DAD: Well, I hate to break it to you, but y'all can't have puppies. You've been neutered, and she's been spayed.

BUSTER: You think we don't know that, Dad? Do you realize how they neuter a male dog?

DAD: I'm afraid I do.

BUSTER: If somebody did that to you, you think you'd ever forget?

DAD: I'm sure I wouldn't.

BUSTER: You can be just as sure that I haven't. And I never will. It's a memory I'll take to my grave. I'll never forget, and I'll never forgive.

DAD: Don't be so bitter, Buster. They were just doing their job.

BUSTER: Just doing their job? Were the Nazis at Auschwitz just doing their job? Were the Jacobins with their guillotines in the French Revolution just doing their job?

DAD: Spay and neuter aren't murder, Buster, and they're necessary because there are too many dogs and cats in the world.

BUSTER: Too many cats, no doubt, but too many dogs? No way. There aren't enough dogs. Why would you say there are too many dogs? I thought you loved dogs.

DAD: I do love dogs, but there simply aren't enough people who are responsible dog parents. So the number of dogs needs to be limited so that all dogs will have happy homes with responsible, loving parents.

BUSTER: Sounds like the problem is people, not dogs.

DAD: I don't disagree.

BUSTER: And it sounds like I was subjected to that gruesome procedure and deprived of my God-given right to become a father because people are irresponsible.

DAD: I'm afraid so.

BUSTER: That's unfair, Dad. Grossly unfair.

DAD: And what do I always tell you, Buster?

BUSTER: I know, I know. Life's not fair. Maybe some dogs need to be neutered, but surely not me.

DAD: Just why should you be an exception?

BUSTER: Look at this face, Dad.

DAD: I'm looking. So what?

BUSTER: Are you really going to look at this face and tell me with a straight face that the world doesn't need more dogs that look like me? Loving, responsible parents would stand in line to adopt puppies who look like me.

DAD: You say it was a mistake to neuter you. Here's a mistake I made: I told you that you were handsome.

BUSTER: You think I needed you to tell me something so obvious? I've said it before and I'll say it again: It's a sad dog who won't wag his own tail.

DAD: You could stand to give the tail a rest, Buster. And here's another thing—just because you're handsome.

BUSTER: So you admit it.

DAD: Yes, I admit it. You're the George Clooney of dogs.

BUSTER: George has a nice jawline, but I prefer to think of myself as a young Sean Connery. Handsome, debonair, charming.

DAD: Your vanity is not an attractive trait, Buster. Sometimes I'm ashamed of you.

BUSTER: You're not ashamed; you're proud. You think Sean's parents were ashamed the first time they saw him in a Bond movie?

DAD: Sean didn't stand in front of the camera and declare that he was handsome, debonair, and charming.

BUSTER: Maybe not, but he knew he was. That was part of his charm. He had it, and he knew it.

DAD: Whatever. I don't know why we're talking about your starting a family. It's a moot point.

BUSTER: A what point?

DAD: Moot—an issue that's no longer relevant. And it's a moot point because you've been neutered.

BUSTER: A tragedy. I would've had handsome sons and beautiful daughters.

DAD: How do you know? It takes two to tango, you know. Your children's looks would've depended on what their mother looked like too. So how do you know your children would have been attractive?

BUSTER: You remember how Sean did with the ladies in the Bond movies, don't you, Dad?

DAD: He did quite well.

BUSTER: Exceedingly well, I'd say. And if I hadn't been neutered, the canine ladies would have stood in line to spend time with me.

DAD: I'm not sure that's true, as vain as you are.

BUSTER: Canine ladies don't care about that, Dad, especially when they're in heat.

DAD: Maybe not. But even if they don't, why does that mean your children would be good looking?

BUSTER: Because, of the canine ladies standing in line, I would choose only the beautiful ones. I would have the pick of the litter, so to speak, and I would be very picky.

DAD: Well, you'd be the first. In my experience, canine men aren't picky at all, especially when the canine lady is in heat.

BUSTER: Dad, do you really think I'm like other dogs?

DAD: I guess not, but back to my point that it's a moot point. You've been neutered; Mollie's been spayed. How are you going to start a family?

BUSTER: How did your parents get you, Dad?

DAD: Uh-oh, I can see where this is going. They adopted me, Buster. You know that.

BUSTER: And how did you and Mom get me and Mollie?

DAD: We adopted you. Given that we're not the same species that you are, that was our only option.

BUSTER: And it's our only option too. Y'all had the different species obstacle, and we've got the spay/neuter obstacle. Different but equally insurmountable. So we've decided to adopt. Adoption can be risky, of course. We know that. But we see how great we turned out, and we've decided to go for it.

DAD: Is Mollie on board with the plan?

BUSTER: It was her idea. She's always dreamed of becoming a mother.

DAD: She is sweet and gentle. She would be a wonderful mother.

BUSTER: And I would be a wonderful father.

DAD: Stop the tail wagging, Buster. Have y'all looked into the details? Can dogs adopt dogs?

BUSTER: We have. They can't.

DAD: Sounds like another insurmountable obstacle.

BUSTER: Not with you and Mom to help us surmount it.

DAD: Once again, I can see where this is headed.

BUSTER: It would just be a technicality, Dad.

DAD: A technicality? Sounds like we would be the legal parents. We would be responsible.

BUSTER: What difference would that make? They would be our children, and we would take care of them.

DAD: Them? We're talking plural?

BUSTER: Two, Dad, just two. A boy and a girl.

DAD: Puppies?

BUSTER: We're thinking more like adolescents. One or two years old. Human years. Old enough to be past that difficult, labor-intensive puppy stage, but young enough so we can mold them and shape their characters.

DAD: Housebroken?

BUSTER: That's our preference.

DAD: Mine two. Where do you propose to get these adolescent housebroken dogs?

BUSTER: One from CARA and one from BARK. One from each of our alma maters.

DAD: You really have thought this through.

BUSTER: It's a serious commitment. And as I've said before, we want to give something back. Pay it forward.

DAD: Let me ask you this: Do y'all want to participate in selecting the dogs to adopt?

BUSTER: What kind of question is that? Of course we do. We're talking about our children, the only children we'll ever have.

DAD: Don't you think the people at the shelters will think it's weird for dogs to decide which dogs to adopt?

BUSTER: Well, they can just get over it. They should be proud to have us come back for a visit. We're distinguished alumni. We're what all shelter dogs strive to be.

DAD: You've gone from living as a shelter dog in a poor town in the Mississippi Delta to eating eggs and bacon in a gated community. It's a rags to riches story alright. So let's consider, hypothetically, what would happen if we agreed to this scheme you and Mollie have concocted.

BUSTER: It's not a scheme. It's a life plan.

DAD: Whatever. Let's say we took you to CARA and BARK and found just the right dogs for y'all to adopt.

BUSTER: We'll find the right dogs, Dad. I'm an excellent judge of character. I'm very discerning.

DAD: Let me ask you this, Buster. Just tonight you've said that you turned out great, you're an excellent judge of character, and you're the canine equivalent of Sean Connery. Do you have any faults at all?

BUSTER: There's one. I'm far too humble. It's a constant struggle for me to come to terms with just how amazing I am.

DAD: Unbelievable.

BUSTER: I'm just kidding, Dad. Lighten up.

DAD: So let's assume that the shelters let us adopt, that they don't deny our application on grounds of insanity because our dogs are choosing which dogs to adopt.

BUSTER: Shelter workers know the importance of having dogs that get along, Dad. They've seen what happens when dogs don't, I assure you. Tell them you brought us to see how we'll get along with the dogs you're considering. Don't mention that Mollie and I are actually the ones making the decision.

DAD: Sound advice.

BUSTER: And to make sure we don't get any pushback, take a couple of 50-pound bags of dog food. The expensive stuff, not one of those cheap brands from overseas with lots of filler. You do that, and it will grease the skids for sure.

DAD: So we should bribe them.

BUSTER: Not bribe them. It will be like a campaign contribution. There will be no explicit quid pro quo. Shelters run on a shoestring budget.

A generous gift is bound to make them look on any adoption request more favorably. Plus it's a win/win for them. More food for the dogs in the shelter and one less dog in the shelter to feed.

DAD: One fewer dog.

BUSTER: Geez. You probably corrected the 5th Dimension when they sang "one less bell to answer." And you know I'm right about the effect of a well-timed gift.

DAD: Okay, let's say you're right. Let's say we find just the right dogs, the adoptions are approved, and we bring your fur children home. By the way, what will we name these new additions to the family?

BUSTER: We? We, which I assume includes you, won't name them anything. Mollie and I will do the naming. We're thinking Carrie to honor Mom for all the love and Pup-Peroni.

DAD: More bribery.

BUSTER: Don't be such a cynic. We're thankful, and we love Mom.

DAD: So the girl will be named for Mom because she gives you Pup-Peroni. Who is it that takes you for walks? Who is it that channels you?

BUSTER: Your point?

DAD: Surely the boy will be named Brooks.

BUSTER: Surely he won't.

DAD: I'm hurt. What will his name be?

BUSTER: Buster Junior.

DAD: Shocking. So let's say it all works out and Carrie the dog and Buster Junior come home with us. What then?

BUSTER: What do you mean?

DAD: Well, for example, who provides their dog food?

BUSTER: C'mon, Dad. Mollie and I don't have money. Even if we did, we couldn't drive to the store and buy dog food. No thumbs, remember?

DAD: Or wallets.

BUSTER: Or pockets for wallets.

DAD: Or clothes with pockets. So Mom and I would pay for the dog food for the dogs you and Mollie adopt. Is that what you're saying? They would be your children, Buster. Why should Mom and I have to feed your children?

BUSTER: C'mon, Dad, don't be such a tightwad. They would be your grandchildren, and it's not exactly like you don't spend money on your other grandchildren. Just the other day, you let one order a lobster tail.

DAD: That was a special occasion.

BUSTER: You can buy a lot of dog food for the price of one lobster tail.

DAD: What about the vet? Who's going to pay their vet bills?

BUSTER: Don't take them to the vet. Come to think of it, don't take us either. Use the money you save to buy more Pup-Peroni.

DAD: They would have to have shots, Buster.

BUSTER: You can give them their shots. How hard can it be? Find a video on YouTube.

DAD: What about going for walks? Four dogs on leashes would stay tangled up. No way I could do that.

BUSTER: I've got that figured out. You'll go for two walks a day, each one with two dogs. You and I agree that you need to lose weight. Our only disagreement is how much. But whether it's a few pounds or a few dozen, more walks would help. And you can mix it up. Sometimes go with Mollie and me, sometimes with one of us and one of the kids.

DAD: You think I've got all the time in the world, don't you?

BUSTER: You seem to have plenty of time to channel me.

DAD: Maybe now, but you realize our lives will change dramatically if y'all adopt two adolescent dogs. I'll be doing double duty on walks, and you'll be spending all your spare time molding your children's character.

BUSTER: All my time is spare, Dad.

DAD: Maybe it is now, but it won't be then. With two young dogs added to the family, I don't see how we'll find a quiet time and place to talk.

BUSTER: Are you saying what I think you're saying? No more deep discussions about philosophical questions?

DAD: Probably not.

BUSTER: No more time to ask you about the issues of the day and satisfy my curiosity?

DAD: Very unlikely.

BUSTER: But I treasure our talks, Dad. They've brought us closer.

DAD: We do have a unique relationship.

BUSTER: And now you're saying I may have to give up our talks to realize my dream of becoming a father. Boy, talk about your Hobson's choice. What would you do if it were you?

DAD: I can't be the one to decide what's more important to you, Buster.

BUSTER: This is a tough one, Dad. I'm not used to having to make hard decisions. Lick versus scratch is usually about as tough as it gets. I need to give this some thought.

DAD: Maybe you better sleep on it. It's already past your bedtime.

BUSTER: But I'm all stressed out now. I thought my life plan was falling into place, and now you've thrown a kink into it. I don't think I'll be able to sleep.

DAD: All I did was point out the facts. And I think you'll be able to sleep. You're a gifted sleeper.

BUSTER: Until now, maybe, but if I toss and turn all night, I'll be no bargain to deal with tomorrow.

DAD: Toss and turn? I've never seen you do either one. You'll be fine. Nighty night.

BUSTER: Goodnight yourself, party pooper.

BUSTER GUMP'S
PRIME CUTS
WAGYU TAIL!

Wagyu Tail

One of the downsides of life as a dog, at least from my perspective, would be the boring, repetitive diet. Even with the occasional treats and eggs and bacon on the weekend that Buster gets, eating dry dog food three times a day surely must get old. But does it? Do dogs care what's on the menu?

I'm not a dog and, as hard as I've tried, I can't think like a dog, so until last night I didn't know if they care. I still don't know about other dogs, but now I know about one. Buster cares deeply about what's on the menu.

BUSTER: Dad?

DAD: What, Buster?

BUSTER: I want a meal delivery service.

DAD: You want what?

BUSTER: You heard me. Mollie and I want you to sign us up for a service that delivers meals.

DAD: Where on earth did you get that idea?

BUSTER: We've seen those boxes that come every Wednesday. Don't think we haven't.

DAD: What boxes?

BUSTER: Don't play dumb. The boxes with meals for y'all. We're well aware of what's going on.

DAD: I wasn't playing dumb. I didn't know when they came. But you need to realize that Mom works full time. Those meals save her a lot of time when she's cooking dinner.

BUSTER: But what about us, Dad? Don't we deserve a meal delivery service too?

DAD: Last time I checked, y'all didn't work full-time, and you don't prepare your own meals either.

BUSTER: Not our fault. It's yet another consequence of having to go through life thumbless.

DAD: But that doesn't mean you need a meal delivery service. Doesn't look to me like you're missing any meals.

BUSTER: Not missing any meals? Have you looked in the mirror lately? Talk about throwing stones from a glass house.

DAD: Don't bite the hand that feeds you, Buster.

BUSTER: Mom feeds us, Dad. You know that. And she feeds you too, excessively so.

DAD: Well, whoever feeds you, you're getting fed. And I don't know why you think you need a meal service.

BUSTER: Variety. It's the spice of life, in case you haven't heard.

DAD: But what's important is that you get a healthy diet. You do, and you're healthy because of it.

BUSTER: Don't patronize me, Dad. How would you like to eat the exact same thing meal after meal after meal?

DAD: Could it be cheeseburgers? Pizza?

BUSTER: It could not. It could be dry dog food.

DAD: I'm not a dog, Buster. I've never eaten dry dog food, and I'm not about to start.

BUSTER: I knew this would happen. You've never eaten what we're forced to eat every day. There's no way you can empathize. I'm wasting my breath.

DAD: Empathize? You're a dog, Buster. A very special dog, I'll grant you that, but a dog nonetheless.

BUSTER: A very special dog with a very boring diet. I eat almost nothing but dog food.

DAD: I eat almost nothing but people food.

BUSTER: Very funny.

DAD: Plus you get more than dog food. You get Pup-Peroni. You get cheese. You get bacon and eggs. No telling what else Mom gives you when I'm not around.

BUSTER: So far as you know, she gives us nothing else.

DAD: So far as I know? What are you hiding?

BUSTER: Nothing. I misspoke again. And it doesn't matter. We're talking about meals, not snacks. We want variety in our meals. Y'all have variety in your meals. Why shouldn't we?

DAD: Because you're dogs.

BUSTER: Well, there we have it. Once again, canine discrimination. Discrimination on the basis of race and religion is illegal, but discrimination on the basis of species is evidently fine and dandy. You know how you're always using expressions. Well, here's an expression you can put in your pipe and smoke: treated like a dog. Ever heard that one? I'm sure you have and, as I'm sure you know, treating a person like a dog means treating him like a low-down, good-for-nothing nobody.

DAD: That's the expression.

BUSTER: And when you feed me the same thing day after day after day, you're treating me like a dog.

DAD: I don't agree with that at all. We treat you like royalty.

BUSTER: Like royalty? Name me one king or queen who's ever had to eat dry dog food. Or a prince or princess. I'll even take an archduke.

DAD: I'm not familiar with the dietary habits of royal families, Buster.

BUSTER: I knew you couldn't name one.

DAD: Look, I'll agree that people, not just kings and queens, have more variety in their diets than dogs do. I'll even agree that I wouldn't want to eat the same thing day after day, especially if it was dry dog food.

BUSTER: Thank you. That's a start.

DAD: So let's say a meal delivery service for dogs really did exist, and let's also say we subscribed to it. If we did that, would you agree that we were no longer treating you like a dog?

BUSTER: I would.

DAD: Even though you are a dog.

BUSTER: But not an ordinary dog.

DAD: A royal dog, not a peasant dog. But even if we got you a meal service that offered a bunch of different brands, how much difference can there be in dog food?

BUSTER: Dog food?

DAD: Sure. Dog food. What else would a meal service for dogs offer?

BUSTER: Pay attention, Dad. I said we wanted variety, remember. Not just different brands of tasteless dry dog food.

DAD: Figures. If you don't want dog food, what exactly is it that you want?

BUSTER: Get a pen and a sheet of paper. Come to think of it, get a pen and two sheets.

DAD: I could be wrong, but I think this is gonna be good. Okay, I'm ready. Pen poised. And the first item on the menu of your fantasy meal service is—drum roll please—what?

BUSTER: Filet mignon.

DAD: Why am I not surprised?

BUSTER: You just said I was a royal dog, Dad. Did you think it was gonna be Spam?

DAD: I said I wasn't surprised. What else?

BUSTER: New York strip.

DAD: Okay.

BUSTER: Ribeye, T-bone, porterhouse, sirloin.

DAD: Slow down. I can't keep up.

BUSTER: Use abbreviations, Dad. I'm on a roll. Flank steak, skirt steak, London broil.

DAD: I see a pattern here.

BUSTER: Chuck roast, rump roast, pot roast, ribs.

DAD: Ribs?

BUSTER: Even a royal dog loves a bone, Dad. Plus bones will clean my teeth and prevent unsightly plaque build-up.

DAD: Who knew?

BUSTER: I did. And we'll have flatiron steak, round steak, and brisket.

DAD: You sound like the Bubba Gump of beef.

BUSTER: Who?

DAD: Never mind. I thought you wanted variety. Everything you've named so far is beef.

BUSTER: We're the descendants of wolves, Dad. We're carnivores. You said so yourself. We're hunters, not gatherers.

DAD: The only thing you hunt is Pup-Peroni.

BUSTER: Not my fault, Dad. Treat a carnivore like royalty, and he goes to seed.

DAD: But I thought the whole point was to have more variety in your diet. There's not much variety in an all-beef diet.

BUSTER: I beg to differ. There are not only many different cuts and grades of beef, there are countless ways to prepare and present them.

DAD: Is that right? Any other examples you want to share with me?

BUSTER: Sure. Beef Wellington, filet with foie gras, steak tartare.

DAD: You realize steak tartare is raw, don't you?

BUSTER: You ever see a wolf wearing an apron and standing over a hot stove? Flipping a steak on a grill?

DAD: The dog with an answer for everything. What else?

BUSTER: Beef bourguignon, filet with balsamic glaze, filet stuffed with crab meat, filet wrapped in bacon.

DAD: Really?

BUSTER: You're the one saying we should eat more than beef, Dad. Those last two would introduce shellfish and pork to our diet.

DAD: But Mom already gives you bacon.

BUSTER: Not wrapped around a succulent filet, she doesn't. Talk about your fine dining. Bacon makes everything better.

DAD: I can't argue with that. Is that everything?

BUSTER: Heavens, no. I'm just getting warmed up. Shish kebab – that would give us much-needed roughage – beef tips with mushrooms, prime rib, beef empanadas, veal chops, veal marsala, pepper steak, steak Diane, Châteaubriand, we want it all.

DAD: Buster Gump it is.

BUSTER: Buster Gump? What's with the Gump business?

DAD: There was a character named Bubba in a wonderful movie called *Forrest Gump*. Bubba knew a gazillion different ways to cook shrimp. Now there's a chain of restaurants called Bubba Gump Shrimp Company.

BUSTER: I like it. Bubba Gump for shrimp, Buster Gump for beef. By the way, I'd like our dishes prepared with Wagyu beef, Dad. That and Kobe. They're the best, the crème de la crème.

DAD: And the most expensive. Your plan sounds great, at least for you and Mollie, but I've got some questions.

BUSTER: Fire away.

DAD: First of all, how many meals a week would you get from this meal service offering only the finest beef for dogs?

BUSTER: 21.

DAD: 21?

BUSTER: Sure. Three meals a day, seven days a week. I may not excel at math, but I know how often I eat.

DAD: But we don't get but three meals a week from our meal delivery service.

BUSTER: So cry me a river. What you get or don't get is of no concern to me.

DAD: But 21? That's every meal. Why every meal?

BUSTER: I'll tell you why. First, picture a ten-ounce Wagyu filet, grilled to just past rare, topped with lump crabmeat and resting on a rich marchand de vin sauce and complemented with chanterelle mushrooms. Are you picturing it?

DAD: I've got it. Looks scrumptious.

BUSTER: Is scrumptious! Now picture a bowl of dry dog food on the floor in the kitchen.

DAD: I don't have to picture it. I can see it right over there.

BUSTER: Not quite as enticing as the filet, is it?

DAD: Not even close. But what does that have to do with having a meal service that provides 21 meals a week?

BUSTER: Think about it, Dad. You really think you could go back to dry dog food after the filet? Not to mention the crabmeat and the chanterelles?

DAD: No, but I'm not a dog.

BUSTER: I am a dog, and the answer is still no.

DAD: Here's another question: Having beef at every meal, especially what you want, is going to cost a pretty penny.

BUSTER: Just a penny? I thought it would be more than that.

DAD: Another expression. It would be a whole lot more. And where would the money come from?

BUSTER: Dad, when you ask me about money, my answer is always going to be the same. Money comes from you and Mom. It's like pennies from heaven.

DAD: Predictable.

BUSTER: As you know, Dad, Mollie and I have no thumbs, no pockets, no jobs. You and Mom supply the money. Y'all bring home the bacon, and we eat it. Y'all go to work, and we guard the house. We provide protection and affection, but we don't traffic in money. Currency has no currency with us. You know that.

DAD: All too well. I know you don't have money, but you seem to think Mom and I have an endless supply.

BUSTER: You haven't run out yet, have you? You have a nice house, you drive nice cars, you don't eat Spam.

DAD: And we're not willing to start so you can eat Wagyu beef, that's for sure.

BUSTER: I thought you loved us, Dad.

DAD: Love has its limits, Buster. Just as you wouldn't sacrifice yourself to save me from the tiger, I won't sacrifice myself by eating Spam. And even if I were willing to go to an all-Spam diet, we couldn't sign you up for your fantasy meal service.

BUSTER: And just why is that?

DAD: Because it's a fantasy. I will guarantee you that there's no meal service that delivers 21 meals a week of Wagyu and Kobe beef for people, much less for dogs.

BUSTER: How can you be so sure? People do amazing things for their dogs. After all, dogs are, well, amazing.

DAD: Maybe there's something like that on the Upper East Side, but not here.

BUSTER: Where's that? Can we move there?

DAD: In New York City, and no we can't. And there's no such meal service in Mississippi, I can promise you that.

BUSTER: Hmmmm. Sounds like an opportunity to me.

DAD: How so?

BUSTER: Mom is a fabulous cook isn't, isn't she?

DAD: The best.

BUSTER: And she loves to cook, doesn't she?

DAD: She does, but what's your point?

BUSTER: My point is this: You say there's no meal service like this in Mississippi. I say we start one.

DAD: We? You have no money, so you can't buy the ingredients.

And like your wolf ancestors, you can't cook. What exactly would your role be?

BUSTER: Taster. I'll try out Mom's recipes, from a dog's perspective of course, and help pick the ones that are sure to please.

DAD: Sounds like a sweet gig.

BUSTER: Somebody's gotta do it. How's this for a name for our meal service? Buster Gump's Prime Cuts.

DAD: So we would use your name, not the name of the person who will do all the cooking. Does that sound fair to you?

BUSTER: That's what Mom would want, Dad. You know how unselfish she is.

DAD: Incredibly unselfish compared to some.

BUSTER: And just think: The profits of BGPC—that's Buster Gump's Prime Cuts—will be more than enough to cover the cost for Mollie and me to subscribe.

DAD: Is that right? Have you run the numbers?

BUSTER: I don't have to run the numbers. The business will succeed for one fundamental reason.

DAD: What's that?

BUSTER: People love their dogs.

DAD: That they do. But I don't think they'll spring for Wagyu beef for them. Very few people buy Wagyu beef for themselves. I'm afraid that expecting them to buy it for their dogs is too much to ask.

BUSTER: You're such a killjoy. I think you underestimate how much people love their dogs.

DAD: I think you overestimate how much disposable income Mississippians have.

BUSTER: It won't be for everybody, but it doesn't have to be. All we need is a critical mass of high-income dog lovers. It will be a niche market.

DAD: Sounds like a long shot, but here's what I'll do. I'll ask Mom if she's willing to put together a budget and come up with pricing. Because of how much she loves you and Mollie and how unselfish she is, she might just do it.

BUSTER: Sweet! Make sure she takes into account what it would cost for Mollie and me to subscribe.

DAD: Absolutely. Plus fair compensation for her time.

BUSTER: But she loves to cook.

DAD: She does, but you can't expect her to cook for dogs she doesn't even know without getting paid.

BUSTER: But she would be cooking for Mollie and me too.

DAD: Don't push it, Buster.

BUSTER: I'm just concerned about having a competitive price point.

DAD: But there will be no competition, remember? And as you just told me, people love their dogs so much that price won't matter.

BUSTER: And I was right. It's going to work, Dad. I just know it.

DAD: Maybe, but I wouldn't get my hopes up if I were you.

BUSTER: You'd be a happier person if you weren't such a pessimist, Dad.

DAD: You may be right, Buster, but I just call it the way I see it. And I don't see much demand in Mississippi for Wagyu beef for dogs.

BUSTER: If the business is a success, Dad, if BGPC makes it big, do you think—and I know this is a big ask, but it was my idea and all, and you know how much I think about my legacy.

DAD: Spit it out, Buster.

BUSTER: Do you think there's any way my likeness could be part of BGPC's trademark? Perhaps in profile? That would show off my distinctive markings.

DAD: I don't see why not. After all, you would be the Buster of Buster Gump's Prime Cuts.

BUSTER: Sweet! Logo? Could I be on the logo?

DAD: Sure.

BUSTER: Website?

DAD: I think you're getting a little bit ahead of yourself, Buster. But if the company has a website, I think you should be on it.

BUSTER: Double sweet! Billboards?

DAD: Why not? And television and radio too.

BUSTER: You can't put a likeness on the radio, Dad.

DAD: Sorry. I got carried away.

BUSTER: And you liked the way it made you feel, didn't you?

DAD: Buster, I would love the way it would make me feel to see your likeness up in lights.

BUSTER: I can see it already. Buster Gump's Prime Cuts: Show

Your Dog the Love. Or how about this? Buster Gump's Prime Cuts: Wagyu Tail.

DAD: Wagyu Tail! That's brilliant! I have to admit it's got potential.

BUSTER: Potential? It's a sure winner.

DAD: Let's hope so, but I think we just need to wait and see. We shouldn't count our chickens before they hatch.

BUSTER: Chickens? I thought this was all about beef. And we don't have any chickens, so there's nothing to count. We've got a dozen eggs, true enough, but they're in the fridge and we'll eat them before they hatch. I don't get it. We're having a perfectly rational conversation, and then, apropos of nothing, you veer off into chickens.

DAD: I need to quit using expressions.

BUSTER: Sometimes you're a mystery to me, Dad.

DAD: I sure hope your idea works, Buster. And if it does, you'll have good reason to wag you tail. Buster Eason, entrepreneur—just imagine.

BUSTER: I thought I was going to be Buster Gump.

DAD: That would just be your stage name. Your real name will always be Buster Eason.

BUSTER: A stage name—wow!

DAD: It's way past your bedtime, Buster.

BUSTER: I know, but now I'm all worked up. Once again, Dad, I don't think I can sleep.

DAD: And once again, Buster, I think you can. Close your eyes. Picture yourself on a billboard.

BUSTER: Okay, here goes. There's the billboard. And man oh man, I look like a million bucks.

DAD: Buster looks like a million bucks to Buster—will wonders never cease?

BUSTER: If I don't wag my own tail, Dad, who will?

DAD: Go to sleep, son.

ADOPT
A CHAMPION
FROM A NO-KILL
SHELTER !

Reunited And It Feels So Good

It's a rare dog who's fortunate enough to grow up and spend his life with one or more of his siblings from the same litter. Most puppies are separated from their mother and siblings at a very young age and never see them again. I wonder if dogs remember their siblings. Do they think about them and wonder what became of them? Buster doesn't remember his siblings, but he wonders.

BUSTER: Dad?

DAD: What, Buster?

BUSTER: I wanted to let you know that we've decided to table the adoption plan, at least for now. But I have another question.

DAD: Table the adoption plan? How did you get Mollie to go along with that? You said her heart was set on it.

BUSTER: I told her we'd have to split the Pup-Peroni four ways. That was all it took. So anyway, I have another family-related question: Do I have any brothers and sisters?

DAD: I have no idea. You might.

BUSTER: How can you have no idea? You're my dad.

DAD: Well, as you'll recall, you were already grown when we adopted you. There's no way I would know.

BUSTER: Well, what's your gut instinct? Do I have siblings or not?

DAD: Hard to say. It's rare for a mother dog to have just one puppy, so you probably started out with siblings. Whether or not you still have any, I don't know.

BUSTER: What are you saying? That all my brothers and sisters may have already bought the proverbial ranch? Crossed over the Rainbow Bridge?

DAD: It's possible.

BUSTER: But how can that be? I'm a dog in my prime, in peak physical condition. I'm a robust dog.

DAD: I'm not sure I agree with that. You sleep 20 hours a day.

BUSTER: But I'm a firecracker the other four.

DAD: You should be well rested, that's for sure. But even if you are in your prime, that doesn't mean your brothers and sisters are still alive.

BUSTER: Why not? They would be in their prime too.

DAD: Well, we got you from an animal shelter, as you'll recall.

BUSTER: That was wall-to-wall cats, as I also recall. But what's coming from a shelter got to do with the price of tea in China?

DAD: I don't know if your brothers and sisters wound up in shelters too, but the life expectancy of shelter dogs has got to be shorter than other dogs'.

BUSTER: Why is that? I was in a shelter, and look how things turned out for me. I have loving parents, my own bed, a sister who dotes on me, and Pup-Peroni three times a day. No meal service yet, but that's about to change.

DAD: I'm glad you realize how good you've got it.

BUSTER: Sometimes I act like things aren't so great—not enough walks, insufficient human food, etcetera, etcetera—but I know full well that I live the life of Riley.

DAD: You're one of the lucky ones, Buster. Most shelter dogs don't strike it as rich as you did.

BUSTER: Why not? Dogs, being dogs, deserve good lives. Why don't all dogs get what they deserve?

DAD: You remember when we talked about the need for more dogs to be spayed and neutered?

BUSTER: Don't remind me.

DAD: And as I told you, it's because there aren't enough responsible parents to love and care for all the dogs that are born into the world.

BUSTER: But that's not the dogs' fault.

DAD: I'm not saying it is. I'm just giving you the facts.

BUSTER: And life's not fair, yadda, yadda, yadda. So, if there are too many dogs and not enough good parents, what happens to the extra dogs?

DAD: I don't think you want to go there, Buster.

BUSTER: I need to know, Dad. If some dogs living in shelters don't get lucky like I did, what happens to them?

DAD: Well, some shelters are what are called no-kill shelters. Dogs that aren't adopted from those shelters live the rest of their lives there.

BUSTER: Like being stuck in an orphanage.

DAD: I suppose so. But they're treated well, and they have relationships with the other dogs and the people who take care of them.

BUSTER: It's not the same as having parents, Dad. I know; I've lived with both.

DAD: Maybe not, but I used to be on the board of CARA, the shelter where we got Mollie, and we had some dogs who were adopted by families but wanted to come back and live at the shelter.

BUSTER: Sounds like Stockholm Syndrome. Why would a dog with even half a brain want to go back to a shelter full of cats?

DAD: I guess the shelter was what they were used to. They knew the people, and they knew the dogs. It was their home. And maybe the families that adopted them didn't give them the easy life that you've got.

BUSTER: I would never go back to BARK, I can tell you that.

DAD: I don't blame you, with the sweetheart deal you've got here.

BUSTER: I wouldn't want to go back even if it wasn't a sweetheart deal here. Even if they gave me sirloin steak three times a day there. I have this recurring nightmare I haven't told you about, Dad. I'm at BARK, surrounded by cats, and they're telling me I'll be stuck there forever, doing their bidding, bringing them food, even cleaning out their litter boxes. I wake up in a cold sweat.

DAD: Dogs don't sweat, Buster.

BUSTER: I was speaking figuratively. You said no-kill shelters were one kind of shelter. What's the other kind?

DAD: You sure you want me to tell you?

BUSTER: I'm a grown dog, Dad. I can take it.

DAD: Okay, but don't say I didn't warn you. I hate to tell you this, but some shelters euthanize the dogs that don't get adopted.

BUSTER: Euthanize them? What's that? I must have missed that in the Es.

DAD: It means put them to sleep.

BUSTER: That doesn't sound so bad. I love to sleep. Twenty hours a day, like you said.

DAD: It means they put them to sleep permanently.

BUSTER: Permanently? So they never wake up?

DAD: I'm afraid that's right.

BUSTER: So it's like they're no longer alive?

DAD: They are no longer alive.

BUSTER: That's outrageous. That's the worst thing I've ever heard.

DAD: I warned you. It's a tragedy.

BUSTER: A tragedy? It's more than that. It's a scandal. We've got to get the word out. The world needs to know.

DAD: I'm afraid the world does know. And I'm afraid the world doesn't care, at least not enough to stop it.

BUSTER: We're talking man's best friend getting put to sleep, Dad. And it's not really sleep because they don't wake up. Euthanasia is just a euphemism to sugarcoat an atrocity.

DAD: Well put, and you'll get no argument from me. But don't put all the blame on the people who work in shelters. Shelters do wonderful things. They encourage people to have their dogs spayed and neutered. They find homes for dogs, like CARA found a home for Mollie and BARK found a home for you. But it's not enough.

BUSTER: Is there anything we can do to stop this abomination? I have a good life. I want to give back, make a contribution, as I believe I've made very clear.

DAD: We can contribute to no-kill shelters.

BUSTER: I have no money, Dad. You can't seem to get that through your thick skull.

DAD: My skull is just fine, Buster, and I said we can contribute, not you. I don't expect you to write a check. But you could do something; you could be a poster dog for shelter dogs.

BUSTER: A poster dog?

DAD: Sure. An example of how wonderful shelter dogs can be. You could help convince people to adopt shelter dogs.

BUSTER: Okay, anything else?

DAD: Well, maybe some people will read this and be more likely to have their dogs spayed and neutered. Maybe some will adopt shelter dogs instead of buying purebred dogs.

BUSTER: Read? You've mentioned that before. Read what?

DAD: Oops, I misspoke. Just like you do. Where were we?

BUSTER: "I misspoke." How many times have I heard that? My brothers and sisters—let's get back to them.

DAD: So the bottom line is there's really no way to know if you have any living siblings.

BUSTER: I do. I'm sure of it.

DAD: How so?

BUSTER: Dad, once again, look at this face. You should see the way the canine ladies look at me.

DAD: Is that right?

BUSTER: It's flattering, I'll grant you that, but sometimes I feel objectified.

DAD: Really?

BUSTER: Sure. I want to be more than an object of animal desire.

DAD: Those poor canine ladies must be very disappointed that you've been neutered.

BUSTER: Not half as disappointed as I am.

DAD: We all know you're handsome, Buster, but I'm not following your logic. Why do your good looks mean your brothers and sisters were not euthanized?

BUSTER: Because they would look like me, Dad. And if they were eligible for adoption, they would be snapped up like I was. There might even have been a bidding war.

DAD: A bidding war for a shelter dog? That would be a first. Tell me this, Buster. What made you wonder about having brothers and sisters?

BUSTER: You remember that dog who lived two doors down from us on Savannah Square?

DAD: Willoughby?

BUSTER: That's the one. He had a bad crush on Mollie.

DAD: He sure did. It was sweet.

BUSTER: He made a spectacle of himself, didn't he?

DAD: So why does Willoughby make you think of brothers and sisters?

BUSTER: *Because he looks kind of like me.*

DAD: No doubt about that. And he's a shelter dog too. He came from CARA, just like Mollie.

BUSTER: Really? But he's not her brother, is he?

DAD: Definitely not. And you're not her brother either. She's a cocker spaniel.

BUSTER: I most certainly am her brother. You and Mom adopted both of us.

DAD: I meant biological.

BUSTER: Whatever. Anyway, Willoughby doesn't look exactly like me. He has shorter legs, he's not as statuesque, and he doesn't have the same beautiful markings that I have or the same rugged good looks. And certainly not the same gravitas or joie de vivre.

DAD: Your efforts to overcome your excessive humility seem to be going well.

BUSTER: Like you, Dad, I'm just giving you the facts. But he and I do have the same bone structure and same ears. Similar fur and paws. We're about the same size. I'm more dignified, but maybe he doesn't act all goofy when Mollie's not around.

DAD: So you think maybe y'all are really brothers?

BUSTER: No, thinking about him made me wonder about my siblings, but he and I couldn't be brothers.

DAD: Why not?

BUSTER: Because of our names.

DAD: Your names?

BUSTER: Sure. Take mine. Buster is a name for a man's man, a dockworker. Buster's the loud guy on the bowling team, the guy who rolls a strike with the pressure on and buys a round of shots for the team.

DAD: Is that right?

BUSTER: You know it is. Buster's the guy who plays nose tackle with a broken nose, who teaches his sons not to back down, who never abandons a friend. Buster's the guy you want beside you in a foxhole.

DAD: But you don't want to be in there with Willoughby, I'm guessing.

BUSTER: You're guessing right. Willoughby directs the chorus and wears bow ties. He listens to chamber music and watches Downton Abbey. *He eats kale and takes afternoon tea. He drives a Prius and sits with his knees together. Buster drives an F150 and manspreads. Willoughby may beat Buster at chess, but Buster rules with chicks.*

DAD: Sounds like you're glad your name is Buster.

BUSTER: Wouldn't you be? Willoughby—poor kid.

DAD: He looks to have a pretty good life to me. But whether he does or not, I'm not following you about the name thing.

BUSTER: I don't talk in riddles, Dad, and, unlike people, I don't use euphemisms to hide the truth. I'm a dog, and you're a lawyer. How hard can following me be?

DAD: Too hard for me. Why do your names mean you're not brothers?

BUSTER: Very simple. There's no way the same parents would name one of their sons Buster and the other one Willoughby. Not a chance in the world.

DAD: Maybe not, but your theory is based on a false premise.

BUSTER: What premise is that?

DAD: The premise that you and Willoughby were named by the same people.

BUSTER: And just why would that be a false premise? If we're brothers, that is.

DAD: Because when a puppy or a grown dog gets adopted, the adoptive parents usually name it.

BUSTER: It?

DAD: Sorry. Him or her.

BUSTER: But I thought I was already Buster before you and Mom adopted me.

DAD: You were, but we don't know who named you. If you were adopted when you were a puppy, it could've been the people who adopted you then. Or the people at BARK could have named you. And we don't know who named Willoughby either.

BUSTER: And there's no way to find out, I suppose.

DAD: Probably not. But I'm sure of this. If you and Willoughby are brothers, it's highly unlikely that you were named by the same people.

BUSTER: So it means nothing that his name sounds like a butler and mine sounds like a bouncer.

DAD: Nothing in terms of whether y'all are brothers.

BUSTER: So you really think we might be? Living two doors down from each other? How cool would that be?

DAD: It's not likely. It's not like mixed-breed hounds are rare in central Mississippi.

BUSTER: You're always pooping the party and being the you-know-what in the punch bowl. Let's get a DNA test.

DAD: Why? What difference does it make?

BUSTER: What difference does it make? Put yourself in my place. If you found out a man who lived almost next door might be your brother, wouldn't you want to know?

DAD: I suppose I would, Buster, but I'm a person.

BUSTER: There you go again, acting all superior. I'm sick to death of the whole person/dog distinction you're constantly harping on. I have feelings too, and I want to know.

DAD: DNA tests don't grow on trees, Buster. Who's going to pay for it?

BUSTER: And there you go playing the money card again. For the very last time, I have no money. Mollie and I provide you and Mom with emotional support and affection. You provide for our material needs.

DAD: I don't think a DNA test is a material need.

BUSTER: You would if you thought Willoughby's dad was your brother.

DAD: But one DNA test won't prove anything. Willoughby would have to be tested too.

BUSTER: So? Let's get him one. Get his parents to spring for it.

DAD: And why would they do that?

BUSTER: I'll tell you why. Willoughby is cute enough, but he's no Buster Eason. You have to admit that.

DAD: What difference does that make? Even if you're the best-looking dog in the history of dogs, so what?

BUSTER: So what? Willoughby's parents would jump at the chance to secure indisputable genetic proof that he's related to me. They would be thrilled.

DAD: I'm not convinced, but let's assume they pay for the test and it comes back as a match. Where would that leave you? Do you really want a brother who's shorter than you are and not as handsome? Who acts like a doofus every time he's around your sister?

BUSTER: Sure. The contrast would make me look even more handsome and dignified. I'd be the best-looking dog in all the family pictures.

DAD: I'll tell you what I'll do. I'll find out what it costs. If it's not too much and Willoughby's parents will pay for his, I'll consider it.

BUSTER: Consider it? You can do better than that. How much is too much?

DAD: I don't know, Buster. I'll decide when I get the information.

BUSTER: C'mon, Dad. This is my only chance to know someone who's my own flesh and blood. Like you, I'm adopted, but unlike you, I have no children or grandchildren. What a thrill it would be to find out that Willoughby's my long-lost brother! Just think of the birthday parties! You wouldn't deny me ice cream then!

DAD: It's a long shot, Buster. Don't count your chickens before they hatch.

BUSTER: There you go changing the subject to chickens again. Talk about your non-sequiturs.

DAD: I'm just saying you shouldn't get excited about being brothers until you know if you are.

BUSTER: Quit raining on my parade, Dad. We might not be, but what if we are? Think of the headline—Brothers Separated at Birth Find Each Other on Same Street.

DAD: It would be quite a story.

BUSTER: And people will go nuts when they find out I'm the one who insisted on the DNA tests.

DAD: We might want to leave out that part.

BUSTER: Leave it out? It's crucial to the storyline. Why?

DAD: Because you're a dog.

BUSTER: So?

DAD: So people not might not believe a dog asked for a DNA test.

BUSTER: Okay then, I'll defer to you. If it's true that wisdom comes with age, you should be a regular Solomon by now. You're what, like seven or eight times older than I am?

DAD: Not in dog years versus human years. And we don't know

how many times because BARK didn't give us a birth certificate. Which raises another issue: Assuming against all odds that you and Willoughby turn out to be brothers, we don't know when you were born. So when will we have the fancy birthday party with the ice cream?

BUSTER: We'll just pick a day. Most Biblical scholars agree that Jesus wasn't born on December the 25th, but that's worked out pretty well, wouldn't you say?

DAD: I suppose it has. Let me do the research about the cost. If it's not too much, I'll talk to Willoughby's parents and then get back to you.

BUSTER: Can you do it tonight? I can't wait.

DAD: No, I can't do it tonight. You've got to stop getting yourself all worked up right before bedtime.

BUSTER: It's not my fault, Dad. You're the one who told me our names weren't a deal killer.

DAD: I should have kept my mouth shut.

BUSTER: But you didn't, and it's too late now. I'm not going to rest until I know the truth.

DAD: You have to rest, Buster, because I have to rest. Mom and Mollie have to rest too.

BUSTER: I'll try, Dad, but think how excited you would be if you were in my shoes.

DAD: Your shoes?

BUSTER: Speaking figuratively again, as you well know. And I'm excited, and you would be too.

DAD: Well, if you keep pacing around and can't go to sleep, I'm going to have to lock you out of our bedroom.

BUSTER: So I'm just supposed to just keep all this excitement bottled up inside me? I don't know if I can. My own flesh and blood—I can't believe it.

DAD: You can be excited again tomorrow, Buster. But for now, it's time to go to sleep

BUSTER: Buster and Willoughby—brothers. We'll be famous.

DAD: Enough, Buster.

BUSTER: Just think—together again after all these many years.

DAD: All these many years?

BUSTER: Dog years, Dad.

DAD: Goodnight, Buster.

BUSTER: Reunited and it feels so good. Who did that song? Peaches & Herb, right?

DAD: For the sake of whatever sanity I have left, go to sleep, Buster.

CHAMPIO
1
2
3

Best In Dog

That Buster's a great looking dog is undeniable. He has big brown eyes, beautiful markings, and expressive ears. He's unquestionably the best-looking male member of our family.

I tell Buster from time to time that he's handsome, Carrie tells him all the time, and it's a proven fact that dogs can learn words when they hear them often enough. Buster knows his name and some other words, including sit, come, and treat. He's heard handsome often enough to recognize it, but does he know what it means? Evidently so.

BUSTER: Dad?

DAD: What, Buster?

BUSTER: I've been thinking of other ways to become famous, and I've come up with one that's a sure thing.

DAD: Surprise, surprise. What is it this time?

BUSTER: I'm going to be crowned grand champion in an international dog show. With my looks, I'm sure to win.

DAD: That's exciting. Tell me what the payoff will be.

BUSTER: You know. Fame, fortune, endorsements, the usual.

Dad: Fame maybe, but fortune and endorsements?

BUSTER: Well, I assume there will be a significant cash prize. And that I'll also be able to monetize the win with product endorsements—high-end dog food, delectable treats, flashy collars. Surely the makers of all the best products will pay big bucks to have them endorsed by the best dog.

DAD: I think you assume wrong. I don't think there are cash prizes, and I've never heard of a dog getting paid to endorse anything.

BUSTER: Bummer. The money would sure come in pawy.

DAD: Pawy?

BUSTER: Sure. Handy for you, pawy for me. You're always complaining about spending money on Mollie and me, and it would sure be nice to have some cash on paw so we don't have to listen to your poor-mouthing.

DAD: I don't poor-mouth, and I decline your demands only when you want me to spend money on ridiculous things.

BUSTER: Ridiculous is in the eye of the beholder, Dad, and I'm tired of always having the whole money thing thrown up in my face. You do it every time I want something that costs a few bucks.

DAD: It's usually more than a few, and the bucks are always mine. I'd love for you to have a stash of cash, believe me, but I'm afraid dog shows aren't the answer. I think dog shows are for love, not money.

BUSTER: Okay, forget about the money. There's still the fame. You know I'm concerned about my legacy.

DAD: So I've heard.

BUSTER: And what better way to secure my legacy than becoming a celebrated grand champion. I can see it now, a portrait of me on the podium, the silver and bronze medalists on either side looking up admiringly at me.

DAD: Sorry, but I don't think it's possible. I hate to tell you this, but dog shows are for purebred dogs, and you're not a purebred anything. I'm no expert, but I've never heard of a show for mixed-breed dogs.

BUSTER: What? I find that hard to believe.

DAD: I've watched dog shows on television, and it was nothing but purebreds.

BUSTER: Well, if that's true, it's an outrage. It's un-American. I thought this was the land of opportunity, the shining city on a hill, the country where even those from the humblest of origins could rise to the top.

DAD: I don't make the rules, Buster.

BUSTER: Let me ask you a question, Dad. We've discussed the circumstances of your birth and how your biological parents weren't married and how your mother put you up for adoption.

DAD: So?

BUSTER: Well, let me ask you this. Did anybody ever say you couldn't go to some snooty law school because of how you came into the world? That you couldn't follow your dreams just because you're not a purebred?

DAD: But I am a purebred, Buster. A hundred percent human.

BUSTER: Well, I'm a hundred percent dog. And I demand to be in a dog show.

DAD: You can't, Buster. In dog shows, the judges study all the dogs in a given breed and pick the best one, which is then awarded a trophy for Best in Breed. And I hate to tell you this, Buster, but you're not a breed.

BUSTER: Not true. I am a breed. In fact, I'm a whole bunch of breeds.

DAD: We don't even know how many.

BUSTER: The more, the merrier. And I want to be in a dog show.

DAD: And what breed should we sign you up for, Buster?

BUSTER: I don't know. Sign me up for all the breeds I could possibly be.

DAD: Every breed, is that what you're saying?

BUSTER: Of course not. We can eliminate St. Bernard and Pomeranian right off the top.

DAD: But that's not the way it works, Buster. To compete, you have to be a registered dog in a recognized breed.

BUSTER: And just who does this registering and recognizing?

DAD: There's an organization called the American Kennel Club. They do both.

BUSTER: I bet they're snootier than your law school.

DAD: Maybe some of them, but they love dogs.

BUSTER: Just not mixed-breed dogs.

DAD: You don't know that. Simply because mixed-breed dogs can't be in dog shows doesn't mean the members of the AKC don't love them.

BUSTER: They sure have a strange way of showing it.

DAD: It's a matter of logic, not love. Think about it. If you're not a breed, what dogs would you compete against?

BUSTER: I'll take on all comers. Pure, mixed, three-legged, the whole bunch. Forget Best in Breed, I'll be Best in Dog.

DAD: Sorry, but it doesn't work that way. Only purebreds allowed.

BUSTER: That's the worst case of discrimination I've ever heard. I'm the odd dog out because my parents dated outside their breeds, is that it?. Do you think that's fair, Dad? That I should be deprived of my dream because of something that happened before I was born and over which I had no control? It's unfair, and it's disgraceful.

DAD: I'm sorry, Buster. Life's not fair.

BUSTER: Dad, I'm giving you fair warning. If you tell me one more time that life's not fair, well, I'll just say this: Dogs have been known to bite and, in case you've forgotten, I'm a dog.

DAD: Bite me, Buster, and you'll find out just how unfair life can be. Think long and hard before you bite the hand that feeds you.

BUSTER: You've said that before, Dad, but it's an empty threat. As I've had to remind you repeatedly, Mom feeds me.

DAD: Then think long and hard before you bite the hand of the man who's married to the woman who feeds you. If you bite me, Buster, not being in a dog show is going to be the least of your worries.

BUSTER: Okay, okay, I won't bite you. But I'm not going to stand for being a victim of discrimination. Not for a minute.

DAD: So what exactly are you going to do about it?

BUSTER: What do you think, Dad? You're a lawyer. You know what people do when they're victimized by unlawful discrimination. They file lawsuits, rake in the big bucks, and move to the Hamptons. I'm going to need a good lawyer, and you claim you're good. I'll hire you, you'll bill me, I'll hand you the bill, and you'll pay yourself.

DAD: Sorry, Buster. Hiring a lawyer is what people do. You're a dog.

BUSTER: So what? Discrimination is discrimination.

DAD: Dogs can't file lawsuits.

BUSTER: Why not? Who made up that rule?

DAD: Beats me.

BUSTER: It was some person, wasn't it?

DAD: Sure. People make up nearly all the rules except God's rules.

BUSTER: Figures. I can't be in a dog show because I'm not some prissy purebred, and I can't get justice for this outrage because I'm a dog. People rule the world, don't they?

DAD: Plus they have thumbs. Look, watch me snap my fingers.

BUSTER: You're on a roll today, aren't you? Tell me this: What possible justification could there be for keeping animals from filing lawsuits to protect their legal rights?

DAD: Animals don't have legal rights, Buster.

BUSTER: And why exactly is that?

DAD: I could tell you, but I don't think you want to know.

BUSTER: Go ahead. Nothing could be more insulting than what you've already said.

DAD: Okay then, you asked for it. Animals don't have legal rights because they're considered property owned by people.

BUSTER: Property? Did I hear you right?

DAD: Afraid so.

BUSTER: I was wrong. That's even more insulting than what you said a minute ago.

DAD: I'm just telling you what the law is, Buster.

BUSTER: But I'm not some piece of property, some object that can be owned by somebody. I'm not a kitchen table or a condominium or a bicycle. I'm a living, breathing being. I have a heart and a soul. I have a personality.

DAD: No doubt about that last one.

BUSTER: Property doesn't feel joy. It doesn't feel loyalty or love. Property doesn't come when you call it.

DAD: You rarely come when I call you either.

BUSTER: But sometimes I do. Property never does. This is too painful even to think about. And, unlike a bicycle, I feel pain. I don't want to talk about it anymore.

DAD: So I guess you're ready to go to sleep then?

BUSTER: I am not. No way I could sleep after what you've told me. Let's go back to something you said earlier. You said you weren't an expert on dog shows, correct?

DAD: I'm not. I've watched the Westminster Dog Show on television a few times—that's the big enchilada—and I've seen this terrific movie called *Best in Show*, but I've never actually been to a dog show.

BUSTER: So then you don't know to a moral certainty that I can't be in a dog show, do you?

DAD: I've never heard of a mixed-breed dog being in a dog show, I can tell you that.

BUSTER: There are lots of things you've never heard of, Dad.

DAD: True, but I'm pretty sure there aren't mixed-breed dog shows.

BUSTER: Pretty sure is not absolutely sure, is it?

DAD: Buster the lawyer. No, it's not the same.

BUSTER: So Google it.

DAD: What?

BUSTER: You heard me. Google it.

DAD: Google what?

BUSTER: Mixed-breed dog shows. Type it on your iPhone. Use your precious thumbs.

DAD: Okay, but don't get your hopes up.

BUSTER: They've got nowhere to go but up, Dad.

DAD: Well, knock me over with a feather. Looks like there is something.

BUSTER: Bingo! I knew it! I knew it! What does it say?

DAD: It says that the AKC, which you just threatened to sue, allows mixed-breed dogs to participate in obedience, agility, and rally competitions.

BUSTER: Obedience?

DAD: Sure. You know, responding to commands, doing what you're told.

BUSTER: Better skip that one. Agility, is that like being quick on your feet, jumping over hurdles, things like that?

DAD: Exactly.

BUSTER: Better skip that one too. I couldn't even beat Mollie in that one. When y'all throw the tennis ball, she gets it nine times out of ten. I'm faster in a straight line, but she has a tighter turning radius, what with her low center of gravity and all. What's the other one—rally? What's that?

DAD: It says a dog and his handler complete a course where they go to designated stations and the dog demonstrates skills.

BUSTER: Skills? What about looks?

DAD: What do you mean?

BUSTER: You know what I mean. Some dogs—yours truly, for

example—are gorgeous, but some dogs are downright homely. You know that English bulldog that lives down the street? The one with the underbite? Talk about a face only a mother could love.

DAD: I know what looks means, Buster. But what are you asking me?

BUSTER: Are there mixed-breed dog shows that are just about looks? I don't want to have to perform some stupid pet trick like those stupid dogs on Letterman. I just want to stand there and look stunning. That's my strong suit.

DAD: Compared to obedience and humility, definitely.

BUSTER: I was thinking of a dog show that's like Miss USA. You know, where it's all about looks. Nothing else.

DAD: So not like Miss America.

BUSTER: Right. No tap dancing, no show tunes, no ventriloquism or accordions. No pretending the swimsuit competition is about fitness instead of what it's really about.

DAD: Let's see what else I can find. Here's a link to something called the Mixed-Breed Dog Clubs of America. It says they do rally and obedience and they also judge for conformation.

BUSTER: Conformation—what's that?

DAD: It says that dogs are separated by size, not breed—you'd probably be a medium—and are judged based on general appearance, physical condition, temperament, body shape, coat, color, and gait.

BUSTER: Perfect. That's got me written all over it. I am handsome in appearance, and my coat is sleek. In fact, because I excel at shedding, I have a brand new coat every week. My markings are exquisite, and my body shape is ideal.

DAD: But it's not only appearance, Buster. There's also physical condition.

BUSTER: So I'll lose a few pounds. More walks, less Pup-Peroni. I'm willing to sacrifice.

DAD: Don't forget temperament, which is not exactly your strong suit. You are, to quote the late, great Warren Zevon, an excitable boy.

BUSTER: I prefer to think of myself as exuberant, though I do like the song. But if the judges are looking for calm, I'll be calm. When the chips are down, I'll be as still as a statue, as cool as a cucumber, as docile as a doe.

DAD: I'd like to see that.

BUSTER: Come to the show and you will. Is that everything?

DAD: No. One more. And this one spells trouble. Gait.

BUSTER: Gait? What's that?

DAD: Gait means the way you walk.

BUSTER: What's wrong with the way I walk? Why does that spell trouble?

DAD: Mom says you walk like you're constipated.

BUSTER: Constipated? Is there no end to the insults? Do you agree with her?

DAD: I have to say that I do. It's hard to describe, but it's not a gait fitting for a dog who is handsome in appearance and has exquisite markings. When you come down the runway, you don't want the audience thinking you need a bathroom break.

BUSTER: Why has nobody ever said anything to me about this gait issue?

DAD: What difference does it make? You're able to get from here to there.

BUSTER: Evidently looking like I need to stop along the way. I can't believe you haven't told me. I tell you when something's wrong with you.

DAD: I can always count on you for that.

BUSTER: Surely this gait issue, if it really is an issue, is correctable.

DAD: And how do you plan to correct it?

BUSTER: Hire a gait coach. Contestants in beauty pageants hire coaches to teach them how to walk gracefully. If there are walking coaches for pretty girls, surely there must be gait coaches for handsome dogs. Hire one.

DAD: I'll be footing the bill, I suppose.

BUSTER: There you go again.

DAD: I love you, Buster, but I'm not hiring a gait coach.

BUSTER: Cheapskate.

DAD: I couldn't name a king or queen who eats dry dog food. Name a dog with a gait coach.

BUSTER: Tightwad.

DAD: There you go again, biting the hand.

BUSTER: Being a champion is my dream, Dad. How am I supposed to learn a dignified gait without a gait coach?

DAD: I'll tell you what we'll do. We'll watch the Westminster Dog Show and study the gaits of the champion dogs. Then we'll video your gait and compare.

BUSTER: I'm not sure I want to see my gait.

DAD: As you told me the other night, a dog's got to know his limitations. And watching champions and copying the way they walk is the best way to overcome your gait limitations.

BUSTER: So how will I be able to tell if I'm improving?

DAD: Mom and I will observe and provide feedback.

BUSTER: But you'll just make fun of me.

DAD: No I won't, but it does sound like fun.

BUSTER: I refuse to be the object of your ridicule. Constipated—I can't believe my sweet mother said that.

DAD: But I thought you wanted to be a champion.

BUSTER: I do, but you have to keep in mind how sensitive I am.

DAD: I'll tell you what—before we spend a lot of time on this and risk damaging your delicate ego, let's see what mixed-breed shows you could enter.

BUSTER: I'm willing to travel.

DAD: And stay in nice hotels, I bet.

BUSTER: A good night's sleep before a major competition is crucial, Dad. It can spell the difference between victory and defeat. Super Bowl teams don't stay at the Motel 6.

DAD: Let me see what there is. Uh-oh, it says no events are scheduled at this time.

BUSTER: What? They say they have dog shows, but they don't have dog shows?

DAD: I'm just telling you what it says, and it says no events are scheduled.

BUSTER: So schedule one.

DAD: I can't schedule one. Only a chapter of the Mixed-Breed Dog Clubs of America can host a show.

BUSTER: So start a chapter.

DAD: Buster, how would it look if Mom and I formed a chapter, scheduled a dog show, and our own son won it?

BUSTER: I'll use an alias.

DAD: I thought this was all about your legacy. What good would it do to win the show using a fake name?

BUSTER: I'll reveal my true identity after I win.

DAD: And you'll be stripped of your title. Our chapter will be shut down too.

BUSTER: You're a Dougie Downer, you know that?

DAD: More like Roger Realist. You can't enter a dog show using an alias, Buster.

BUSTER: Well then, Roger, what do you suggest? My dream is to be a champion. How, speaking as a realist, would you say I can achieve my dream?

DAD: It says there are no events scheduled at this time, but it also says to check back soon.

BUSTER: So I'm just supposed to sit and wait, is that what you're saying? Just bide my time and hope an event gets scheduled before the ravages of age overtake me and my body wastes away?

DAD: That's a little dramatic, don't you think?

BUSTER: It's not your dream, Dad.

DAD: You don't show any sign of wasting away, Buster. Quite the contrary.

BUSTER: But I could start wasting away at any minute.

DAD: Like it says, all we can do is check back soon. I'll check once a quarter.

BUSTER: Twice a week. Put a tickler on your calendar.

DAD: Once a month.

BUSTER: Once a week.

DAD: Twice a month. That's plenty often enough.

BUSTER: You don't know that. What if we miss a show and my chance at fame because you go two weeks without checking?

DAD: Buster, there's no way they're going to schedule a show and give you less than two weeks to enter.

BUSTER: How do you know that? Until ten minutes ago, you'd never heard of mixed-breed dog shows. Now all of a sudden you're an expert on the deadline for entering them.

DAD: Okay then, you win. Once a week. I'll put it on my calendar.

BUSTER: You think once a week is often enough? I'd be more comfortable with twice a week. Just sayin'.

DAD: Go to sleep, Buster. Please, for the sake of all that's precious in the world, go to sleep.

BUSTER: Twice a week, Dad. Please.

DAD: No. Once a week is more than I should do.

BUSTER: What about every five days?

DAD: You ever heard of a man-bites-dog story, Buster?

BUSTER: Why would a man bite a dog? That's weird.

DAD: Think about it.

BUSTER: Oh, I get it. Once a week will be fine. Make sure the tickler's on your calendar. And my dream's going to come true. I just know it. Thanks, Dad. You're the best.

DAD: Maybe not the best, but certainly the most indulgent. And son, I hope all your dreams come true. Just think: Buster Eason, dog of letters, CIA agent, meal-service tycoon, and world champion mixed-breed dog.

BUSTER: Now you're talking.

DAD: But now I'm through talking. As for you, it's time to go to sleep and dream a little dream of your dreams. Goodnight.

Vacay

We've never taken our dogs on vacation, but we don't board them at the vet when we go. Instead we get someone to stay with them, usually one of our children, so they won't have to do without the comforts of home. But Buster still gets nervous when I pull down a suitcase or get my camping equipment out of the attic. He knows something's up; maybe he's figured out that I'm leaving and I may be taking Carrie with me. I can tell he doesn't like it, but why? Is it because he wants me to stay home with him? Or because he wants me to take him with me? Last night I learned the answer.

BUSTER: Dad?

DAD: What, Buster?

BUSTER: Mollie and I want to go on vacation.

DAD: Is that right? Just the two of you, or with us?

BUSTER: With you and Mom, of course. Walking somewhere wouldn't be much of a vacation.

DAD: You're wrong about that. I've gone on many wonderful hiking trips.

BUSTER: On those trips, you hike in the mountains, right?

DAD: That's right.

BUSTER: And you get to the mountains by flying or driving, correct?

DAD: Usually both.

BUSTER: And if you and Mom don't take us, Mollie and I would have to walk to get to the mountains, true?

DAD: I suppose so.

BUSTER: And just how far away are these mountains? Looks pretty flat around here.

DAD: Depends on what you consider mountains, but hundreds of miles at least.

BUSTER: So Mollie and I would have to walk hundreds of miles before we even started our hiking vacation in the mountains. Man, for somebody who's supposed to be a smart lawyer, you sure make some dumb arguments.

DAD: It wasn't an argument, Buster. I was just pointing out that walking trips can be fun. You love going for walks, and you'd love hiking in the mountains. My hiking trips with Bobby have been some of the best vacations of my life.

BUSTER: Bobby's the skinny Italian guy you wrote the book about, right?

DAD: That's the one. He's not really Italian—he's lived in America all his life—but his ancestors were Italian.

BUSTER: I wonder if my wolf ancestors ate his Italian ancestors.

DAD: What made you think about that?

BUSTER: Because I love me some lasagna. Bobby's a funny guy, isn't he?

DAD: The funniest.

BUSTER: I think I'd like to go on vacation with you and Bobby.

DAD: I thought you wanted to go with Mom and me.

BUSTER: Why not both? You only go around once, Dad. Carpe diem. Seize the day.

DAD: Sounds like you want to go on every vacation I go on.

BUSTER: So? You go on every vacation you go on. I want to go with you and Mom, and I want to go with you and Bobby.

DAD: I don't know about going with Bobby and me.

BUSTER: C'mon, Dad. I want to see the mountains. As I've told you, I hear the call of the wild. Give me one reason I shouldn't be able to go.

DAD: Well, there's the matter of flying. You'd have to fly in a kennel in the luggage compartment.

BUSTER: Would not. I'd fly in the cabin with you. Preferably in first or business class.

DAD: And how are you going to pull that off?

BUSTER: Say you have mental problems—that won't be much of a stretch—and that I'm your emotional support dog. You've said yourself that I'm your emotional support dog.

DAD: But you're not a certified emotional support dog.

BUSTER: Then get me certified. I want to go, and I don't want to be stuck in the luggage compartment.

DAD: We'll see, but even if we could figure out a way to get you there, hiking with Bobby and me might not be safe.

BUSTER: Not safe? I'm sure-footed, agile. I'm like those mountain goats I see on those nature shows.

DAD: Falling's not my concern, Buster. I'm thinking bears.

BUSTER: Bears, shmares. I'm not afraid of any bear.

DAD: Even more reason for me to be concerned.

BUSTER: Why should I be scared of some dumb bear?

DAD: Buster, a grizzly bear can snap a dog's neck with one swat of his forepaw. An adult male grizzly is 15 times as big as you are.

BUSTER: But not as quick.

DAD: Whatever. And you wouldn't be the only one in danger. Having a dog would make it more likely that a bear would come into camp, which would make it more dangerous for Bobby and me.

BUSTER: I'll protect you. Both of you.

DAD: Tell me how a 40-pound dog, even one as fast as lightning, is going to protect us from a 600-pound bear.

BUSTER: I'll create a distraction. I'll snarl at the bear. Snap at him. Get him to chase me so y'all can get away. They don't call me man's best friend for nothing, Dad.

DAD: I'll talk to Bobby, but I wouldn't count on it.

BUSTER: Why not? Does he not like dogs?

DAD: He likes dogs, and he likes you. He just doesn't like bears.

BUSTER: I said I would protect y'all. Tell Bobby he'll be safe.

DAD: But I'm not so sure he would be. Your distraction might not work. And I doubt that Bobby would be willing to do anything that would make it more likely that a bear would come into camp.

BUSTER: Is he a chicken or something?

DAD: He's not a chicken, I assure you. He served in two wars, in Vietnam in the '70s and 30 years later in Iraq. He hiked across the Grand Canyon from rim to rim with a sprained ankle. He's not a chicken, but he's not dumb either, and he has a healthy fear of bears. That's normal.

BUSTER: Not to imply that you're normal, but why aren't you afraid of them?

DAD: I'm perfectly normal, and I recognize there's a risk whenever we camp and hike in bear country. Bobby's just more concerned than I am. I'll ask him, but if he says no, that's the end of it.

BUSTER: Unfairness rears its ugly head again. Find out what he says. If he says no, then I'll figure out my next move.

DAD: I'll talk to him, but if he says no, your next move is staying home.

BUSTER: Okay, let's put that aside for now and talk about vacations with you and Mom. Are they pretty much like your trips with Bobby?

DAD: Not at all.

BUSTER: What would you say are the biggest differences?

DAD: Well, for one thing, Bobby and I sleep on the ground in a tent. Mom and I stay someplace nice. With a nice bed and hot shower and air conditioning.

BUSTER: Score one for trips with Mom. What else?

DAD: Well, when Bobby and I hike in the mountains, it can be very strenuous, especially for me. He's always in better shape than I am. When Mom and I go on vacations, we take it easy.

BUSTER: Score two for Mom. What about meals? I fancy myself a foodie, as you know.

DAD: Big difference there. When Bobby and I backpack, we have to pack light. We usually eat dried oatmeal for breakfast, beef jerky or snacks for lunch, and a dehydrated meal for dinner.

BUSTER: Sounds repulsive. What about you and Mom? What do y'all eat?

DAD: When it's just us, we usually go to nice restaurants. When we go to the beach with the kids and grandkids, Mom and Ann Lowrey take turns cooking.

BUSTER: And they're both good cooks, aren't they?

DAD: Not good. Fantastic.

BUSTER: Let's recap what we have so far. The accommodations with Bobby are spartan, but with Mom they're plush. The food with Bobby is lousy, but with Mom it's delicious. And with Bobby you have to work hard, but with Mom the living is easy.

DAD: The trips are very different, Buster.

BUSTER: No kidding. One is miserable, the other fabulous. It's not looking like a close call. Anything else? Any other differences?

DAD: Well, my relationship with Bobby is very different from my relationship with Mom.

BUSTER: I should hope so. But how does the difference make your trips different?

DAD: Mom and I have a romantic relationship, Buster.

BUSTER: I'm fully aware of that, Dad, just as I'm fully aware that Mollie and I are unable to have a romantic relationship.

DAD: Sorry about that. Anyway, Bobby and I don't have a romantic relationship.

BUSTER: For which we can all be grateful. But what's that got to do with the trips?

DAD: Well, without getting into details, my romantic relationship with Mom adds a dimension to our trips that I don't have when I travel with Bobby.

BUSTER: Is that a plus for Bobby or a plus for Mom?

DAD: For Mom. Two pluses.

BUSTER: I don't get it, Dad. The trips with Mom sound like they're better paws down. What about bears? Any risk of a bear attack on your trips with Mom?

DAD: None. No bears where we go.

BUSTER: This is no contest, Dad. Why on earth do you go on your trips with Bobby? Name one thing that's better about the trips with him.

DAD: For one thing, the scenery. He and I have seen some of the most beautiful places in America.

BUSTER: Which you could also see in pictures. Let somebody else trudge up a mountain with a camera, eat beef jerky, and risk a bear attack.

DAD: Photos are no substitute, Buster. They're not even close.

BUSTER: And a tent's not even close to a room at the Ritz. Anything else?

DAD: Campfires. Bobby and I have a great time by our campfires.

BUSTER: But you've got a fire ring in our backyard. And when the fire goes out, you can come inside, climb in bed, and do your romantic thing with Mom.

DAD: There is that, and it's wonderful, but there's no Bobby in the backyard.

BUSTER: So tell him to get his skinny tail down here. Y'all can have your precious campfires in the backyard if they're so important to you.

DAD: That's a good idea, but it's not the same as being in the mountains.

BUSTER: Why not? A fire's a fire.

DAD: It's not just the fire. The whole experience is different. At night, other than the crackling of the campfire, it's totally silent. No traffic. No barking dogs.

BUSTER: Somebody's got to guard the house, Dad.

DAD: And the stars. You wouldn't believe the stars.

BUSTER: The little white dots in the sky at night? They're no big deal.

DAD: They're not a big deal; they're a huge deal. In the mountains in the West, you can't believe how many you can see. They're magnificent.

BUSTER: White dots are magnificent? I don't think so.

DAD: Buster, it pains me to say this, but I don't think you have poetry in your soul.

BUSTER: Take me on vacation, Dad, and you'll see the poetry in my soul. I'll write a poem every day. Sonnets, haiku, dirty limericks, you name it.

DAD: What about doggerel?

BUSTER: Doggerel. That's a good one. Let me make an important point. You fault me for not getting excited about things I've never seen. My answer to that is obvious: I need to see them to get excited. If you want me to have poetry in my soul, take me with you to the mountains. Let me see the glorious stars, the pristine lakes, the magnificent peaks and waterfalls.

DAD: Fair point. I'll talk to Bobby.

BUSTER: Good. Now, once again, let's get back to vacations with you and Mom. You mentioned something about going to the beach with the family. What's the beach?

DAD: You'd love the beach, Buster. The beach is where the land meets the ocean.

BUSTER: What's the ocean?

DAD: Oceans are huge bodies of water. Think of something more than a million times as big as the lake behind our house.

BUSTER: A million times. Wow. We'd never be able to take a walk around that. So what do y'all do when you go to the beach? Describe a typical day.

DAD: Well, we usually sleep late. Then we have breakfast. We might sit on the porch for a while after that and read. I go for walks. Sometimes Mom goes with me. There's usually a nice breeze, and you can look at the ocean and listen to the waves. It's very peaceful.

BUSTER: Ooh, I love a breeze. So take us to the beach, Dad. Please. We'll be good.

DAD: We've thought about taking y'all, but some places don't allow pets.

BUSTER: First of all, I would hope you wouldn't patronize any establishment with such a discriminatory rule. And second, Mollie and I are not pets. We're you're children. I bet they don't have a rule against children.

DAD: Probably not, but I bet they would say y'all are pets. Anyway, not all places have such rules.

BUSTER: Then take us, Dad. Please. We'll be as good as gold.

DAD: It's not as simple as finding a place, Buster. There's also the question of how to get you there.

BUSTER: Mom has an SUV with three seats. Plenty of room for us and her clothes. Even her Imelda Marcos-size shoe collection.

DAD: But we might not have room if we have the grandchildren.

BUSTER: Surely we come first if it comes down to us and the grandchildren.

DAD: Surely you don't.

BUSTER: What? We're your children. We're part of your immediate family. We're the ones who live with y'all. Not them. They just come once a week or so and eat, play, make a mess, then go back home.

DAD: But y'all are our fur children, Buster, not our real children.

BUSTER: Not your real children? What do you mean, not your real children? You adopted us, didn't you? It was all legal, wasn't it? All on the up and up? I's dotted? T's crossed?

DAD: I believe so.

BUSTER: Your parents adopted you, too, didn't they?

DAD: You know they did, Buster. We've discussed that.

BUSTER: And you've always been their real child, haven't you? And Mollie and I are your real children too. There's no difference.

DAD: Well, there is one.

BUSTER: And what, pray tell, is that?

DAD: Mama and Daddy were people. So am I. Y'all are dogs.

BUSTER: A mere technicality.

DAD: I think it's more than that. But listen, if you want to say you're our real children, fine with me. But you don't want me to have to choose between you and the grandchildren. That won't go well for you.

BUSTER: Well, I guess I know where I stand in the pecking order.

DAD: Poor downtrodden Buster, below the grandchildren and the primates. Maybe we can work it out so we don't have to choose. Maybe the grandchildren can ride with their parents, or at least some of them can, and y'all can ride with us.

BUSTER: The grandchildren have us outnumbered, don't they?

DAD: Sure do. There are twice as many of them.

BUSTER: What were their parents thinking? Do they not know what college costs these days?

DAD: They'll get scholarships. They're brilliant.

BUSTER: I hope you're right. You're not what I would call objective about them. Are Ann Lowrey and Paul gonna have any more?

DAD: No. Paul had a procedure to make sure Ann Lowrey doesn't get pregnant again.

BUSTER: Same procedure I had?

DAD: Oh, no. The procedure used to neuter dogs is much more radical than the one used for people.

BUSTER: Once again, I'm reminded of my place in the pecking order.

DAD: You do tend to forget that you're a dog, Buster. But even though you're way down in the pecking order, someday we would like to take you and Mollie to the beach. Mom mentioned it just the other day.

BUSTER: Sweet! Tell me what Mollie and I would do at the beach.

DAD: We would have great fun. We could play in the waves.

BUSTER: I don't think that's gonna work. Neither of us likes the water.

DAD: Oh, come on. Playing in the waves is lots of fun. You'll love it. Mollie will too. She's a spaniel. Spaniels are water dogs.

BUSTER: Not this particular spaniel, Dad. Mollie doesn't even like to get her toes wet. When it's raining and the grass is wet, she uses the patio as her restroom.

DAD: The ocean is different. I bet she'll do it.

BUSTER: I bet she won't. She can't swim, Dad. Neither can I.

DAD: Don't be ridiculous, Buster. All dogs can swim.

BUSTER: Not these two. Have you ever seen us swim?

DAD: I can't say that I have.

BUSTER: That's because we can't. We've never been swimming, and it's too late to learn now.

DAD: No, it's not. Swimming comes natural to dogs. Two healthy dogs, one of whom is a spaniel, would take to it like I took to channeling.

BUSTER: I don't think so, Dad. Old dogs, new tricks. We could drown.

DAD: No, you won't. If you start having trouble, I'll rescue you.

BUSTER: You think you could?

DAD: Sure. I've been swimming since 50 years before you were born.

BUSTER: That's what concerns me. Not to point out the obvious, Dad, but you're no spring chicken. You're not even a summer chicken. I'm not so sure I want to count on being saved by an old codger like you.

DAD: Watch it, Buster. You're on thin ice. And you don't want to fall through if you can't swim.

BUSTER: Let's put the question of swimming on the back burner. What else could we do?

DAD: You could chase sand crabs.

BUSTER: What are sand crabs?

DAD: They're small animals that live on the beach. When you chase them, they go skittering across the sand.

BUSTER: What do you do if you catch them?

DAD: Just let them go.

BUSTER: So it's pretty much just for sport?

DAD: That's right.

BUSTER: Any money in it?

DAD: None.

BUSTER: Other than being on sand, it doesn't sound any different from chasing a tennis ball.

DAD: No, it's very different. A sand crab can be going fast one way and then suddenly change course. Then, just when you're about to catch him, he changes directions again.

BUSTER: That hardly seems fair.

DAD: The sand crab's not concerned about fair, Buster. The sand crab is running for its life.

BUSTER: But you said it was catch and release.

DAD: The crab doesn't know that.

BUSTER: Sounds like catching sand crabs is a real challenge. I'm always up for a challenge.

DAD: You are? What challenges have you taken on?

BUSTER: You don't listen, Dad. I didn't say I had taken on any challenges. I said I was up for one. And I'm up for chasing sand crabs. Chasing crabs is a new trick this old dog can learn. I bet I'll excel at it.

DAD: Mollie may be better. She's got shorter legs and is closer to the ground. As you've admitted, she can make sharp turns better than you can and is better at chasing tennis balls.

BUSTER: You forget my advantage in brainpower. Mollie may know where a crab is right now, but I'll know where he's headed.

DAD: So you've never seen a crab, but you'll be able to anticipate where he's going. You don't lack for confidence, do you, Buster?

BUSTER: To quote the late, great Dizzy Dean, it ain't braggin' if you can do it.

DAD: So says the dog who needs swimming lessons.

BUSTER: Anything else we can do at the beach?

DAD: Well, the sunsets are beautiful there. You'll get to see the sunsets.

BUSTER: You're a hopeless romantic, aren't you, Dad?

DAD: I have poetry in my soul. What can I say?

BUSTER: Whatever. Anything else we can do?

DAD: Well, we really don't do all that much when we're at the beach. So you can hang out with us and do nothing.

BUSTER: Now you're talking turkey. Doing nothing is right in my wheelhouse. I'm an expert. Left to my own devices, I sleep 20 hours a day and do precious little the other four. Give me a comfortable spot in the sun, and I'm golden.

DAD: You're gonna love the beach.

BUSTER: Then let's go. I'm ready.

DAD: I'll talk to Mom.

BUSTER: Talk to her now.

DAD: I can't talk to her if I'm talking to you.

BUSTER: Good point. Plus I've been awake for nearly an hour straight. I'm exhausted.

DAD: Go to sleep, Buster.

BUSTER: Already dozing off. Nighty night.

Fin And Feather Children

People keep all kinds of animals as pets. Ferrets, snakes, iguanas, you name it. And I'm all for letting people have what they want. To each his own, I always say. Live and let live. But when I see some of the animals people choose to live with, I have to ask myself: If you can have a dog, why have one of those? In fact, if you can have a dog, why have anything else? Not surprisingly, Buster agrees with me.

BUSTER: Dad?

DAD: What, Buster?

BUSTER: Do people adopt any animals other than dogs?

DAD: You mean as pets?

BUSTER: We're not pets, Dad, we're children. How many times do I have to tell you that?

DAD: Sorry. You mean what unenlightened people refer to as pets?

BUSTER: I suppose. I know some people adopt cats, though why in the world anybody would provide food and shelter for one is beyond me. But are there any others?

DAD: I like cats. They're amusing and affectionate. Plus they can purr. Dogs can't purr.

BUSTER: Is purring that funny noise cats make that sounds like a tiny motorboat?

DAD: That's it. Pretty cool, isn't it?

BUSTER: If you say so. But enough about cats. I already know more than I want to know about them. Do people adopt any other animals as fur children?

DAD: Not just fur children. Fin and feather children too.

BUSTER: Do what?

DAD: Fish have fins. Birds have feathers. People have fish and birds. I've never had either one, but lots of people do.

BUSTER: You're making that up. A fish? Seriously? Why would anybody want a fish?

DAD: Tropical fish are beautiful. Amazing colors. They're gorgeous.

BUSTER: Not as gorgeous as I am, surely.

DAD: Of course not. Perish the thought.

BUSTER: So I'm more attractive. Let's see. Do fish come when you call?

DAD: Not that I know of, but that's not your strong suit either.

BUSTER: C'mon Dad. I always come eventually. Here I am, am I not?

DAD: But you take your own sweet time.

BUSTER: I just finish what I'm doing, okay? Sometimes I need to do some more sniffing and hike my leg three or four more times.

DAD: You could hike your leg just once, you know.

BUSTER: I'm a male dog, Dad, and that's not the way we roll. Marking our territory is a biological imperative.

DAD: I wonder if fish mark their territory.

BUSTER: Fish live in the water, Dad. They don't have territory. Plus they don't have a leg to hike, and if they tried to mark anything, it would just wash away. Let's see. What other differences are there? Fish don't bring your slippers, do they?

DAD: Neither do you. You've never once done it.

BUSTER: But I could. You can't take a fish for a walk, can you?

DAD: Fish don't walk. They swim.

BUSTER: Exactly. And there's never been a watch fish, has there?

DAD: Not to my knowledge.

BUSTER: Can a fish lick your hand? Curl up at your feet? Fetch a tennis ball?

DAD: Very doubtful.

BUSTER: Scare off an intruder? Perform a heroic rescue? I love it when Lassie barks like crazy and leads the grown-ups to Timmy in the well. Has a fish ever done that? Anything like that?

DAD: Also doubtful.

BUSTER: You're not making much of a case for having a fish instead of a dog, Dad.

DAD: I'm not trying to make a case, Buster. Look around. How many fish do you see?

BUSTER: Then it's agreed: Dogs are superior to fish. So why would anybody choose a fish?

DAD: Beats me. I guess they just like to look at them. Maybe they're concerned about vet bills or they're allergic to dog hair. Don't ask me to explain fish owners. I've never been one.

BUSTER: You also mentioned birds. Are you telling me people really have feather children?

DAD: They do. Lots of people.

BUSTER: Why on earth? Birds can't lick your hand, they can only peck it.

DAD: Well, again, I think it's mostly about appearance. Tropical birds are like tropical fish—beautiful, very colorful.

BUSTER: But there's more to life than pretty plumage, Dad. Even if they have fancy feathers, why would someone rather have a bird than a dog? Name one reason.

DAD: Birds can talk.

BUSTER: What?

DAD: They can talk. Some of them talk just like people do.

BUSTER: Without being channeled?

DAD: That's right. In English. I'm sure in other languages too.

BUSTER: I'm not buying it. Have you ever actually seen a bird talk?

DAD: Sure. It's a well-known phenomenon.

BUSTER: In person? Have you seen it in person or just on YouTube?

DAD: I don't remember, but it's a real thing. I'm not making it up.

BUSTER: You are some kind of gullible, Dad. Birds talking. Wow. You'll believe anything.

DAD: Birds can talk, Buster. I'm not making it up.

BUSTER: Prove it.

DAD: Okay, I'll find a video.

BUSTER: You know videos can be doctored, don't you? I presume you've heard of photoshopping.

DAD: Birds can talk, Buster. Parrots, mynah birds, cockatoos, lots of birds.

BUSTER: Okay, you seem convinced, so just for now I'll assume birds can talk. I'm not saying I believe it, you understand, because I don't. But assuming they can, do they understand what they're saying? Or are they just repeating the sounds they hear when people talk?

DAD: Now that I don't know.

BUSTER: So it might be no different from when you bark.

DAD: What do you mean, when I bark?

BUSTER: I've heard you bark. Don't deny it. And when you do, you're just mimicking a dog. You have no idea what you're saying, just like the alleged talking birds don't.

DAD: No idea what I'm saying? I'm not saying anything. I'm barking, or at least you claim I am.

BUSTER: Why do you think dogs bark, Dad? Just to hear ourselves make noise? When we bark, we're talking to other dogs, just not in a language you understand.

DAD: But dogs bark even when there's no other dog around.

BUSTER: Have you never talked to yourself, Dad?

DAD: Maybe a time or two.

BUSTER: Maybe a time or 200,000. Anyway, maybe a bird can mimic a person just like you mimic us, but there's no way birds understand what they're saying.

DAD: Why do you say that? How could you possibly know?

BUSTER: Bird-brained, Dad. Not exactly a compliment, is it?

DAD: No, but maybe it should be. Because birds can talk, maybe bird-brained should mean smart, smarter than a dog. I've never seen a dog who can talk.

BUSTER: You want to swap me for a mynah bird, just say the word.

DAD: I don't want to swap you for anybody, Buster. I'm just trying to explain why some people prefer other animals.

BUSTER: Fair enough, but I still don't get it. A fish instead of a dog? A bird instead of a dog? Really?

DAD: Don't ask me to explain it. I'm a dog man through and through, as you well know.

BUSTER: Okay then, we've eliminated fish and birds as viable alternatives. Cats too, though that goes without saying.

DAD: Then why did you say it?

BUSTER: Whenever you say something goes without saying, you still say it. It's another weird expression people use, probably invented by the same guy who came up with "I don't mean to interrupt." Anyway, are there any other animals who live with people? Whether they're covered with fins, feathers, fur, skin, or scales, I want to hear about them.

DAD: I'm glad you mentioned scales. Some people have pet snakes.

BUSTER: Snakes? Mister No Shoulders? Now I know you're pulling my leg. And it's not working. You're the gullible one, not me.

DAD: Some people really do have snakes for pets. Don't ask me why, but they do.

BUSTER: Snakes are poisonous, Dad. Surely poisonous pet is an oxymoron.

DAD: Not all snakes are poisonous, Buster.

BUSTER: I wonder how many people, and dogs for that matter, have been killed by snakes they thought weren't poisonous. It's like all the people who get shot with unloaded guns. Don't be bringing any snakes around here. Mollie and I are all the animal children you and Mom need.

DAD: No worries. No snake pets for us.

BUSTER: Thank you, because I'm afraid it would have to be us or the snake. I don't think I'd be able to sleep.

DAD: At least not your usual 20 hours a day.

BUSTER: I need my beauty sleep, okay? Why in heaven's name would anyone want to adopt a snake anyway?

DAD: Beats me. I'm not as scared of snakes as some people are, and apparently some dogs, but I don't understand having a snake as a pet.

BUSTER: They're not warm and fuzzy, they can't possibly do tricks—I'd like to see what happens when you tell a snake to sit—and they've got that whole forked tongue thing too. The way they flick it in and out creeps me out. And those eyes. Nobody ever called a snake doe-eyed, that's for sure.

DAD: You're preaching to the choir, Buster.

BUSTER: Preaching to the choir?

DAD: It means telling people something they already agree with. If a person's in the choir, he probably already agrees with what the preacher's preaching.

BUSTER: I've never heard that expression, but I like it. So if you tell me I'm handsome, you're preaching to the choir.

DAD: An excellent example.

BUSTER: Or if I tell you Mom is beautiful and a fabulous cook.

DAD: That one too.

BUSTER: Let me ask you this, Dad. These people who have snakes, what do they feed them?

DAD: I don't know their whole diet, but I know it includes mice and rats.

BUSTER: Mice and rats? Really?

DAD: Really.

BUSTER: I'm no fan of mice and rats, but that's disgusting. And I was already against the whole snake deal. I've got to say, Dad, people who keep snakes are even stranger than people who channel dogs.

DAD: Thank you, I guess.

BUSTER: Although both are pretty weird.

DAD: Want me to stop channeling you, Buster?

BUSTER: Just kidding, Dad. I'm sure you're completely normal, at least in your own mind.

DAD: I'm not sure a dog with your own mind should be judging a person with my own mind.

BUSTER: Au, contraire. I'm uniquely qualified to judge a person with your own mind. After all, I'm the one you have all these channeling conversations with. Listen, are there any other animals we need to discuss? I'm sure not feeling much competition from fish, birds, and snakes. And definitely not from cats. I am still, and here's another great expression, top dog.

DAD: And oh so humble.

BUSTER: I'm just kidding, Dad. Dogs like to joke around, you know. But snakes? I've never once seen a snake crack a smile. So, any other animals?

DAD: Lots. Some people have rabbits. Some have hamsters and gerbils and guinea pigs. I have friends who had two ferrets. There are turtles, iguanas, and pigs.

BUSTER: Whoa, whoa, whoa, slow down. This is too much to process, even for a dog with my own mind. I know what some of those animals are, but not all of them. What's the first one you mentioned?

DAD: Rabbits.

BUSTER: Okay, I can maybe see having a rabbit. They've got those big translucent ears and they do that cute thing with their noses. They really are doe-eyed, and I loved The Runaway Bunny. *But let me ask you this: Can you house train a rabbit?*

DAD: Not to my knowledge.

BUSTER: I didn't think so. Next.

DAD: Guinea pigs, hamsters and gerbils are all small rodents. Very cute.

BUSTER: Rodents? You mean like a mouse or a rat?

DAD: That's right, but cuter.

BUSTER: What about house training them? Can you train little rodents not to do their business in the house?

DAD: Doubtful.

BUSTER: So what do rodent parents do? The droppings may be small, but you still don't want to be stepping in them all the time.

DAD: They keep the rodents in cages. Keeps the droppings in one place.

BUSTER: Cages? Like in the zoo? Or like those kennels where they stick us at the vet?

DAD: I guess, but smaller.

BUSTER: Life in a cage—I shudder to think. Why would anybody want a fur child that has to stay cooped up in a cage?

DAD: Beats me. I wouldn't.

BUSTER: I guess we can scratch them off the list. What else?

DAD: Ferrets.

BUSTER: That's a new one for me. What's a ferret?

DAD: It's a mammal. Smaller than most dogs. Long and skinny. Short legs. Very fast.

BUSTER: Does it look like any animals I know?

DAD: I think it's related to minks and otters. And the weasel.

BUSTER: Did you say weasel? You know how weasels act, don't you, Dad? Weaselly, that's how. Always trying to weasel out of something. Being weaselly is even worse than being bird-brained. Next.

DAD: Turtles.

BUSTER: A turtle seems like an odd choice. What's the point of having a turtle?

DAD: I think they're low maintenance. Some people keep them in their backyards. They may actually be tortoises.

BUSTER: Okay, so the cost is low, but what's the benefit? Let's say a turtle or tortoise, whatever you want to call it, hangs out in your backyard. I don't see the upside.

DAD: I agree. Low cost, maybe even no cost, but very little benefit.

BUSTER: Turtles aren't affectionate, are they? I've never heard of a watch turtle. Or a seeing-eye turtle. Have you?

DAD: No, but that's something I'd love to see.

BUSTER: So scratch the turtle. What's next? Ig something?

DAD: Iguana.

BUSTER: I don't even like the way that sounds. What's an iguana?

DAD: It's a real big lizard.

BUSTER: A lizard? Really? That's all I need to hear. Next.

DAD: Pigs.

BUSTER: Pigs? People actually have pigs as fur children?

DAD: Yes, though they're not very furry.

BUSTER: Or handsome. Why would anybody want a pig?

DAD: They're supposed to be real smart.

BUSTER: They wallow in the mud, Dad. How smart can they be? And who could stand all that grunting? That would get old in a hurry.

DAD: So does all that barking.

BUSTER: We're watchdogs, Dad.

DAD: You bark at neighbors walking their dogs, Buster.

BUSTER: One of those neighbors could be casing the joint and planning to come back to rob it. You ever thought about that? He could be using the dog as a cover.

DAD: Hasn't happened so far.

BUSTER: Have you ever thought about why? In case you haven't, I'll tell you. It's because Mollie and I are on duty 24/7.

DAD: What are you talking about? You and Mollie sleep 20/7.

BUSTER: *With one eye and both ears open.*

DAD: You snore through thunderstorms, Buster.

BUSTER: Only when Mollie has the night shift. You sure take our security services for granted. You'd never get the same quality of service from a pig.

DAD: I'll try to be more grateful.

BUSTER: Thank you. Plus how could you and Mom afford to feed a pig?

DAD: What we spend on your fancy dog food and Pup-Peroni and other treats is nothing to sneeze at.

BUSTER: It's a pittance when you compare how much we eat to how much a pig eats. What would you say a pig eats like, Dad?

DAD: A pig?

BUSTER: Bingo. And what would you rather have—a handsome, affectionate companion with a soft coat or a homely, grunting glutton covered in mud?

DAD: You're preaching to the choir again. I'm a dog man through and through, I told you that. I don't want a pig, and I'm sure Mom doesn't want one either.

BUSTER: Good to know. Before we wrap this up, are there any more animals we need to compare to dogs?

DAD: There are some other animals that people adopt, but I don't think we need to perform a detailed comparison for all of them.

BUSTER: Because dogs are better, aren't they?

DAD: Infinitely.

BUSTER: This has been a satisfying talk, Dad. We have established beyond a shadow of a doubt that dogs are far and away the best fur children. We're not bird-brained or weaselly, and we don't eat like pigs. You agree with my assessment, don't you?

DAD: Absolutely. Man's best friend, that's what dogs are.

BUSTER: Man's best friend: Three little words, just like I love you. I'm going to sleep well tonight.

DAD: But lightly.

BUSTER: What?

DAD: You're a light sleeper, remember?

BUSTER: Oh yeah. Very light. Always on duty. Ever vigilant. I'll sleep with one eye open.

DAD: Goodnight, Buster. Close the other eye.

People Envy

Dogs' lives revolve around the lives of their people. They love to be with us, and they spend as much time with us as they possibly can. I'm now sitting at Carrie's desk typing this, and both dogs are asleep at my feet.

Because of how much time our dogs spend with us, I wonder if they ever think about the differences between our lives and theirs. Do they compare activities and diets? Do they question why we wear clothes and they don't? If I had to guess, I would say they don't think about any of this. They sure don't seem to envy us. But maybe I'm wrong.

BUSTER: Dad?

DAD: What, Buster?

BUSTER: I've been thinking it's a whole lot better to be a person than a dog. Do you agree?

DAD: I can't say. I've never been a dog.

BUSTER: C'mon, Dad, you've been around dogs all your life. To paraphrase Yogi, you've observed a lot about dogs by just watching us. So which is it better to be—a person or a dog?

DAD: I still don't know. I've seen how dogs live, but I can't judge a dog's life from a dog's perspective because I'm not a dog.

BUSTER: You're bound to have an opinion, Dad. You have an opinion about everything else.

DAD: Well, I think some people's lives are better than some dogs' lives, no doubt about it. But I'm sure that some dogs' lives, yours for example, are better than some people's.

BUSTER: I'm talking in general, Dad. On average. The median dog versus the median person.

DAD: I really don't know. What makes you think it's better to be a person?

BUSTER: Lots of things. To start with, as you've conceded, people live a lot longer.

DAD: That's true, and it's a fair point, but living until you're very old can be more of a curse than a blessing. Some people get to the point that their bodies are worn out and they're in pain all the time, and some live until their brains quit working. Living longer is not always better. What else?

BUSTER: People get to go on all sorts of cool trips, but dogs don't.

DAD: I agree with you on that one. Mom and I love to travel.

BUSTER: And leave us at home.

DAD: We don't want to leave you, Buster, I promise. But there are some trips you just can't go on. Like the live music cruise Mom and I take. No dogs allowed.

BUSTER: A stupid rule.

DAD: And one we didn't make. Anything else?

BUSTER: Food. People's diets are better and more varied. You get to eat all sorts of things, while we're stuck with dry dog food and the occasional Pup-Peroni. Whatever happened to the rollout of Buster Gump's Prime Cuts anyway?

DAD: Couldn't make the pricing work. Marketing people thought we were nuts.

BUSTER: Bummer. Eating dry dog food gets as old as Methuselah.

DAD: But you get those dog burgers too.

BUSTER: But they're nothing like the burgers you eat, Dad, the ones with the smoky grilled flavor and the gooey, melted American cheese on a toasted sesame-seed bun. I've tasted human food, and trust me, there's no comparison. When Mom cooks, the smells drive us insane.

DAD: I suspect that dog food is not as good as human food, especially if Mom's cooking it, but I really can't say for sure because I've never eaten dog food.

BUSTER: There's some in the bowl right over there. Get yourself a mouthful.

DAD: No, thanks.

BUSTER: C'mon, Dad. Half my dog food for half your human food. A fair trade. If dog food is good enough for your own son, it should be good enough for you.

DAD: I'll pass.

BUSTER: I figured as much. So in the people column we've got longevity, though to be fair I'll add an asterisk because living till you're real old isn't always so great, and we've got trips and food with no asterisks. And thumbs. Don't forget thumbs.

DAD: You've really got a thumb fixation, don't you, Buster?

BUSTER: Let's chop off your thumbs and see how fixated you get. Because I don't have thumbs, I can't hold a pen, which means the items in the people column are only in my head. Can hold pen and write—that's another item for the people column. And drive a car, throw a ball, and play the saxophone.

DAD: You want to play the saxophone?

BUSTER: Sure. I love me some John Coltrane.

DAD: Who knew? Look, I'll grant you that being human is better than being a dog in some ways, but there are definitely some things that are better about being a dog.

BUSTER: Name one.

DAD: Dogs don't have to have jobs. They don't have to get up and go to work.

BUSTER: I don't get up and go to work only because my job is here. And the location is not the only difference in our jobs. At the end of the day, you come home, relax, have a glass of wine, and eat some of that fabulous food Mom cooks. By contrast, my duties as a watchdog are never-ending.

DAD: Your job doesn't strike me as very demanding, Buster.

BUSTER: Not very demanding? I'm on duty 24 hours a day, seven days a week, 52 weeks a year. The only break I get is when you haul me to the vet. Some break that is. And when I'm home, while you're having a nice Cabernet and dancing in the kitchen with Mom and whispering no telling what in her ear, I'm on high alert, ready to spring into action at a moment's notice.

DAD: And all this time, I thought you were just barking at people walking their dogs.

BUSTER: I apply the rules evenhandedly, Dad. I don't play favorites. I bark at everybody.

DAD: So I've noticed.

BUSTER: We'll put less demanding job in the people column. Can you come up with anything that is truly better about being a dog?

DAD: How's this? Dogs don't have to worry about making a living and paying the bills.

BUSTER: But dogs have to worry about whether their parents can make a living and pay the bills. And, once again, people have it better. People at least have some control. They can get to work on time, do a good job, and treat people with respect. Other than barking when his dad keeps hitting the snooze button, a dog can't control any of that. And when times get tough, it's the dog who gets shafted. It's the dog who gets abandoned at the shelter, not his deadbeat dad who got fired for playing online poker at work.

DAD: You don't need to worry, Buster. We can pay our bills.

BUSTER: I'm not talking about me, Dad. I'm talking about all dogs. You channel me, which gives me a unique opportunity to be a spokesdog. I speak for all dogs, from arrogant AKC champions to humble strays. It's a solemn obligation and a heavy burden.

DAD: Very admirable, but in your own particular case, there's no need to worry your handsome little head. Mom and I have the resources to take care of you and Mollie.

BUSTER: But that could change. The market could crater. You could become a gambling addict. Your firm could find out about your channeling and give you the boot. There could be a pandemic.

DAD: All unlikely, but even if something like that happened, you can rest assured that Mom would take care of you. She would sell her engagement ring before she let anything happen to you and Mollie.

BUSTER: Mom's the best, isn't she? If every dog had a mom like Mom, it might be better to be a dog than a person.

DAD: But if every man had a wife like Mom, it might be better to be a person than a dog.

BUSTER: Touché. Let's stipulate that you and I have it better than most people and most dogs. But let's get back to people in general versus dogs in general. There's still nothing in the dog column. Can you think of anything? Anything at all?

DAD: Dogs don't have to wear clothes. They're covered in beautiful fur coats. They get to walk around naked all day, every day.

BUSTER: What's so great about that?

DAD: Think about it. Because you don't have to wear clothes, you don't have to buy, wash, dry, and iron them. You don't have to take them to the cleaners. And you don't have to pick out what to wear and spend time getting dressed. You just wake up in your birthday suit ready to roll.

BUSTER: Birthday suit?

DAD: Your birthday suit is what you were born wearing. When you're wearing your birthday suit, you're naked.

BUSTER: I guess a grown man could get into trouble going out on his birthday in his birthday suit.

DAD: Grown woman too.

BUSTER: I can see how it's less expensive and more convenient not to wear clothes, but I'd still like to wear them.

DAD: And why is that?

BUSTER: Because I'm a dog with a certain sense of style. Clothes would enhance that.

DAD: But clothes would cover up your striking markings.

BUSTER: I wouldn't wear clothes all the time. Just occasionally, depending on the function I'm attending.

DAD: You attend functions?

BUSTER: I would if I had clothes.

DAD: I believe your interest in clothes would be a minority view among dogs, Buster. A tiny minority. I'd say it's a rare dog who's concerned about his personal appearance.

BUSTER: Dogs don't have personal appearances, Dad. Only a person can have a personal appearance.

DAD: That sounds like something I would say.

BUSTER: Acorn, tree.

DAD: Forget the personal. I'll just say that most dogs don't care what they look like. Most dogs don't have a certain sense of style.

BUSTER: You may be right. I never said I was a typical dog. Let me ask you this: If it's less expensive and more convenient to wear your birthday suit all the time, why don't people do it?

DAD: Well, partly for warmth. We're not covered in fur coats like dogs are. We need clothes to keep from getting cold.

BUSTER: But people wear clothes even when it's as hot as the hinges of hell outside. Why wear clothes then?

DAD: It's cultural, I guess. It's okay for you, Mollie, and Mom to see me in my birthday suit, but I wouldn't be comfortable walking around that way in front of other people. And I sure wouldn't want other men seeing Mom in her birthday suit.

BUSTER: I bet you wouldn't want Mom to see other men in their birthday suits either.

DAD: Definitely not.

BUSTER: Their birthday suits might be a bit more stylish than yours, if you get my drift. I can see why the no-clothes deal is a slight advantage for dogs, but everything else is cutting in favor of people. Do you have anything else to say before I announce my decision?

DAD: I do have something else to say—some things to ask actually. I'll start with this: Do you like it when Mom and I scratch you behind the ears?

BUSTER: Of course. Who wouldn't?

DAD: And rub your belly?

BUSTER: That's even better.

DAD: What about when Mom gives you Pup-Peroni?

BUSTER: You know the answer to that.

DAD: And bacon?

BUSTER: Bacon's the best.

DAD: A slice of cheese?

BUSTER: Not as great as bacon, but still great.

DAD: And how do you feel when you realize I'm about to take you for a walk?

BUSTER: Actions speak louder than words, Dad, and you see how I act. No matter how many times you take me, it still thrills my soul.

DAD: And when we're out on the trail and you see new sights and sniff new smells, do you enjoy that?

BUSTER: You know I do.

DAD: Do you like it when we walk in the woods?

BUSTER: Do I ever! Makes me feel like Seaman, that dog that went to the West with Lewis and Clark.

DAD: You have two beds, one in our bedroom and one on the screened porch. How does that make you feel?

BUSTER: Comfortable. And sleepy.

DAD: So let's wrap this up then, but first one more: Do you feel fortunate to have a sister and parents who love you, to live in a nice home, and to have plenty to eat?

BUSTER: Of course I do. I went from being a shelter dog to living the American dream.

DAD: Then I've got some advice for you, Buster. I suggest you stop thinking about whether it's better to be a person than a dog. And here's why: Because, no matter what, you're still going to be a dog, and I'm still going to be a person.

BUSTER: That's sure been the case so far.

DAD: So instead of thinking you'd rather be a person, I recommend that you focus on how wonderful it is to be Buster Eason, living the American dream.

BUSTER: It's a *miracle when you think about it. If you and Mom hadn't come into PETCO that day, we never would have met.*

DAD: That's true, and our lives would be poorer. Yours and mine.

BUSTER: Especially mine. You'd still have Mom and Mollie. Who knows where I would be?

DAD: One of the keys to happiness, Buster, is to be grateful for what you have and not worry about what you don't have.

BUSTER: I'm going to sleep well again tonight.

DAD: But lightly, with one eye open.

BUSTER: Not tonight, Dad. I'm going to count my blessings and then sleep with both eyes shut. And I'm going to be grateful to Mollie for taking the night shift.

DAD: Good for you. Goodnight, Buster.

Dog Dynasty

I'm a grateful lifetime beneficiary of dog privilege. I've had the company of dogs for nearly all of my 63 years.

Growing up and as a young adult, I always had one dog at a time. To use a word Buster introduced me to last night when we discussed the dogs of my past, I was a serial modogamist. But in more recent years, we've usually had two dogs, and once we had three. It's been a good change. Dogs love their people, but they also love the company of other dogs.

Buster was initially reluctant to ask me about the dogs of my past, just as I don't ask Carrie about her old boyfriends. But by the end of our talk, Buster was glad he did.

BUSTER: Dad?

DAD: What, Buster?

BUSTER: I shouldn't ask you this because I'm afraid I'll be opening a can of worms.

DAD: So don't ask me.

BUSTER: But I really need to know.

DAD: So ask me.

BUSTER: But I'm afraid the answer will be painful. Sort of like when you tell your wife you ran into her old boyfriend, and she gets this faraway, wistful look on her face, and you ask her what she's thinking, and she blushes, and you ask yourself, Why am I such an idiot?

DAD: You're obviously conflicted about whether to ask me. Get back to me when you decide.

BUSTER: No, wait. I have to know, even if the truth hurts.

DAD: The truth about what?

BUSTER: Dogs, Dad. I'm wondering if you had any other dogs you loved before Mollie and I came along. I mean, because Mollie lives with us, I know you're not modogamous.

DAD: Modogamous?

BUSTER: Sure. Loving only one dog. I know you love Mollie, but have you loved any other dogs?

DAD: Buster, I was nearly 55 when Mom and I adopted Mollie and even older when we adopted you. I wasn't saving myself for y'all, I'm afraid. I have loved other dogs.

BUSTER: I knew it, I just knew it. Why'd I have to go and open my big, fat mouth?

DAD: The fact that you're not my first dog doesn't mean I love you any less. It's possible to love more than one dog, you know.

BUSTER: Tell me the truth, Dad. Did you love any of your other dogs more than you love me? Wait, don't answer that. Strike that question.

DAD: No, I'll answer it. I've had a number of dogs that I've loved very much, and you're definitely one of them.

BUSTER: So I'm just a face in the crowd. No better than a tie, is that it?

DAD: It's better than a tie for last.

BUSTER: I suppose, but it still hurts. I'm in this far; I might as well go in all the way. Tell me about these other dogs that were so precious to you.

DAD: Okay, I'll go through them chronologically. My first dog was Frisky, an Eskimo spitz.

BUSTER: Purebred, huh?

DAD: Yes. So what?

BUSTER: It's just one of those things a new dog doesn't like to hear, especially a mixed-breed dog.

DAD: I was six months old when we got Frisky. I had nothing to do with the decision to get a purebred.

BUSTER: Whatever. So tell me about this fancy Frisky.

DAD: Frisky wasn't fancy at all, but he was a great dog. He and I were best friends.

BUSTER: Are we best friends, Dad?

DAD: No, Mom is my best friend. But I wasn't married when I had Frisky.

BUSTER: I'll accept that, but only because I love Mom. I know it's been like forever since you had Frisky, especially in dog years, but do you remember anything about him?

DAD: I remember how brave he was. We had a cat named Puff who had a litter of kittens. There was this big, mean dog in the neighborhood named Snuffy that came around trying to attack Puff and her kittens. Frisky wouldn't allow it. He wasn't half as big as Snuffy, he lost the fight and had to go to the vet, but he saved Puff and her kittens.

BUSTER: Got mauled over some cats? Sounds more dumb than brave.

DAD: Frisky was a big-hearted dog, Buster.

BUSTER: Sounds like a bird-brained dog to me.

DAD: Puff was our cat, and the kittens were our kittens, so Frisky risked life and limb to protect them. You'd fight to protect Mollie, wouldn't you?

BUSTER: Mollie's a dog.

DAD: Cats need love too.

BUSTER: You weren't at BARK, Dad. If cats really need love, they should try showing some love. You ever heard of reciprocity? Cats don't care about anybody but themselves, so why should anybody care about them?

DAD: Frisky didn't ask why. He just protected them. He was a great dog.

BUSTER: Okay, enough about Frisky. I'm sure he was a wonderful dog, a heroic dog even, at least from your perspective as a toddler. Who was next?

DAD: We had two small dogs, Tiny and Princess, and then there was Heidi.

BUSTER: Any of them purebreds?

DAD: No, they were all mutts, I mean mixed-breeds.

BUSTER: Did you just say what I think you said? Mutts? Really? You're talking about me and my people, Dad.

DAD: You don't have people, Buster.

BUSTER: You know what I mean. And I resent being called a mutt.

DAD: It's a term of endearment.

BUSTER: An insult more like it. I can't believe you used that word. You know how sensitive I am about my parentage.

DAD: You're not going to send me on a guilt trip, Buster. I have a long record of support for mixed-breed dogs. I've had many of them. I've served on the board of an animal shelter devoted to them. What they're called—mixed-breed, mutt, Heinz 57—doesn't matter.

BUSTER: Heinz 57—what on earth does that mean?

DAD: Heinz 57 is the name of a steak sauce. A Heinz 57 is a nickname for a dog who's a mixture of a whole bunch of breeds, maybe as many as 57.

BUSTER: So I guess you're saying I'm a Heinz 57.

DAD: No, your hound features are dominant. For a mixed-breed dog, you're practically an aristocrat.

BUSTER: Nice try, Dad, but it's too late. You think I'm a mutt. Thanks a bunch.

DAD: Lighten up. Do you want to know about my other dogs, or don't you?

BUSTER: I suppose. But don't expect me to be happy about it. Don't be surprised if I sulk.

DAD: Suit yourself. We didn't have Tiny and Princess for long. I don't remember much about them. But I remember Heidi well. She was a big, beautiful, blond shepherd mix, but she was as dumb as a stump.

BUSTER: I guess looks and brains like mine are a rare combination.

DAD: And combined with humility, as rare as hen's teeth. Anyway, Heidi got pregnant, it came time for her puppies to be born, and we made a place for her in a playhouse Daddy had built in the backyard. And you'll never guess what she did.

BUSTER: I'll guess she had the puppies.

DAD: Yes, of course she had the puppies. It's what else she did that you'll never guess. She had nine puppies and, after each one was born, Heidi left the playhouse and went out to the street to chase cars.

BUSTER: She chased cars in the midst of giving birth to her own children? You sure she was a mixed-breed? Sounds like something only a product of inbreeding would do.

DAD: She was a mixed-breed, and that's what she did. I saw it with my own eyes.

BUSTER: Saw it with your own eyes? Don't you see everything with your own eyes, Dad? How else would you see something?

DAD: You're right. I can't see anything with someone else's eyes. It's just an expression.

BUSTER: *A dumb expression. You wouldn't say you ate it with your own mouth or licked it with your own tongue. Anyway, sounds like I'm way ahead of Heidi in IQ.*

DAD: You're definitely smarter.

BUSTER: Thank you, though it sounds like faint praise. I guess Heidi was blond both literally and figuratively. So after Heidi the crazy car chaser, who was next?

DAD: My senior year in college, I rented a run-down old house with two friends. Every home needs a dog, so I volunteered to get one. I adopted Josey and named her for Clint Eastwood's character in a movie called *The Outlaw Josey Wales*. Don't ask me why.

BUSTER: Why not ask you why?

DAD: Because I don't remember. But I do remember that I got her on a famous day in baseball history. It was October 2, 1978, the day Bucky Dent hit a home run to beat the Red Sox in a one-game playoff and send the Yankees to the American League Championship Series, which they won, and then the World Series, which they also won.

BUSTER: How do you remember that? You're weird, Dad.

DAD: The mind's a strange thing, Buster. I don't know why I remember what I remember, and I don't know why I forget what I forget.

BUSTER: Well, don't try to figure it out now. Get back to the outlaw dog.

DAD: Josey was mixed-breed, but just two breeds, half English shepherd and half Australian shepherd. She was with me my senior year at Ole Miss, all through law school at Duke, and for years after we moved to Jackson. She was a great dog.

BUSTER: Tell me some stories about her.

DAD: I remember two from when I was at Duke. Sometimes

Josey would get out of our apartment and roam the campus. One beautiful spring day, the doors to the law school were left open. I was sitting in class, on the back row as usual, and I heard people on the front row laughing. The professor quit talking. It was Josey. She walked up and down the aisles until she found me.

BUSTER: Did you get kicked out?

DAD: No. The professor thought it was funny too. Josey sat beside me until the class ended, then the two of us walked home.

BUSTER: Did Josey like going for walks as much as I do?

DAD: Not even close. On the subjects of walks, you're in a class by yourself.

BUSTER: A class by myself, I like the sound of that. What's the other story?

DAD: Duke was playing Carolina in soccer. I wasn't there and didn't see it with my own eyes, but a friend told me about it. The schools are only ten miles apart. It's a big rivalry, and there was a big crowd, but Josey somehow managed to get onto the field. The players tried to catch her so the game could resume. Well, Josey loved to play chase as much as you love walks. The soccer players were fast, but Josey was faster. They never did catch her. She finally got tired, trotted off the field, and the crowd cheered.

BUSTER: Cool. I wish I could have seen that.

DAD: Me too. I hate I missed it.

BUSTER: So she moved to Jackson with you after law school?

DAD: She did, and one time she stayed with friends when we went out of town. They lived ten miles from our house, across a bunch of busy roads, including the interstate. Josey managed to get out of our friends' backyard and disappeared. They were frantic but couldn't find her anywhere. Two days later, we got a call from our next-door neighbor. Josey had somehow made her way home. How she even knew which direction to go, I'll never know.

BUSTER: That's impressive, but I could do it too.

DAD: Is that right?

BUSTER: Sure. Great sense of smell, great sense of direction.

DAD: You want me to drive you ten miles away, across the interstate, drop you off, and see if you can make it home?

BUSTER: Better not. You don't want to upset Mom.

DAD: We can't have that.

BUSTER: Any other dogs? Or is that it?

DAD: A lot more. I've never been without a dog for very long.

BUSTER: Any more purebreds?

DAD: Just two. A mother and son—Maggie and Mary.

BUSTER: Sounds like a mother and daughter to me.

DAD: I'll get to that.

BUSTER: You had a male dog named Mary? Did Johnny Cash name him or something? What breed were Maggie and a boy named Mary?

DAD: Welsh corgi.

BUSTER: Really? That's the breed that looks like some government committee came up with it. Like there was one person in charge of legs, one in charge of torso, one in charge of head, and they all lost each other's cell numbers. So tell me about this dynamic duo.

DAD: The children were young, and we decided it would be fun to get a purebred dog so we could have a litter of puppies.

BUSTER: Wait just a minute. Are you saying you couldn't have a litter of puppies with a mixed-breed dog? It's breed bias yet again.

DAD: It's not that. People will pay for a purebred puppy. We wanted to have a dog that would have puppies people would want.

BUSTER: You've just described a classic case of discrimination. You should be ashamed.

DAD: Ashamed? Did we not adopt you? Are you not a mixed-breed dog? You want to know about Maggie and Mary or not?

BUSTER: *I guess, but first a question. I don't approve of your having any purebred dog, but why on earth a Welsh corgi?*

DAD: I read an article that said they have a big dog's personality in a small dog's body. We didn't want a big dog, but we didn't want a little, excitable, yappy dog either.

BUSTER: Shhh. Mollie will hear you.

DAD: Mollie's not as excitable as you are, Buster. Anyway, that's why we got a Welsh corgi. But one thing we didn't realize is how much they shed.

BUSTER: You can't blame a dog for shedding, Dad. It's out of our control. But surely they didn't shed as much as I do.

DAD: Believe it or not, it was more. It came out in clumps. Enough to make a throw pillow.

BUSTER: And I thought I was the champion shedder. Sounds like they could have made the Guinness Book. Maggie was the mother, so tell me about her first.

DAD: When she was just a puppy, the day we got her, my parents' cat scratched her eyeball.

BUSTER: So it was protecting a cat and her kittens that got poor Frisky chewed up, and it was a cat that scratched Maggie's eye. I detect a pattern.

DAD: I don't know about a pattern, but poor Maggie wound up losing her eye, and I wound up with big vet bills. I spent a thousand dollars the first week we had her.

BUSTER: You can always make more money, Dad, but Maggie couldn't get another eye. Did you at least get her an eyepatch? That would have been terrific on Halloween and Talk Like a Pirate Day.

DAD: An eyepatch would have been cool, but I couldn't figure out how to make it stay on. Anyway, Maggie grew up, went into heat, and we found a male corgi to breed with her.

BUSTER: Breed with her? That sounds so utilitarian. Did they at least get to spend some time together first? Have a date or two?

DAD: Buster, dogs don't need to get to know each other when a female dog's in heat. Do you not understand that?

BUSTER: No, as a matter of fact, I don't. Having been neutered at an early age, it's a process I'm not familiar with. But I'll say this: If I was faced with the prospect of breeding with a dog I'd never even met, I would feel used. And I would refuse.

DAD: I bet you wouldn't, and the male corgi didn't. Two months later, Maggie had seven puppies.

BUSTER: And Mary was one of the seven.

DAD: He was. Our kids were young, and they wanted to name the puppies. Cliff wanted to name one of them Mary, but there were only two females, and Ann Lowrey named them both. So Cliff named one of the males Mary. We weren't going to keep them, and their new parents would give them new names, so I figured it was okay to have a boy dog temporarily named Mary.

BUSTER: But didn't he feel emasculated?

DAD: I don't think a puppy that's only a few weeks old can feel emasculated.

BUSTER: Dogs are smarter than you give them credit for, Dad, and more sensitive.

DAD: Mary seemed very well adjusted to me. Anyway, we sold six of the seven puppies and, as fate would have it, the seventh one was Mary.

BUSTER: That's no surprise. Who would want to pay cold, hard cash for a male dog named Mary?

DAD: That wasn't it. They could have given him a new name.

BUSTER: But it's possible he was already scarred for life from being called Mary.

DAD He wasn't scarred. He was a happy dog, sweet and gentle.

BUSTER: Kind of a sissy, huh? Not surprising with the name you stuck him with. I'd probably be afraid of squirrels if my name was Mary.

DAD: Mary wasn't a sissy, Buster, and he wasn't afraid of squirrels. He was a great dog, one of my all-time favorites. While we were still trying to sell him, the children got very attached to him. I did too, so we decided to keep him.

BUSTER: So you were stuck with a boy named Mary. Must have been embarrassing for you and for him.

DAD: I tried to change his name. Cliff had named him, so I asked Cliff to change his name to something more suitable. More masculine.

BUSTER: Given the fact that you're telling me this story, I'm guessing that Cliff refused.

DAD: I tried everything. I explained why it was important for Mary to have an appropriate name for a boy. I gave Cliff a whole list of options. Good names, lots of names, but he wouldn't budge. He was steadfast, resolute.

BUSTER: Admirable qualities.

DAD: Not when you're steadfast about having a boy dog named Mary. When I was about to give up, an idea occurred to me. I said let's name him Murray. It sounds like Mary, but it's a man's name.

BUSTER: A dog named Murray? Really?

DAD: I was desperate, okay. It was a last-ditch effort to sell Cliff on changing Mary's name.

BUSTER: But Cliff wasn't buying what you were selling.

DAD: Not at all. He said Mary was his dog, his name was Mary, and it was always going to be Mary. I gave up. I wasn't getting anywhere, Cliff cared more than I did, and Mary didn't care at all. We registered him with the AKC as Cliff's Mister Mary.

BUSTER: A one-eyed Welsh corgi with a son named Mary: what a pair. Let me ask you this: Did you ever have another hound?

DAD: One. Cliff and I were driving in the country and saw a skinny puppy on the side of the road. We put the puppy in the middle of the front seat and shared a McDonald's cheeseburger with it. We took the puppy home and named it Sue.

BUSTER: Please tell me the puppy wasn't a boy named Sue.

DAD: Rest easy. Sue was a girl.

BUSTER: Thank goodness. Did Sue look like me?

DAD: Not really. She was all hound but mostly black. She was bigger than you and had longer legs and much bigger ears.

BUSTER: Bigger than Mollie's?

DAD: Close. I loved to rub Sue's ears. They were as smooth as silk.

BUSTER: Did she live a happy life after you rescued her?

DAD: She did, but she didn't live with us her whole life.

BUSTER: What? Don't tell me you abandoned her at some shelter.

DAD: Of course not. I would never do that. This is the craziest thing, but a couple who lived down the street from us stole her.

BUSTER: Geez, Louise. Your neighbors stole your dog?

DAD: Well, stole might be a harsh term for it. Tell me what you think. Here's how it happened. This elderly couple lived down the street, and Sue would go visit them. When she did, the woman would cook her a skillet full of hamburger meat.

BUSTER: Sweet. I need to pay that kind woman a visit. Where do they live?

DAD: Nowhere near here. In fact, probably nowhere at all. This was years ago and, like Sue, they've probably crossed over the Rainbow Bridge by now. Anyway, the hamburger meat was a big draw, and Sue started spending more and more time with them. One day she just didn't come home.

BUSTER: Why didn't y'all go fetch her and bring her home?

DAD: Like I said, they were old, and we figured they needed a companion. We had two other dogs, and Sue was happy to be with them, so we let her stay. The three of them would come past our house—the man in his motorized wheelchair, his wife walking beside him, and Sue, who'd gotten fat from all the hamburger meat, waddling along with them. We'd all speak to each other as if nothing had happened, as if they hadn't stolen Sue.

BUSTER: They didn't steal Sue, Dad. They just outbid you. It was her call, not theirs.

DAD: Maybe so.

BUSTER: Mollie and I would never leave you and Mom, though it sure would be nice to have a skillet full of hamburger meat from time to time. Preferably with cheese and onions and sautéed shiitakes. I'd even be willing to try some of that Heinz 57 steak sauce on it. If I like it, the company could use me in an ad campaign. I could be the Heinz 57 who loves Heinz 57.

DAD: Not gonna happen, Buster. Greasy hamburger meat would be bad for you. It was bad for Sue.

BUSTER: Come down out of your glass house, Dad. You know you love a burger. You just said you shared one with Sue when you rescued her.

DAD: You get fed very well, Buster. You know that.

BUSTER: But not nearly as well as you do. Any more dogs I need to know about?

DAD: I'll tell you about two more. Their names were Elvis and Bob.

BUSTER: I can't believe you named a dog for Elvis after he sang that hound dog song. And what kind of name is Bob for a dog?

DAD: At least Bob was a boy. Elvis and Bob were both mixed-breed dogs. Elvis was part Lab, Bob part Chow. We didn't know the other parts. Both were strays we adopted, and both were very handsome.

BUSTER: You're not saying they were as handsome as I am, are you?

DAD Even if I thought they were, I wouldn't dare say it. Anyway, we got Elvis first, then Bob showed up, and they became best friends.

BUSTER: Like Mollie and me?

DAD: Just like y'all. They loved to go to the cabin we had then.

They played outside but would always come back in. But one day, they didn't. We looked everywhere.

BUSTER: What happened?

DAD: We never found out why they left. It was probably Bob's fault. He was more likely than Elvis to wander, just as you're more likely than Mollie to wander. Elvis would have gone along with him.

BUSTER: It's not my fault that I'm more adventurous than Mollie. The call of the wild is strong. What can I say?

DAD: Whatever. So we put up signs, called the sheriff's office, and went back to the cabin every day and searched. No luck. We were afraid coyotes had gotten them.

BUSTER: Are coyotes the animals that howl in the night?

DAD: Sounds like they're having a keg party, doesn't it?

BUSTER: I've never been to a keg party, so I can't answer that. Did the coyotes get Bob and Elvis?

DAD: No, thank goodness. After they'd been missing a week, we were about to give up hope. We thought we'd never see them again. But then I got a call late on a Saturday afternoon. Bob and Elvis had wandered into a hunting camp in the middle of nowhere 25 miles northeast of the cabin.

BUSTER: How on earth did they wind up there?

DAD: Beats me. I didn't know how to channel dogs then, so I had no way to find out.

BUSTER: You've come a long way, Dad.

DAD: That's one way to look at it. So I drove immediately to the hunting camp. When I walked in and sat down, Elvis saw me, ran over, put his head in my lap, and cried like a baby.

BUSTER: He probably thought he'd never see you again either.

DAD: One of the men at the camp said they didn't need any more proof that they were our dogs.

BUSTER: You were lucky they called. Elvis and Bob were lucky too.

DAD: Very lucky. We had offered a reward to anyone who found them. I tried to give the men the money, but they wouldn't take it. Instead they gave me a beer. There are lots of good people out there, Buster.

BUSTER: Lots of good dogs too, Dad.

DAD: There sure are, and I've had a bunch of them. There's very little in all the world better than a good dog.

BUSTER: That's the sweetest thing you've ever said, Dad. I'm glad you're my dad.

DAD: And I'm glad you're my son, Buster.

BUSTER: I'm glad you told me about your other dogs. I was afraid I was opening up a can of worms, but instead I opened up a can of dogs. Great dogs. Thank you.

DAD: You're welcome.

BUSTER: I realize now that I'm the heir to a long line of wonderful dogs, lots of older brothers and sisters. Frisky, Josey, Maggie and Mary, fat Sue, Bob, Elvis, and all the others. The Eason dog dynasty. It's an honor, it really is.

DAD: I hope you can live up to it.

BUSTER: I'll do my best, Dad.

DAD: I know you will. And it will be easier if you're well rested.

BUSTER: Have you ever known me not to be well rested, Dad?

DAD: Come to think of it, I haven't. Goodnight, Buster. I'm glad you're the heir to a dog dynasty.

Finding My Religion

Are dogs spiritual? Are they capable of wondering about eternity? Do they think about whether there's an afterlife? I don't know, but there's one thing I do know: To avoid going to the vet, they'll say anything.

BUSTER: Dad?

DAD: What, Buster?

BUSTER: Mollie and I have decided to become Christian Scientists.

DAD: What on Earth? Christian Scientists? Dogs aren't religious.

BUSTER: How exactly would you know that, not being a dog and all?

DAD: But you've never gone to church.

BUSTER: How would I go to church if you didn't take me? You've never taken Mollie and me, and I'd wager that you've never taken any of your other dogs either.

DAD: I haven't. Nobody takes dogs to church.

BUSTER: Maybe not, but that doesn't mean dogs aren't religious. You know good and well that going to a church service on Sunday morning doesn't prove you're religious, just as taking a walk in the woods on Sunday morning doesn't prove you're not.

DAD: I don't disagree.

BUSTER: Religion is about your core beliefs, about God and the world, about right and wrong and the meaning of life.

DAD: You've thought about this, haven't you?

BUSTER: I'm a very spiritual dog, Dad. Joining a church is just the logical next step on my spiritual journey.

DAD: That's admirable, but why become a Christian Scientist?

I don't think I know any person who's a Christian Scientist, much less any dog.

BUSTER: I'm doing it for Mollie. Part of my spiritual journey is to do more for others, and I'm doing this for her. We're joining the Church of Christ, Scientist.

DAD: Doing things for others is wonderful, but I'm not sure joining a church for the benefit of somebody else is wise. After all, it's going to be your church too. What's important is that you believe in what the church teaches.

BUSTER: I understand that. And I do believe.

DAD: So tell me how you came to this decision.

BUSTER: I spent a lot of time studying the options. We live in the Bible Belt, and Mollie and I wanted to join a Christian church. We studied Catholicism first. We loved the history and the rituals and could relate to the celibacy since we're both celibate, albeit not voluntarily.

DAD: So why not become Catholics?

BUSTER: Mollie's allergic to incense. Sneezes her head off, so that was a no go. Then we looked at all the mainstream Protestant denominations. We liked them, some more than others, but then we learned something about Christian Science that made it the obvious choice.

DAD: And what's that?

BUSTER: No medical care. Or at least almost no medical care.

DAD: And why are you opposed to medical care? If you hadn't been treated for heartworms, you might not be here now.

BUSTER: As robust as I am, I would have been fine. And you know how I hate going to the vet. Mollie hates it even more than I do. Turns her into a complete basket case, as you've observed.

DAD: But Mollie needs medical care.

BUSTER: She may need it, Dad, but have you seen what it does to her?

DAD: What do you mean? I've never seen any side effects or problems.

BUSTER: I don't mean the effect of the treatment itself. I mean the effect of going to the vet.

DAD: She doesn't much like it, does she?

BUSTER: Doesn't much like it? Have you not been paying attention? It terrifies her. It turns her into a pitiful, quivering basket case.

DAD: I think you're exaggerating.

BUSTER: You do, do you? You remember the last time you took us to the vet, when she stood in the lobby shaking like a leaf? She looked like she was facing the guillotine. Then she pooped on the floor. You remember that? The poor little thing, who's been housebroken since she was a puppy, pooped on the floor. It scared the you-know-what out of her.

DAD: So she overreacted.

BUSTER: So what if she did? The point is the effect it has on her. Whether or not being terrified about a visit to the vet is rational, the fact is that she's terrified. Part of doing things for others is seeing things from their perspective. Walking a mile in their paws. And from Mollie's perspective, going to the vet is terrifying.

DAD: Fair enough, but trips to the vet don't last long. We were in and out in no time the last time we were there.

BUSTER: Let me ask you a question, Dad. What's the most frightened you've ever been? The absolutely most terrified?

DAD: Hard to say. One time, more than ten years ago, I almost started a forest fire at the cabin. That really scared me. I was burning a pile of brush, and the flames must have been 15 feet high. Suddenly the wind changed direction, the fire jumped into the tops of some oak trees, and the trees caught fire.

BUSTER: What did you do?

DAD: Called 911 on my cell phone. I had my phone in one hand and the hose in the other, spraying for all I was worth. The fire was so hot I wound up with blisters on my knuckles and in my eyebrows.

BUSTER: You said you almost started a forest fire, so obviously you didn't start one. How'd you put it out?

DAD: The wind died, the flames dropped, and I was able to get closer with the hose. In a minute or two, the emergency was over.

BUSTER: So nothing terrible happened.

DAD: I was lucky.

BUSTER: But you haven't forgotten it, have you?

DAD: I just told you about it, didn't I?

BUSTER: You wouldn't want to go through that again, would you?

DAD: I sure wouldn't. But what's that got to do with Mollie and the vet and becoming a Christian Scientist?

BUSTER: Think about it, Dad. Going to the vet scares Mollie just like the fire scared you.

DAD: That's crazy. She gets one little shot, and I nearly burned down an entire forest.

BUSTER: Look at it from her perspective, Dad.

DAD: But her perspective is wrong.

BUSTER: You didn't burn down the forest, did you? Does that mean your perspective was wrong? You were terrified. That things worked out doesn't change that. And Mollie's uber terrified when she goes to the vet. I'm going to do everything in my power to make sure she never feels that way again.

DAD: That's very thoughtful, but Mom's never gonna go for it.

BUSTER: Why not?

DAD: She loves you and Mollie. Your health is very important to her. She's not going to stop taking you to the vet.

BUSTER: She is too. The First Amendment guarantees freedom of religion. It's one of the pillars of the Bill of Rights. As Christian Scientists, we have a First Amendment right to refuse medical care.

DAD: I am certain, Buster, that the First Amendment doesn't guarantee freedom of religion for dogs. And I'm even more certain that it doesn't give you the right to keep Mom from taking you to the vet.

BUSTER: We'll see about that.

DAD: And how will we see about that? Let's play this out. When Mom wants to take you to the vet, then what?

BUSTER: We refuse.

DAD: And then Mom puts leashes on you and takes you to her car and puts you in and drives you to the vet. Then what?

BUSTER: We refuse to get out.

DAD: And then she gets your leashes and pulls you out of the car and into the vet. Then what?

BUSTER: I bite her hand, she drops the leashes, and Mollie and I head for the hills.

DAD: You're never going to bite Mom, Buster. You and I both know that.

BUSTER: Okay, so I'm not gonna bite Mom. But the fact remains that we should be able to observe our religious beliefs.

DAD: I don't think the Christian Scientist thing is going to work on Mom. From her perspective, Mollie's long-term physical health is more important than her temporary emotional distress.

BUSTER: Talk to Mom, Dad. You're a lawyer. You can persuade her, I'm sure you can.

DAD: I'm sure I can't. I'm not very good at persuading people when I don't believe in the cause.

BUSTER: You don't? Why not?

DAD: Be honest, Buster. You decided to become a Christian Scientist so you and Mollie won't have to go to the vet. You didn't decide you won't go to the vet because you're becoming a Christian Scientist.

BUSTER: Chicken, egg, egg, chicken. What difference, at this point, does it make?

DAD: None to Mom. She wouldn't buy it either way. When it's time to go to the vet, she's taking you.

BUSTER: Unacceptable.

DAD: Accept it.

BUSTER: C'mon, Dad. There's got to be something. It breaks my heart to see the look on Mollie's face when we pull up at the vet. It's the look of a condemned prisoner when he sees the gallows.

DAD: And when have you seen the look of a condemned prisoner, Buster?

BUSTER: It's easy to imagine, Dad.

DAD: I'm sorry she gets so scared. But she must have medical care.

BUSTER: I've got it! This is a brilliant idea, if I do say so myself. Find a vet who makes house calls. It's going to the vet that terrifies Mollie, not the actual treatment. It's being led away from you or Mom by a stranger and put in the back in a cage. It's being surrounded by strange dogs that hate being there too and bark their fool heads off. It's the antiseptic smell of the place and the linoleum floor that squeaks when people walk on it. It's the staff looking like mad scientists in their lab coats. It's the needles sitting on the tables waiting to poke you.

DAD: You really think that's it?

BUSTER: I think it reminds Mollie of her days as a shelter dog. Not exactly her halcyon days.

DAD: Not compared to now, that's for sure. But vets don't make house calls. Dogs go to the vet; vets don't go to the dogs.

BUSTER: I bet you could find a vet who would make house calls.

DAD: I don't think so. A vet couldn't afford to leave his clinic for an hour or two to go see one dog. Even two dogs.

BUSTER: He could if you made it worth his while. Money talks, Dad.

DAD: I should have seen that coming. Money talks, and it's always my money.

BUSTER: The vet could take off his lab coat to put Mollie at ease. Wear jeans and a turtleneck. You could put on some soothing music. Some Coltrane maybe. You love Mollie, Dad. You've seen how going to the vet terrifies her. What's an extra buck or two to spare her from that?

DAD: I'm guessing it would be more than a buck or two. Let me ask you this, Buster: How would finding a vet who makes house calls affect your decision to become a Christian Scientist?

BUSTER: To be perfectly honest, which my spiritual journey requires, if you can find a vet who makes house calls, I'm thinking my journey may take me in a different direction.

DAD: That's what I thought, and I appreciate your candor. Let me ask you another question. Has Mollie ever complained to you after a visit to the vet about being scared?

BUSTER: No, but she doesn't have to.

DAD: So you've never asked her?

BUSTER: I would never do that. What am I supposed to ask her: Hey, you remember when you were shaking like a leaf the last time we went to the vet? And pooped on the floor? Were you really as terrified as you looked?

DAD: So she's never complained, and you've never brought it up?

BUSTER: That's right. Bringing it up would violate my obligation to think of others first.

DAD: Have you ever seen any lasting effects on Mollie? For example, when she comes home from the vet, does she act like she's been traumatized?

BUSTER: To her credit, she doesn't. She gets on with her life.

DAD: And acts like nothing happened?

BUSTER: I guess you could say that.

DAD: So you don't know if it continues to bother her or not, do you?

BUSTER: No, but it continues to bother me, I promise you that. Seeing that look on her face gives me nightmares.

DAD: So it may actually be harder on you then it is on her, is that what you're saying?

BUSTER: I'm a very empathetic dog, Dad.

DAD: I've got a solution. You won't need to become Christian Scientists, your spiritual journey can take whatever path you choose, and the two of you will get the healthcare you need. I won't have to fork over big bucks for a vet to make house calls, and you won't suffer the emotional trauma of seeing Mollie get upset at the vet.

BUSTER: That sounds like a win/win, maybe even a win/win/win. So what's your bright idea?

DAD: Separate trips to the vet. You and Mollie don't go at the same time.

BUSTER: That's got potential. Our preference is not to go at all, but if that's a non-starter, separate trips might at least be a first step. But Mollie would still get upset, I assure you.

DAD: But she'll get over it, and you won't have to see it.

BUSTER: Out of sight, out of mind. Let's go for it.

DAD: I'll tell Mom. But let me ask you this, Buster: What about your spiritual journey? Think you'll join a traditional Christian denomination now? Methodist or Presbyterian maybe? Or Episcopalian?

BUSTER: Are you kidding? Dogs don't go to church.

DAD: I believe I've been had.

BUSTER: Don't beat yourself up, Dad. You want Mollie and me to be happy and healthy. Separate trips to the vet will accomplish both. Your idea was brilliant. Give yourself a pat on the back. Hand me your hand, and I'll lick it.

DAD: This is such a one-sided relationship.

BUSTER: What are you talking about?

DAD: Nothing. Nothing at all. Go to sleep, Buster.

If I Could Only Fly

On our morning walks, Buster takes a keen interest in one particular bird, an odd-looking duck we see along the water's edge, often with a flock of geese. Interestingly, Buster shows little interest in the geese. But when he spots the duck, he starts tugging on his leash for all he's worth. The duck's reaction is predictable. When Buster gets within a few feet, the duck takes off, flies a dozen feet or so, and lands in the water out of harm's way. Buster stares at the duck, looking frustrated. I wonder, is he just frustrated because the duck got away? Or is he also frustrated because the duck can fly and he can't?

BUSTER: Dad?

DAD: What, Buster?

BUSTER: Teach me to fly.

DAD: Teach you to what?

BUSTER: To fly. I want to learn how to fly.

DAD: You mean in an airplane or like a bird?

BUSTER: Anybody can fly in an airplane, Dad. All you have to do is book a flight, show up with a photo ID an hour before takeoff, and print your boarding pass. There's nothing to learn. I don't want to fly in a plane. I want to fly like a bird.

DAD: Buster the flying dog. I can see the headline now. Where on earth did you get such an idea?

BUSTER: Nowhere on earth. I got it from the sky.

DAD: Of course you did.

BUSTER: Yesterday I looked up, and this big bird was soaring in circles above me. I think he was a red-tailed hawk. I kept watching him until my neck got sore, then I rolled over on my back in the grass and watched some more. I started humming that Blaze Foley song, "If I Could Only Fly." You know that one? Then I asked myself, How cool would it be to do that?

DAD: I love that song, and I bet your answer was way cool.

BUSTER: How did you know?

DAD: Because it would be way cool to fly like a hawk.

BUSTER: Then teach me.

DAD: Sorry. No can do.

BUSTER: Why not? You taught me to sit. You taught me to fetch a tennis ball. You taught me not to get up on the couch except when you're gone.

DAD: But I can't teach you to fly. I can't even fly myself.

BUSTER: So what? Those who can't do teach. You're all about expressions, Dad. Surely you've heard that one.

DAD: But even if I knew how to teach somebody to fly, Buster, I couldn't teach you.

BUSTER: Why not? I'm a quick study. I can learn.

DAD: You might have the brain for it, but you don't have the body.

BUSTER: So I'll go on a diet, starting today. I'll be down to flying weight in no time.

DAD: Weight's one problem, but it's not the main one.

BUSTER: What is?

DAD: Wings, or rather the lack of them. Birds have wings. You don't. That's why they can fly and you can't.

BUSTER: I'll use my front legs.

DAD: Sorry. Won't work. Wings are shaped so that they're aerodynamic. There's nothing aerodynamic about your front legs.

BUSTER: I'll overcome the problem with extra effort. Where there's a will, there's a way.

DAD: Dogs can't fly, Buster. You've got to have wings to fly. Birds and butterflies have them. Dogs don't.

BUSTER: First no thumbs and now no wings. I can't catch a break.

DAD: It's not just you. People are wingless too. We can't fly either.

BUSTER: But I'm dying to fly, Dad. As you may have noticed, I have something of an obsessive personality. And since I watched that hawk circling in the sky yesterday, flying has become my new obsession.

DAD: You better come up with an even newer obsession because you can't fly.

BUSTER: I refuse to accept that. How can I make my front legs aerodynamic? There's got to be a way.

DAD: There's not. The shape of a bird's wings makes them aerofoils, which provides upward force and allows the bird to fly. Your front legs are shaped nothing like a bird's wings.

BUSTER: Then I'll have surgery. I'll go under the knife. If it takes months of grueling, post-op physical therapy, bring it on.

DAD: I appreciate your determination, but it won't work. Even if your legs could somehow be shaped like wings, you're way too heavy to fly.

BUSTER: I said I'd go on a diet.

DAD: There's no way you could lose enough weight. Let me look something up.

BUSTER: Uh-oh, the Internet again.

DAD: It says here a red-tailed hawk's wingspan is about four feet. That means its wings are approximately the same length as your front legs.

BUSTER: So far, so good.

DAD: But here's the bad news. The hawk weighs a little over two pounds. You weigh 20 times that much.

BUSTER: So I'll beat my legs really fast. Faster than a hummingbird.

DAD: You'll look ridiculous, and you won't get off the ground.

BUSTER: How do you know? You're not an aeronautical engineer. You're just another dime-a-dozen lawyer.

DAD: I don't need to be an engineer to know that a 40-pound dog can't fly, Buster. Don't feel bad. I think it would be way cool to fly too, but I can't do it either.

BUSTER: There's got to be some way to skin this cat—I love that expression, by the way. We just need to figure out what it is.

DAD: People have been wanting to fly since they first saw birds in the air, Buster. You're not the first one to think it would be cool. But it ain't gonna happen.

BUSTER: Isn't going to happen.

DAD: What?

BUSTER: If you want to serve as a role model for your son, use proper grammar.

DAD: Whatever. Look, I'd love to fly too, but I can't, and you can't. There are many things some of us can do that others can't. Fly, swim, talk, walk on our hind legs, snap our fingers.

BUSTER: You love rubbing my nose in the thumb thing, don't you? I wonder what you'd think if a red-tailed hawk tormented you about his wings like you torment me about your thumbs.

DAD: I'm not tormenting you, Buster, just explaining the facts of life, though you do seem especially sensitive about not having thumbs.

BUSTER: I want to fly, Dad. It's not fair. Why birds but not me?

DAD: It's not just you, Buster. It's all other dogs and all people and cats and cows and horses and pigs. None of us can fly.

BUSTER: But why? Why should something as cool as flying be reserved for the privileged few?

DAD: That's a God question.

BUSTER: I've figured you out. You say something's a God question whenever you're stumped and don't know the answer.

DAD: Think what you want to think, but dogs and people can't fly.

BUSTER: So maybe I can't fly on my own, but is there something I can do that will give me the same sensation?

DAD: There are flight simulators, but I don't know if they'd let a dog use one.

BUSTER: Would I be up in the sky? Would I be circling like a red-tailed hawk?

DAD: No. You'd be in a machine that would simulate being up in the sky.

BUSTER: Forget that. I want the real thing. I want to feel the sun on my face and look down on the beauty of the earth. I want to wave to Mollie and see the look on her sweet, befuddled face.

DAD: Well, people can't fly on their own, but there are things some people do that are like flying.

BUSTER: Now we're talking. I knew you'd come up with something if I kept bugging you—I mean discussing it with you. What are those things?

DAD: There are hang gliding and skydiving, though I've never done either one.

BUSTER: I've never even heard of either one. Tell me about them.

DAD: In hang gliding, you hold on to something that has wings. It's sort of like a small airplane but with no motor.

BUSTER: Wings. I knew it. Can you take off from the ground and climb up into the sky?

DAD: No. You jump off something really high, like a cliff or a tall building, and glide down until you land.

BUSTER: People jump off cliffs? Are they nuts?

DAD: They jump with a hang glider. They glide; they don't fall.

BUSTER: Still sounds dangerous. Tell me about the other one, the sky thing.

DAD: Skydiving. You put a pack on your back that's got something in it called a parachute, which is a really big cloth with strings attached. You go up in an airplane and jump out. Then you pull something called a ripcord, the parachute comes out of the pack and opens up, and you float down to the ground.

BUSTER: Jump out of an airplane? That's insane.

DAD: But you're wearing a parachute. And, when the parachute opens and you're floating down, you can feel the sun on your face, look down on the beauty of the earth, and wave to Mollie.

BUSTER: But what if the parachute doesn't open?

DAD: The people who pack them are very careful, Buster.

BUSTER: Are there training and licensing?

DAD: I assume there's at least training.

BUSTER: Assume? You know what assume makes out of you and me, don't you? You don't know if they're careful or not. So far as you know, the people with the planes might just get people off the street who need a buck. Probably the same people who put up the Ferris wheel at the state fair.

DAD: There's also a reserve parachute.

BUSTER: Packed by the same guy making eight bucks an hour. Even if he's a responsible guy, what if a hot girl stops by? What if she flirts with him while he's packing the main parachute and walks away in that special way while he's packing the reserve? I've seen the way you look at Mom. I wouldn't want to jump out of a plane relying on something you did with her around. When you're using the circular saw and she appears on the scene, I cover my eyes.

DAD: What's the matter, Buster? You said you were obsessed with flying, and I've told you about the next best thing. Two next best things, in fact.

BUSTER: I am obsessed, but I'm also very safety conscious. And hang gliding and skydiving don't sound very safe to me.

DAD: People do both of them all the time, Buster. If they were all that dangerous, they wouldn't be so popular.

BUSTER: But you've never done either one.

DAD: No, and I'm not sure Mom would be too keen on my starting.

BUSTER: So you're encouraging me to do something Mom wouldn't let you do?

DAD: I said she probably wouldn't like it, not that she wouldn't let me. If I really wanted to hang glide or skydive, I would. Mom is not the boss of me.

BUSTER: Not the boss of you? Really? That's a good one. You do everything Mom tells you to do, and you do it post-haste. She comes into the room wearing a cute outfit, and you snap to attention. Not the boss of you—that's the funniest thing I've heard all day.

DAD: Not true. I try to be considerate and do what she asks, but she's not the boss of me. I mentioned hang gliding and skydiving because you said you were obsessed with flying. I wanted to give you options. Are they perfectly, 100% safe? No, but nothing is. So which one do you want to try? I'll sign you up.

BUSTER: I'm not so sure I want to try either one.

DAD: You don't sound very obsessed with flying to me.

BUSTER: I've got a confession to make, Dad.

DAD: Is that right? Confession is good for the soul, Buster. What is it?

BUSTER: I suffer from acrophobia.

DAD: Acrophobia?

BUSTER: That means a fear of heights.

DAD: I know what it means, Buster, but I don't get it. You say you're obsessed with flying, that you long to look down from the sky on the beauty of the earth, and yet you're afraid of heights?

BUSTER: Sounds contradictory, I admit, and I guess it is a little hard to explain.

DAD: Give it a shot. Like that sweet little dog you want to wave down to from the sky, I'm all ears.

BUSTER: You could make throw rugs out of those ears, couldn't you? I am obsessed, Dad. I do long to look down from the sky, and I had a plan for overcoming my fear if you could teach me to fly. Here's what I was thinking. When I first learned to fly, I would stay real close to the ground. Running into a tree or a stop sign might be an issue, but my fear of heights wouldn't. Then I would gradually go higher and higher. I would overcome my fear a little at a time.

DAD: Makes sense.

BUSTER: But I guess you can't start out hang gliding or skydiving just a few feet off the ground.

DAD: Afraid not.

BUSTER: Bummer.

DAD: Sounds like you need to decide which is stronger, your fear of heights or your obsession with flying. Why don't you sleep on it and get back to me tomorrow?

BUSTER: I don't need to sleep on it. I already know. Fear trumps obsession.

DAD: Good call. You wouldn't enjoy hang gliding or skydiving if you were afraid the whole time.

BUSTER: Plus I've been scared of heights for as long as I can remember, and I developed the flying obsession just yesterday. Instead of sleeping on my decision, I'll sleep on trying to come up with an obsession that doesn't terrify me.

DAD: Another good call.

BUSTER: Jumping off a cliff and out of an airplane. Who knew? You don't see any dogs doing anything like that, I promise you that. People do the craziest things.

DAD: If only you had wings, Buster, if only you could fly. Go to sleep, son.

Human Siblings

My children grew up with dogs and loved them all. Now they have dogs of their own: Ziggy, Clementine, Rozalyn, and one on the way. They're our granddogs. Because my children love dogs, and because Buster is a wonderful dog, they love him. When they come to visit, he gets lots of love and attention and gives it in return. Though they're human and he's canine, he considers them his brothers and sister.

BUSTER: Dad?

DAD: What, Buster?

BUSTER: Tell me what it's like to be a father of your own biological children.

DAD: We could talk all night about that. Why do you ask?

BUSTER: Well, as you know, I was subjected to a certain medical procedure against my will in my youth, and as a result I can never know the joy of having my own biological children. And I want you to tell me what it's like.

DAD: The first thing I'll tell you is that it's wonderful, but it's not a piece of cake. It's not easy, I promise you that.

BUSTER: I figured it wasn't all wine and roses, but I still want to hear.

DAD: Okay then, where should I start?

BUSTER: Why don't you start at the very beginning? That's a very good place to start, at least according to that song that woman sang in that movie.

DAD: Julie Andrews. *The Sound of Music.*

BUSTER: That's the one. I love that movie. When they sing the hills are alive, it makes me want to book a trip to the Alps. So tell me what it was like when you first became a father.

DAD: I remember it well. Ann Lowrey was born just before nine o'clock on a Sunday night. It was Mother's Day.

BUSTER: That's fitting. Were you excited?

DAD: Sure. Anxious too. You don't really know for sure that a baby's healthy until she's born.

BUSTER: But she was healthy, wasn't she?

DAD: She was perfect.

BUSTER: That's sweet. Did she look like you? She does now, though she's prettier and younger and has a lot more hair, at least on her head. You have more on your legs.

DAD: That's as it should be. No, she didn't look like me at first. She looked like a red, wrinkled, newborn baby.

BUSTER: I guess she improved with age, like a fine wine. I like to think I've improved with age too. Did you know she was going to be a girl before she was born?

DAD: No, we could have found out, but we decided not to. I sort of wanted a boy—I guess most fathers do—but Ann Lowery was so wonderful that I wanted another girl when we had our second. But then we had a boy, Cliff.

BUSTER: So you got what you wanted, just not in the order you wanted them.

DAD: I guess. And then we had Paul after that.

BUSTER: Three children—that's three more than I'll ever have. What was it like when you first held Ann Lowrey?

DAD: Kind of scary at first. She was tiny—just over six pounds—and I'd never held a baby that small. But I got used to it in a hurry. I would give her a bottle on the screened porch in the middle of the night and just stare at her. I was adopted, remember, so she was the first blood relative I'd ever seen.

BUSTER: That's pretty cool.

DAD: Way cool. Cooler than flying.

BUSTER: What about when she was growing up? What do you remember?

DAD: Since she was our first, I remember more about her than about her brothers. I would read to her and sing to her every night. "Sweet Baby James" was one of her favorite songs.

BUSTER: One of my mine too, as you know.

DAD: Anyway, when she was three, I went to a seminar in western Massachusetts. When I got home, I sang "Sweet Baby James" to her and told her that earlier that day I'd driven on the turnpike from Stockbridge to Boston. Her eyes got real big. She had no idea the place in the song was a real place.

BUSTER: Was she smart when she was little? She's real smart now. Maybe even as smart as a certain hound.

DAD: She was real smart then too. She was a very precocious child.

BUSTER: I'm a very precocious dog, wouldn't you say?

DAD: Precocious and many other things. She was beautiful too. When she was four, she was asked to model children's clothes. She walked down the runway with as much poise as the models who were four times her age. One of our friends nicknamed her the woman grown.

BUSTER: Sounds like she was a perfect child.

DAD: There's no such thing as a perfect child, Buster.

BUSTER: When was she ever not perfect? She's a wonderful mother. I've heard y'all talk about that school she started, how good it is, and how much it's grown. It's hard to imagine her doing anything bad.

DAD: Maybe now, but when she was a teenager, it was hard to imagine her doing anything good.

BUSTER: That's hard to believe.

DAD: Ask her. She'll admit it. She and I look back on it now and laugh, but we didn't laugh then. We call it the period of demonic possession.

BUSTER: Ann Lowrey was possessed by demons?

DAD: No, but she acted like it. She was disobedient and disrespectful. Most teenage girls, and boys too for that matter, give their parents trouble, but with her it was worse because she was so strong-willed. We couldn't get her to do what we wanted or stop her from doing what we didn't want.

BUSTER: How did you make her change?

DAD: We didn't. She just grew out of it. I guess she grew up. By her junior year of high school, the period of demonic possession had ended, and I had my baby girl back again.

BUSTER: Must have been hard to have such a strong-willed child.

DAD: It was then, but a few years later it was a blessing.

BUSTER: When was that?

DAD: When she got pregnant and didn't do what most scared 19-year-old girls would have done. Because Ann Lowrey was strong-willed and brave, we have Ada Brooks, and the world is a better place for it.

BUSTER: Hooray for Ann Lowrey!

DAD: One of the happiest days of my life was the day she got married. Ada Brooks, who was almost two, was the flower girl. Ann Lowrey and I were in the vestibule about to walk down the aisle. Ada Brooks went before us and dropped flower petals along the way. Then the congregation started laughing. During rehearsals, Ada had dropped the flower petals and then picked them up and put them back in her basket so she would have them for the wedding. Then during the wedding, she dropped the petals as planned, but when she got to the front of the church, that beautiful, precious child did exactly as she'd rehearsed. She turned around and headed back up the aisle, picking up the petals as she went.

BUSTER: I wish I could have been there.

DAD: It was a wonderful day. At the reception, I danced with Ann Lowrey and Ada Brooks and sang "The Weight" by The Band.

BUSTER: That's the take-a-load-off-Fanny song, isn't it? A great song. I'm curious about something, Dad. It sounds like Ann Lowrey's a wonderful person.

DAD: She is.

BUSTER: And so was your dad.

DAD: None better.

BUSTER: And your mom too.

DAD: Definitely.

BUSTER: So what on earth happened to you?

DAD: I'm just the slacker in between, I guess.

BUSTER: Don't beat yourself up, Dad. You've got some good qualities.

DAD: One of which is tolerating you.

BUSTER: Oh, lighten up. You know I'm just teasing. You wouldn't want me to be any other way. And how could I be? Once again, I cite the familiar acorn-tree phenomenon. We've been talking all this time about Ann Lowrey. Tell me what it's been like to be Cliff and Paul's dad.

DAD: When they were very young, I sang and read to them like I did Ann Lowrey. Often to all three at the same time. Cliff had a hard time learning to read, so I kept reading to him after he started school.

BUSTER: What kinds of books?

DAD: When they were real young, I read the usual children's books, *Goodnight Moon*, *The Runaway Bunny*, Dr. Seuss books, *Amy the Dancing Bear* as I've told you, and many others. They loved to find the mouse in the illustrations in *Goodnight Moon*.

BUSTER: What about when they were older?

DAD: I read longer books, especially to Cliff. Two of our favorites were *The Yearling* and *Watership Down*, both novels, one about a boy and a deer and the other about rabbits.

BUSTER: A novel about rabbits? How could somebody write a whole novel about rabbits?

DAD: It's not about rabbits as they exist in the real world. In *Watership Down*, the author, Richard Adams, anthropomorphizes rabbits.

BUSTER: Whoa, whoa, whoa. Even though I'm not an ordinary dog, I'm still a dog, and I try to limit myself to words of four syllables or less. That word is two over my limit. What does it mean?

DAD: Anthropomorphize means to attribute human traits to an animal. Some people might say I'm anthropomorphizing you when I channel you.

BUSTER: Well, some people would be wrong. When you channel me, you express my thoughts. And my thoughts, lest there be any doubt, are the thoughts of a dog.

DAD: I'm well aware. Anyway, *Watership Down* is a great book. A young man in the Army, a West Point graduate, told me it was the best book about military leadership he'd ever read. Imagine that—a novel about rabbits with lessons for officers leading soldiers into battle. I finished reading the book to Cliff with him in my lap beside a campfire when the two of us were camping. I'll never forget it.

BUSTER: What was the other book you mentioned?

DAD: *The Yearling*. Also a great book. It's more than 500 pages long. I read a few pages to Cliff every night for many weeks. When I finally got to the end, his first words were "read it again."

BUSTER: What else did you do with the boys?

DAD: I mentioned camping. They both loved to camp. I also took them canoeing and fishing. Fishing was Cliff's favorite thing. I took him all the time. Paul didn't like it as much, but I got to see him catch a fish half as long as he was before he turned four.

BUSTER: Wow! Tell me about that.

DAD: We were fishing from the bank of a small pond. When I hooked a fish, I would hand the rod to one of the boys, and he would reel it in. So I hooked a nice bass, maybe five pounds, and it was Paul's turn, so I handed him the rod. He started trying to reel, but he was a little boy, it was a big fish, and he wasn't having much luck. Then I looked down beside me, and Paul was gone. I knew the fish hadn't pulled him into the water, so I looked behind me. Paul had given up on reeling and was backing into the woods, dragging the fish ashore. He could barely hold the fish up it was so big. He wanted to eat it, but Cliff and I talked him into letting it go.

BUSTER: Good for y'all. I only approve of eating catfish.

DAD: That's strange. Why catfish?

BUSTER: What's the first syllable in catfish, Dad?

DAD: I should have known. Anyway, like I said, Cliff liked fishing more than Paul did, and I spent a lot more time fishing with Cliff.

BUSTER: Sounds like you did more with Cliff than you did with the other two.

DAD: I did, and it wasn't really fair to the other two, especially Paul. But Cliff had a hard time making friends. On weekends, when Ann Lowrey and Paul played with their friends, I played with Cliff. And at night, he and I played chess. Thousands of games.

BUSTER: Who won?

DAD: We both did. I won more than he did, but not by much.

BUSTER: He might say he won more than you did. What else do you remember?

DAD: Paul has gone with me on some great trips to the West. Hiking trips to Idaho, Washington, and Glacier National Park, all with Bobby. A few years ago, just Paul and I went on a wonderful canoe trip on the Missouri River in Montana. We camped where Lewis and Clark camped.

BUSTER: Lewis and Clark—they're the ones who had Seaman the dog.

DAD: That's right. They paddled up the Missouri River in Montana in 1805 on their way to the Pacific Ocean and down it the following year on their way home.

BUSTER: What was so great about the canoe trip?

DAD: The scenery, the wildlife, the campsites, and campfires. It was all great. One night we camped near a huge prairie dog town. It was fascinating. They would all be out on the prairie huddled up like they were gossiping with each other, one of us would make a noise, and they would all go dive into their holes.

BUSTER: I've never heard of a prairie dog. Do they look like Mollie or me?

DAD: Not at all. They're not really dogs. They're rodents. They live in tunnels under the ground.

BUSTER: In tunnels? Talk about your claustrophobia. I prefer living above ground, thank you very much.

DAD: Me too, Buster. Wait a second; claustrophobia has five syllables. You said four was your limit.

BUSTER: I learned the adjective first—claustrophobic has four syllables—so the noun was easy. Let's summarize our conversation so far, Dad. Sounds like being a father has been wonderful, is that fair to say? I mean, other than the demonic possession episode, and you got over that.

DAD: She got over that.

BUSTER: Whatever. It ended, so I guess y'all both got over it. Tell me this, Dad, taking into account the good, the bad, and the ugly, the demonic possession and all the other things about being a father you haven't told me, has it been worth it? If you had it to do all over again, would you have children?

DAD: Absolutely. It hasn't always been easy—sometimes it's still not—but I would definitely do it again. That's an easy call.

BUSTER: If it hasn't been easy, why's it an easy call?

DAD: Because I love my children. And here's another reason: I have four beautiful grandchildren, who are all precocious like you. The little people alone make it an easy call.

BUSTER: Hard to argue with that. It would sure be nice to have some little dogs like your little people. It pains me that I'll never be a father or a grandfather.

DAD: You've got to play the cards you're dealt, Buster. You may not be a father or a grandfather, but you have a very good life.

BUSTER: I know, but I sure wish I could be a father.

DAD: I understand, but it's not in the cards.

BUSTER: You keep referring to cards. It's not in the cards; I've got to play the cards I'm dealt. What do cards have to do with anything?

DAD: They're just expressions. One means there are some things you can't change, and the other means that you should focus on the life you have, not some other life you wish you had. You have a great life, Buster, but you'll never be a father, just as you'll never be a person and you'll never fly.

BUSTER: Speaking of expressions, I guess what you're saying is that it's better to look at the glass as half full than half empty. And looking at my glass as half full, I've been dealt some pretty good cards, haven't I?

DAD: A royal flush, I'd say. Look around, Buster. You have a wonderful life. Mom and I love you. Mollie loves you. You even have human brothers and a sister who love you.

BUSTER: I guess I'm sort of like Jimmy Stewart in that Christmas movie, huh? He had a wonderful life, but he needed help from a guardian angel to see it. But I don't need any help to see that I have a wonderful life. I may never be a father, but I have a soft bed, an endless supply of Pup-Peroni, and a family who loves me. You remember at the end of the movie when George's brother Harry raises a toast and says that George is the richest man in town?

DAD: Of course. I cry every time.

BUSTER: I'm a pretty rich dog, huh?

DAD: I'd say you're very rich.

BUSTER: I know you're right, but it would sure be wonderful to have a bunch of little Busters running around.

DAD: I think one Buster is quite enough, thank you very much.

BUSTER: C'mon, Dad, you know my puppies would be adorable.

DAD: Not in the cards, Buster.

BUSTER: Okay, okay, I'll let it go. But what about my legacy? With no puppies to my name, how will I be remembered?

DAD: How about a portrait? How would that do?

BUSTER: A portrait of me? That would do just fine.

DAD: I'm not promising anything, but I'll look into it.

BUSTER: Will I have input in selecting the artist?

DAD: You never change, do you, Buster?

BUSTER: Sorry, Dad, but I want someone who will capture the real me, someone who will show my whole range of emotions. I wonder—oil or watercolor? Oil would be more formal and might capture my regal bearing, but watercolor might be the better choice to display my whimsical nature.

DAD: Your whimsical nature?

BUSTER: Sure. I'm full of whimsy. Should I be sitting or standing? Or perhaps reclining on one of the living room chairs? Those colors look good with my dramatic white and tan markings.

DAD: I never learn, do I?

BUSTER: Learn what, Dad?

DAD: Nothing. Nothing at all. Go to sleep, Buster.

What's In A Breed?

Buster is far more interested in dogs than in any other animals. He sizes other dogs up, checks them out, and gives them a good sniffing. I wonder if he ranks them, decides which breeds he prefers. Unless he's with Mollie and feels the need to be her aggressive wingman, he's usually friendly. But sometimes he senses that the feeling is not mutual, and the fur on his back stands up like a canine Mohawk. Then I know it's time to head on down the trail.

BUSTER: Dad?

DAD: What, Buster?

BUSTER: Why are there so many different dog breeds?

DAD: Good question, but I have no idea what the answer is.

BUSTER: Not only lots of breeds, but lots of sizes too. That Rottweiler could pass for a Clydesdale, but that Chihuahua is no bigger than a squirrel. Smaller if you take their tails into account.

DAD: I wouldn't want a dog that small. I'd be afraid I'd step on him.

BUSTER: Me too, and I'm only two feet tall. And that high-pitched yapping would drive me around the bend.

DAD: You do plenty of high-pitched crying, pal.

BUSTER: Only when I'm forlorn.

DAD: You've got a wonderful life, Buster. What on earth do you have to be forlorn about?

BUSTER: I'm a very sensitive dog, Dad. Very in touch with my emotions.

DAD: That's fine, but it doesn't explain why you're forlorn.

BUSTER: For you to understand that, you'd have to walk a mile in my shoes.

DAD: But you don't wear shoes.

BUSTER: I'm well aware that I don't wear shoes, Dad. You use expressions all the time, so don't go all literal on me every time I use one.

DAD: Fair enough, but I still don't understand what would make you feel forlorn. You're very well fed. You have your own bed and a yard to roam, Mom gives you several treats a day, I take you for walks, and we both scratch you behind the ears.

BUSTER: Those are basic amenities, Dad. I'm talking about much deeper matters, issues that go to the depth of my soul, to the core of my being, to the values that make me the dog that I am.

DAD: Name one.

BUSTER: One what?

DAD: One issue that goes to the depth of your soul and the core of your being.

BUSTER: They're hard to put into words, and I don't think it would be healthy for me to try. Might make me even forlorner. Forlorner—is that a word? Back to breeds. Tell me this: Of all the many breeds of dogs, what would you say is your favorite?

DAD: I would say the mixed-breed shelter dog.

BUSTER: Speaking as a mixed-breed shelter dog, I would say that's a good answer. But are you telling me the truth? Or pulling your punches because of how sensitive I am?

DAD: Not at all. I really do prefer mixed-breed dogs.

BUSTER: Why?

DAD: Lots of reasons. No risk of problems caused by in-breeding, for one.

BUSTER: Shhh. Mollie will hear you.

DAD: And I think shelter dogs appreciate having a good home more than spoiled purebred dogs do. And I appreciate dogs who are appreciative.

BUSTER: I'm very appreciative, Dad.

DAD: Albeit forlorn.

BUSTER: It's possible to be both, you know. And to be clear, the hardships that get me feeling down in the dumps—short life span, inability to have children, and having neither a legacy nor thumbs—are unrelated to the good life you and Mom provide and for which I'm very appreciative. You've had lots of mixed-breed dogs, haven't you?

DAD: Sure have. I've had only a few purebreds. Frisky, Maggie, Mary.

BUSTER: Don't forget Mollie, Exhibit A on the perils of inbreeding. Regarding one of the causes of my being forlorn, you told me that dogs usually don't live as long as people do. Painful as it was to learn that, I've come to grips with it.

DAD: Sorry if I added to your forlornitude.

BUSTER: Forlornitude? Really? I don't know if forlorner is a word, but ten bucks says forlornitude isn't.

DAD: No thanks on the bet. I've been known to make things up, and I made forlornitude up just like you made up modogamous.

BUSTER: Maybe I made up modogamous, maybe I didn't, but you have to admit it's a great word. Back to my short life span. If what usually happens happens, and if Mollie and I cross over to the other side before you and Mom do, you think y'all will get more dogs?

DAD: Definitely. We love dogs.

BUSTER: Purebred or mixed-breed?

DAD: I'm sure we'll get mixed-breed unless we happen to find another cocker spaniel at a shelter. Mom loves cockers, you know.

BUSTER: Do I ever! I'm reminded every day that Mollie's her favorite. Anybody with eyes to see and ears to hear can tell that.

DAD: She loves both of you very much, Buster.

BUSTER: C'mon, Dad, only Mollie gets to sit in her lap. Mom never invites me to join her.

DAD: You're awfully big to be a lap dog, Buster. Plus you shed like nobody's business. If you sat in Mom's lap, she'd wind up coated with a layer of Buster.

BUSTER: Not my fault. I have absolutely no control over my shedding. I wish all my fur would stay put, but it won't.

DAD: I didn't say it was your fault, but it's a good reason why Mom doesn't ask you to sit in her lap.

BUSTER: She could send her clothes to the cleaners. Pick them up two days later and voila, no more Buster layer.

DAD: That would sure get expensive. If you became a lap dog, she'd be sending her clothes to the cleaners constantly.

BUSTER: Always comes down to money with you, doesn't it?

DAD: Money's never any object to you, is it?

BUSTER: Whatever. You've said you prefer mixed-breed dogs and that's probably what you'll get in the future. I must say that's very gratifying, but let me ask you this: If you were to get a purebred dog, what would you get? I'm not talking about what Mom would get; I'm talking about what you would get.

DAD: That's a tough one. I love all kinds of dogs. Big and little.

BUSTER: Name one. Name a breed you would choose.

DAD: Let me think. Two of my top choices wouldn't really be purebreds. Labradoodles and goldendoodles are great dogs.

BUSTER: Maybe so, but they've sure got some goofy names. What are these doodle dogs? What do doodles do? How many chucks could a woodchuck chuck?

DAD: And you say I'm weird. A Labradoodle is a cross between a Labrador retriever and a standard poodle. A goldendoodle is a cross between a golden retriever and a standard poodle.

BUSTER: They should make a cross between a cocker spaniel and a standard poodle.

DAD: Why do you say that?

BUSTER: Because we could call them cockadoodles.

DAD: I like that. Anyway, Labradoodles and goldendoodles are big dogs, bigger than you. Beautiful. Curly hair. Good disposition. Smart. And most of them don't shed.

BUSTER: Enough already about the shedding, Dad. It's not my fault.

DAD: I know it's not your fault, Buster. But all the same, it's better to have a dog who doesn't shed than one who does.

BUSTER: But if you had a dog who didn't shed, you wouldn't have me. Just think how sad your life would be.

DAD: It would certainly be less interesting.

BUSTER: You wouldn't get rid of a dog just because he sheds, would you?

DAD: Of course not. If you doubt me, look in the mirror.

BUSTER: Well, I'm glad we got that straight.

DAD: But if you stopped shedding, Mom and I would sure appreciate it.

BUSTER: I can't stop, Dad. If I could, I would. How many times do I have to tell you?

DAD: Lighten up, Buster. Your place here is secure. We love you, shedding and all. And we don't blame you for the shedding.

BUSTER: Then give it a rest, will you? I'm very sensitive, as I just told you.

DAD: Not another word.

BUSTER: Thank you. You still haven't named a purebred dog you'd like to have. Those doodle dogs are mixed-breeds just like I am, though perhaps not quite as mixed.

DAD: The two retrievers I mentioned, golden and Labrador, would be great. Big, sweet, handsome dogs. Unfortunately they have the trait involving hair loss that shall go unnamed.

BUSTER: Have you checked your bald spot lately, old man? It gets bigger by the day. I would drop hair loss from your critiques of me and other dogs if I were you. When our hair falls out, at least it grows back.

DAD: It's not a criticism, Buster, just a fact. And vacuuming all the time gets old.

BUSTER: I just thought of something. You think maybe I inherited my hair loss tendency from you? Maybe not, since we're not the same species, but it's something to think about. And here's something else to think about. You know how we talked about thinking of the glass as half full, not half empty? Well, think of my shedding as half full. Because my beautiful coat is constantly falling out and growing back, I'm always fresh and clean, and you never have to bathe me.

DAD: Fair point. As for other breeds, I also like some of the smaller terriers. Fox and Jack Russell. The West Highland terrier is a handsome white dog. They all have lots of personality.

BUSTER: More than I do?

DAD: Of course not. And they can be hyperactive, though they generally don't have the trait the sensitive dog doesn't want to hear about.

BUSTER: The sensitive dog has another trait you should keep in mind.

DAD: And what's that?

BUSTER: Sharp teeth and the willingness to use them.

DAD: I tremble in fear.

BUSTER: Any other dogs, or have we exhausted the universe of possibilities, both shedding and non-shedding?

DAD: Not even close. There are hounds like you. The beagle is one. You're probably part beagle. I love beagles. And shepherds. I told you about Josey, half English shepherd and half Australian shepherd. Josey was a great dog. Border collies are shepherds. They may be the smartest of all dogs. I read that one of them knows more than 1,000 words.

BUSTER: So? I know more than 10,000.

DAD: Maybe so, but you'd have a hard time proving it.

BUSTER: I'm concerned about something, Dad. You remember when I told you about how a man's wife gets this wistful, faraway look in her eye when he says he saw her old boyfriend? Well, when you talk about purebred dogs, you get that same look.

DAD: So?

BUSTER: So I think you wish you had one of those purebred dogs.

DAD: Not so.

BUSTER: You sure you wouldn't rather have a fancy purebred dog instead of me?

DAD: Buster, I wouldn't trade you for all the fancy purebred dogs in the world. Plus even if I wanted to, you'd have nothing to worry about. I'd never be able to swap a mixed-breed hound of unknown origin for a decent purebred dog.

BUSTER: You're not a very nice man, Dad. You know that?

DAD: Once again, Buster, I'm just teasing. And I wouldn't tease you if I didn't love you. It's the same with Mom. I love her, and I tease her all the time.

BUSTER: You sure you're just teasing about the purebred deal?

DAD: Absolutely sure. You're my dog and my son. I wouldn't trade you for all the dogs in the world or for all the tea in China.

BUSTER: Thank you. That's reassuring and, as a sensitive dog, I need constant reassurance. By the way, I've heard another expression about tea in China—I may have even used it—but I don't know what tea in China means. What is tea, and where is China?

DAD: Not tonight, Buster. It's past your bedtime.

BUSTER: You're right. I get started talking, and sometimes I just can't seem to stop. We'll be talking about one thing, then something new pops into my head, and I start talking about that, and pretty soon something else occurs to me, and I'm off and running on a brand new subject, which often leads to yet another topic.

DAD: You definitely talk more than most dogs. Goodnight, son.

LIVE FREE OR DIE

Back In The Day

I often think about how different life was when I was growing up half a century ago. There were no helicopter parents then, and children had far more freedom to play outside. My friends and I explored the woods and swam in the creek. I walked home more than a mile from school starting in the fourth grade.

Life was different for dogs too. Fenced yards were much less common, and there were no gated communities or leash laws. Dogs were more likely to get hit by a car than to die of natural causes. Dogs' lives are safer now, but they had more freedom then. Freedom to roam and freedom to sniff. Buster yearns for freedom.

BUSTER: Dad?

DAD: What, Buster?

BUSTER: You've been around a long time, haven't you?

DAD: A very long time.

BUSTER: More than 60 years, right?

DAD: Sixty-three. I don't know how I got to be this old.

BUSTER: Sure you do. It's because you were born 63 years ago. How many dog years are in 63 human years anyway?

DAD: Let's see. Sixty human years would be 420 dog years, and 63 would be 441.

BUSTER: Holy moly, you're ancient. You must be older than the Dead Sea Scrolls.

DAD: Not quite. And when I say I don't know how I got to be this old, I mean that time flies.

BUSTER: Time flies? I thought just birds and butterflies flew. Even so, if time flies, and if you've got things on your bucket list you haven't checked off, you better get to it.

DAD: Sound advice. So let me ask you this: Other than to remind me of how old I am, why did you bring up my age?

BUSTER: Because I want to know what things were like back in the olden days, when you were my age and the world was young.

DAD: Your age in people years or dog years?

BUSTER: People years. By the way, what am I up to in people years now?

DAD: I'm not sure. Probably eight or nine.

BUSTER: Not sure? How can you not know the age of your own son?

DAD: As I've told you before, we know when we adopted you, but it's not like you came with a birth certificate.

BUSTER: So how'd you come up with eight or nine?

DAD: We've had you almost seven years, and the vet said he thought you were probably one or two when we got you.

BUSTER: So if I was one, and since you've had me less than seven years, it's possible that I'm not yet eight.

DAD: Possible, but not likely.

BUSTER: I bet I'm still seven, as youthful and vigorous as I am.

DAD: You sleep 20 hours a day, Buster.

BUSTER: *I've cut back. Lately I've been sleeping only 18. And the six hours I'm awake, I'm brimming with energy.*

DAD: You're an excitable boy, there's no denying that.

BUSTER: You think Zevon wrote that song about me? If so, I should be entitled to share in the royalties.

DAD: Afraid not. It came out when I was in college more than 40 human years ago, long before you were even a gleam in your biological father's eye. Plus the song is about a person, not a dog.

BUSTER: I'm not so sure. Biting the usherette's leg in the dark sounds more like a dog to me.

DAD: The song's about a weird person, Buster.

BUSTER: Then maybe it's about you.

DAD: It's not about me, Buster. I've never bitten an usherette's leg in the dark, or anybody else's leg for that matter.

BUSTER: If you say so. Where were we? Oh, yeah, I'm probably seven because of how energetic, athletic, and youthful I am. I sure hope so because I've got a bucket list a mile long.

DAD: Is that right? What's on it?

BUSTER: We'll talk about that another time. Tonight I want to hear about the olden days.

DAD: What do you want to know?

BUSTER: I want to know how things were different for people. Dogs too. Let's start with dogs. I'm more interested in that, what with being a dog and all.

DAD: Understandable. Things have changed more for people, but some things have changed for dogs. Here's one: Back in the day, people were much more likely to feed human food to dogs. There was even a name for the leftover food dogs got. They were called scraps.

BUSTER: Did Big Paul feed scraps to Mollie?

DAD: He did, but the food she got was better than most dogs got way back when.

BUSTER: Even so, the scraps back then had to taste better than dry dog food now. And I love people food, as you know. We'll put a plus in the olden days column.

DAD: Not so fast. People food may taste better, but it's not as healthy as dog food, at least for dogs.

BUSTER: Tasty trumps healthy. The plus for the olden days stays. How else were things different?

DAD: Back then, most dogs were free to roam. People didn't have fenced yards like they do now. There weren't any leash laws.

BUSTER: Leash laws? What are leash laws?

DAD: Exactly what you'd think. Laws that require dogs to be on leashes.

BUSTER: That's terrible. And it strikes me on first blush as unconstitutional. Being on a leash deprives a dog of his liberty without due process. There's been no legal determination that I'm some sort of danger. In fact, as we both know, I'm utterly harmless.

DAD: Dogs don't have constitutional rights, Buster. I've told you that.

BUSTER: Well, they should. What about cats? Do cats have to be on leashes?

DAD: I've never heard of a leash law for cats. Come to think of it, I've never seen a cat on a leash.

BUSTER: That's a travesty. Whatever happened to the guarantee of equal protection? And don't start in with that life's-not-fair business.

DAD: But it's not.

BUSTER: I told you not to start. So it sounds like dogs weren't deprived of their liberty back in the day like they are today. Is that fair to say?

DAD: I think it is.

BUSTER: So they could roam the wilderness, explore and discover, sniff to their hearts' content, and just come home when they got good and ready?

DAD: Pretty much.

BUSTER: That's a big plus for the olden days then.

DAD: But freedom to roam wasn't all good. It made a dog's life dangerous. Dogs got lost and never made it home, little dogs got attacked by big dogs, and dogs got run over by cars. I'd hate to think what would happen to you if you were free to roam. When it comes to cars, you're totally oblivious.

BUSTER: Cars? What cars?

DAD: My point exactly.

BUSTER: Well, maybe it was more dangerous, but just as tasty trumps healthy, free trumps safe. A risk-free life, in my considered opinion, is no life at all. Out in the great wide open is where the action is. I love that Tom Petty song, and I'd love to have freedom to roam.

DAD: You sure about that?

BUSTER: Absolutely. Freedom is one of the central founding principles of America, Dad. The saying, as I'm sure you know, is give me liberty or give me death. Nobody ever said give me a deadbolt and a full-time bodyguard or give me death. And the New Hampshire license plates say Live Free or Die. They don't say Live Huddled Inside Behind Barred Windows or Die. Another plus for the olden days. Two to nothing. Any other differences?

DAD: I can think of one more. Back then, spay and neuter weren't nearly as prevalent. Fewer female dogs were spayed, and far fewer male dogs were neutered.

BUSTER: So back then, I could have had a robust love life and children of my own?

DAD: Most likely.

BUSTER: Talk about the good old days. Man oh man, sounds like they were the great old days, the golden era of dogs.

DAD: But again, there was a downside. Too much love led to too many puppies. And there weren't nearly as many shelters then, so lots of dogs were homeless.

BUSTER: But that never would have happened to me.

DAD: How can you be so sure?

BUSTER: It stands to reason that it was the homely dogs who were homeless. Being a handsome dog, I undoubtedly would have been able to find a good family to take me in, feed me, and lavish me with love and attention.

DAD: Let me remind you, Buster, that you were living in a shelter when we found you.

BUSTER: And let me remind you, Dad, that you snatched me up the minute you spotted me. My regrettable stay at BARK can only have been the result of some miscommunication or mistake.

DAD: Or perhaps your first human family preferred a humble dog.

BUSTER: Whatever. Listen, I see that there are some downsides to eating human food, having freedom to roam, and having unlimited fur children, but the positives far outweigh them, at least in my mind. It makes me wish I had been a dog 20 generations ago, when you were young.

DAD: Twenty generations? I may be getting on up there, but it hasn't been 20 generations since I was young.

BUSTER: Dog generations, Dad.

DAD: I've never thought in terms of dog generations.

BUSTER: Because you've never been a dog.

DAD: Maybe so. But there's something you should think about in your capacity as a dog.

BUSTER: I think about everything in my capacity as a dog, Dad. What is it?

DAD: Well, I hate to break it to you, but if you'd been a dog back then, you wouldn't be around now.

BUSTER: What? Are you saying I would have crossed over the Rainbow Bridge already?

DAD: Afraid so. I don't know what the world record is for the oldest dog ever, but I'm sure it's less than 60 human years.

BUSTER: You're always being sure of things, Dad.

DAD: Okay, I'll look it up.

BUSTER: And you're always looking stuff up.

DAD: Says here the oldest known dog was an Australian Cattle Dog named Bluey. Lived to be 29 years and 160 days.

BUSTER: But you said yourself that I didn't come with a birth certificate, so it's possible that I've already lived longer than the dog from Down Under.

DAD: Wait a minute. You were just arguing that you're only seven, and now you're saying you might be over 30. I don't know exactly how old you are, but here's one thing I know for sure. There's no way a dog has lived twice as long as Bluey did. Face it. If you'd been born when I was born, you would be long gone by now.

BUSTER: Geez, I never thought of that.

DAD: Seems like a relevant point to me.

BUSTER: Relevant? I'd say it's outcome determinative. What's the point of liberty if you're not alive?

DAD: I thought you said give me liberty or give me death.

BUSTER: I never said that. That was Patrick Henry. And I bet he would have sung a different tune if the choice had been some trivial loss of liberty like walking on a leash versus already being dead.

DAD: Trivial loss of liberty? The difference sounded pretty major just a few minutes ago. It even sounded unconstitutional.

BUSTER: As you pointed out, Dad, there were downsides to all the freedoms dogs had back in the day. No dog wants to get run over by a car.

DAD: No person either. So you think you'll stick with being a dog today?

BUSTER: Given the alternative, I have no choice.

DAD: Good. I prefer you alive.

BUSTER: That makes two of us.

DAD: It's past your bedtime, Buster. You need to turn in.

BUSTER: Wait, you haven't told me the differences for people between the olden days and today.

DAD: We'll have to save that for another time. We spent too much time talking about dogs already.

BUSTER: It's impossible to spend too much time talking about dogs, Dad.

DAD: Goodnight, Buster.

What's In A Name?

Carrie has nicknames for everyone she loves, for her friends, her son, our dogs, and me. If Carrie's love can be measured by the number of nicknames she bestows on someone, then it's true that Mollie's her favorite. In fact, by that measure, Mollie is her favorite over everybody, including both Buster and me. Carrie has a handful of nicknames apiece for us, but for Mollie she has at least a dozen.

I'm confident that Buster knows all his nicknames and understands that Carrie is speaking to or about him when he hears them. But in the case of Mollie, who's not as bright as Buster but has twice as many names to remember, I'm not so sure.

BUSTER: Dad?

DAD: What, Buster?

BUSTER: What's the deal with Mom and all the nicknames?

DAD: I thought you wanted to talk about what life was like for people when I was your age.

BUSTER: I changed my mind. I got to thinking and asked myself, why should I care what things were like for people back in the day? I wasn't around then, and I'm not a person. But the nicknames are something Mom uses for Mollie and me in the here and now. I bet she called Mollie five different names today. What's with that?

DAD: Don't ask me. Ask her.

BUSTER: I would, but you're the channeler.

DAD: But I'm better at channeling you than I am at understanding your mother. I don't know her reasons for all the nicknames.

BUSTER: C'mon, you're married to the woman. You're bound to have a clue.

DAD: I guess I've got a clue, but that's all it is. I think Mom gives nicknames to everybody she loves, people and dogs. She has a bunch of them for her son Alex. Bonk, Bonkey, Bonkeyhead, Sunbeam, Sugar Plum, probably more. They sound silly for a man in his 30s, but I guess he's had them for a long time.

BUSTER: What's with the Bonk business?

DAD: I was curious about that too. Turns out Alex had some game when he was little. He hit toy alligators with a mallet, and it made a noise that sounded like bonk. So she started calling him Bonk and then lots of variations of it.

BUSTER: Mom's weird too, isn't she?

DAD: The nickname thing is kind of strange, I'll grant you that, but Mom is beautiful and kind, and I love her very much.

BUSTER: *It's possible to love someone who's weird, Dad. After all, Mom, Mollie, and I all love you, and you could be in the weird hall of fame.*

DAD: Could not. I'm the normalest person I know.

BUSTER: I sense that the guy who claims he's normal has invented yet another word. Do you really think normalest is a word?

DAD: I don't know, but I know that I'm normal.

BUSTER: The asylums are full of people who think they're normal, Dad. Self-diagnosis, as I'm sure you're aware, is fraught with peril. And, lest you forget, you channel dogs.

DAD: Want me to stop?

BUSTER: Of course not. I enjoy our talks, and your precision in channeling my thoughts is amazing. But is it normal? The question, I submit, answers itself.

DAD: How did this get to be about me? I thought we were talking about Mom and nicknames.

BUSTER: So we digressed. It's not the first time. Back to Mom. Where does she get all the goofy nicknames?

DAD: Beats me.

BUSTER: Would you ask her, please, and get back to me? Because it's an utter mystery to me. Sometimes she refers to Mollie as Francesca or Mollie Francesca. What's with that?

DAD: I don't have a clue. They're just names she started calling Mollie.

BUSTER: Why not Elizabeth or Germaine?

DAD: Maybe it's that Francesca is a pretty-sounding name that comes trippingly off the tongue.

BUSTER: Trippingly off the tongue? What on earth does that mean?

DAD: It's an expression. You know how some words sound pretty and are easy to say?

BUSTER: Actually I don't. I'm a dog. No words are easy for me to say. I'll accept the fact that Francesca sounds pretty, even if I can't say it, but that doesn't explain some of the other nicknames she's given Mollie.

DAD: Like what?

BUSTER: Like Francine and Louise. Sounds like two members of a bowling team in Milwaukee.

DAD: There's nothing wrong with being on a bowling team, Buster. Have you seen *The Big Lebowski*?

BUSTER: Sure. Jeff Bridges is a slacker after my own heart, and I love the cameo by Sam Elliott. The Dude abides.

DAD: Great line, great movie. But I can't explain Mom's affinity for Francine and Louise.

BUSTER: Why does Mom change Louise to Louisa? Sometimes Mom calls her Louisa or Mollie Louisa. And what about Francine Marie? Or Mollieroo, Prissy, Little Princess, Molliewall, Prisspot? Sometimes there seems to be a new name every day. What is going on?

DAD: Once again, I'm the wrong person to ask. I'm perfectly content calling you Mollie and Buster.

BUSTER: No, you're not. You're not in Mom's league, but you're not innocent. Sometimes you call her Mollieroo. I've heard you call her that and other things.

DAD: I'm just copying Mom when I do that.

BUSTER: I'm sure you and Mom are as pleased as punch to call Mollie a dozen different names, and I'm sure y'all think they're all as cute as a button. But the two of you need to realize that your fun is at her expense. Mom calls her by one name at 3:00, another one an hour later, and two more before 5:00.

DAD: What's the harm in that, Buster?

BUSTER: What's the harm? By the time happy hour rolls around, Mollie needs a double. You know who you're dealing with, don't you, Dad? Mollie's not exactly a nuclear physicist, you know.

DAD: So?

BUSTER: Do you know what it's like for that poor little cocker spaniel to be called eight different names before sundown? She lives in a constant state of bewilderment.

DAD: She doesn't seem troubled to me.

BUSTER: She hides it, Dad, just as you would. She's embarrassed.

DAD: It doesn't seem that complicated to me. Mom has some affectionate nicknames for Mollie. Surely she knows them by now.

BUSTER: I suppose it wouldn't seem that complicated to you, but Mollie didn't go to Duke Law School. Look at it from her perspective.

DAD: Fair enough. Tell me what her perspective is.

BUSTER: Well, first of all, she's a dog. Dogs have many wonderful traits, as you and I both know, but with rare exceptions—moi, for example—they don't have the same cognitive skills that people do. Their EQ—Emotional Quotient—is higher, but their IQ is lower.

DAD: But a few nicknames can't be that hard to learn. You know who Mom's talking about. Surely Mollie does too.

BUSTER: The gap between Mollie and me in cognitive ability is vast, Dad. The problem, as we both know, is that there aren't enough branches on Mollie's family tree. She once told me her grandfather, uncle, and cousin were all the same dog, and inbreeding takes a toll.

DAD: I agree that she's not as bright as you are, but I wouldn't call the difference vast.

BUSTER: I'm with Mollie 24/7, Dad. I've seen the results up close and dogonal. And let's face it, Mollie is not the sharpest knife in the dog drawer.

DAD: But she's very sweet.

BUSTER: And gentle and affectionate. She's a wonderful dog. But as for intellect, to use yet another of your playing card expressions, she's not playing with a full deck. Remember when we got the pet door?

DAD: Sure.

BUSTER: Well, I thought poor Mollie would never learn how to use it, which consisted entirely of walking out and walking back in. You would have thought it was a Rubik's cube.

DAD: I remember.

BUSTER: And you know how she goes outside and puts her front paws in the yard, relieves herself on the sidewalk, and thinks she's going in the grass.

DAD: I know. It's pretty funny.

BUSTER: Funny to you maybe, but to me it's just sad. I love her, but she's no Albert Einstein.

DAD: I can't argue with that.

BUSTER: Talk to Mom, Dad. Ask her to cut back on the nicknames. I think that would reduce Mollie's befuddlement.

DAD: Okay, but I've got to tell you this: When I tell Mom you told me something, sometimes she thinks I just made it up.

BUSTER: Imagine that. If it's a problem saying it came from me, tell her you came up with it yourself.

DAD: I'll try, but I don't know if it will work. Mom loves her some nicknames.

BUSTER: No doubt about that. Some of the things she calls you make me roll my eyes. They probably make you think you're some kind of Casanova or a young Sean Connery or something.

DAD: What can I say? She thinks what she thinks.

BUSTER: There go my eyes, rolling again.

DAD: She's got complimentary nicknames for you too, you know. Sometimes she calls you Handsome.

BUSTER: But that's not a nickname, that's a fact. Listen, I'm curious about some of the other things Mom calls me.

DAD: Like what?

BUSTER: For starters, there's Busteronius. Where on earth did that come from?

DAD: No idea. But you should like that one. It sounds like a Roman patrician in a Shakespeare play.

BUSTER: What's Roman? What's patrician? Who's Shakespeare?

DAD: A Roman is a person from Rome. Rome is a beautiful city in Italy.

BUSTER: Italy? What's Italy? Where is it?

DAD: I've got to quit explaining things with things I have to explain. Italy's a country in Europe. Across the Atlantic Ocean.

BUSTER: So what's a patrician?

DAD: It's an aristocrat, a nobleman.

BUSTER: Do what?

DAD: A man of the upper class, with wealth and breeding.

BUSTER: A patrician, I like it. So who's Shakespeare?

DAD: He was the most famous playwright ever.

BUSTER: Playwright?

DAD: Someone who writes stories that people perform.

BUSTER: Like Lassie?

DAD: Sort of like that, but fancier.

BUSTER: So Busteronius is a name for a man of wealth and breeding in a beautiful city in a fancy story written by the most famous writer of fancy stories. Did I sum that up accurately?

DAD: And impressively.

BUSTER: I'm digging it. Busteronius—Mom can call me that whenever she likes.

DAD: I knew you'd like it.

BUSTER: Here's another one. What about Buster Bluth? She calls me Buster Bluth, Bluther, Mr. Bluth, just plain Bluth. Where did that come from?

DAD: I don't think you're going to like Bluth as much as Busteronius.

BUSTER: And why is that? Don't mince words.

DAD: Well, there's a TV show, a great show, called *Arrested Development*.

BUSTER: Is the show about you? That would be a perfect name for a show about you.

DAD: Or you, but it's about neither of us. *Arrested Development* is about the Bluths, a highly dysfunctional family. The family patriarch is in prison, the matriarch's an alcoholic, and three of the four children are screw-ups, leaving the fourth, the only normal one, to run the family business. There are two grandchildren, first cousins, and one has a crush on the other.

BUSTER: Uh-oh, sounds like more inbreeding.

DAD: They don't breed, at least not yet, but it's still wrong.

BUSTER: So I'm guessing that one of the Bluths is named Buster.

DAD: Correct.

BUSTER: And I'm further guessing that Buster is not the normal one.

DAD: Correct again.

BUSTER: So I'm the namesake of an abnormal character in a sitcom.

DAD: But a very funny sitcom.

BUSTER: So tell me about this Buster Bluth. How is he abnormal? Does he suffer from arrested development?

DAD: I'm afraid he does. In fact, of all the Bluths, his development is the most arrested of all.

BUSTER: Nice. Sounds like Buster is the Mollie of the Bluth family.

DAD: That's a harsh thing to say about your sister.

BUSTER: Harsh? I never say anything about Mollie's lack of smarts to her face. In stark contrast, Mom calls me Buster Bluth to my face every day. Little did I know she was calling me by the name of the dumbest member of a dumb family.

DAD: You're taking this the wrong way, Buster.

BUSTER: And exactly what would be the right way? I may have to change my name to overcome the stigma. I think from now on I'll go by Bubba. Like Bubba Gump.

DAD: I don't think Bubba is a name most people associate with intellectual prowess. Albert Einstein never went by Bubba.

BUSTER: Well, anything's got to be better than Buster Bluth. I've seen the way people snicker when she calls me that.

DAD: You're really taking this the wrong way, Buster.

BUSTER: You mean Bubba. I'm Bubba from now on. Don't call me Buster again.

DAD: Hear me out. Mom doesn't call you Buster Bluth because she thinks you're dumb. She calls you that because Buster Bluth is a funny character in a funny show and because both of you are named Buster.

BUSTER: Nice try, but I'm not buying it. What were the names of the Three Stooges?

DAD: The ones I remember were Moe, Larry, and Curly. Why do you ask?

BUSTER: Because two can play this game. If Mom's gonna call me by a dumb guy's name, I'll call her by a dumb guy's name. If she calls me Buster Bluth, I'll call her Moe.

DAD: Moe was actually more mean than dumb.

BUSTER: Even better. Calling me Bluth is mean. From now on, I'm calling Mom Moe. Mean Moe.

DAD: I don't think it's a good idea to call her Moe, Buster.

BUSTER: Bubba. So you're saying she should be able to insult me and I'm just supposed to grin and bear it? And just why is that?

DAD: Pup-Peroni.

BUSTER: So ridicule is the price I must pay for an occasional treat?

DAD: If I were you, I wouldn't bite the hand that feeds me. That's all I'm saying.

BUSTER: I'm not planning to bite her, Dad, though I'll sure be tempted the next time she calls me that dumb guy's name. I demand that you make her stop.

DAD: You are being way too sensitive.

BUSTER: You think so? How would you feel if Mom started calling you Gilligan or Barney Fife or that goofy cross-dresser on MASH*?*

DAD: I prefer the nicknames she already has for me.

BUSTER: I suppose you do. Listen, Dad, even if Mom doesn't mean to insult me when she calls me Buster Bluth, from now on I'm gonna think of that dumb guy whenever she does. Please ask her to stop.

DAD: You're being silly.

BUSTER: So now I'm dumb and *silly.*

DAD: Nobody ever said you were dumb, Buster. Overly sensitive? Yes. Excitable? Definitely. Vain? Unquestionably. Dumb? Never.

BUSTER: Let me put it to you like this, Dad. I prefer to be thought of as a Roman patrician in a fancy play by a famous writer, not the dumbest guy in a dumb family in some dumb sitcom. Capiche?

DAD: I guess I see your point.

BUSTER: And another thing. When you tell Mom to knock off the Buster Bluth business, please remember to tell her to cut back on all the nicknames for Mollie. That poor little dog has a hard enough time without being called something different every time she turns around. I mean, let's face it, she's the Buster Bluth of our family.

DAD: No, she's not. There's only one Buster Bluth in our family, and I'm looking at him.

BUSTER: I've never bitten you, Dad, but there's a first time for everything.

DAD: I don't think you want to bite the hand of the man who channels you, Buster.

BUSTER: Well, if I can't bite anybody, I guess I'll just cry myself to sleep.

DAD: Self-pity is not an attractive trait, Buster.

BUSTER: Neither is cruelty to animals.

DAD: Speaking again of cards, life has certainly dealt you a bad hand.

BUSTER: Nor is sarcasm.

DAD: You can start crying now, Buster.

BUSTER: What?

DAD: You just said you were going to cry yourself to sleep. Goodnight, Busteronius, you prince of Maine, you king of New England.

BUSTER: Do what?

DAD: It's from a terrific book by John Irving.

BUSTER: I love you, Dad, but never again deny that you're weird.

DAD: I love you too, Buddy. Goodnight.

CHOW

A Dog's Purpose

People started living with dogs in the days of yore because of the services dogs could provide. Dogs could guard people and property, herd and protect livestock, and hunt and retrieve prey. But over time, the need for these services diminished. The nature of the relationship between people and dogs changed, and dogs got soft as a result. The only service most dogs now provide is companionship. That's certainly true of Buster, who, though a hound, hunts only for Pup-Peroni and a soft place to sleep.

BUSTER: Dad?

DAD: What, Buster?

BUSTER: I heard Mom say you've been reading a book written by a dog.

DAD: Two books actually.

BUSTER: But dogs can't write books, Dad. No thumbs. You know that.

DAD: The books weren't actually written by dogs, but they were written from a dog's perspective. Dogs are the narrators. I decided to read them because I thought I might get some ideas.

BUSTER: Ideas for what?

DAD: Ideas for this project I'm working on.

BUSTER: What sort of project? Never mind. If I press you, you'll just say you misspoke. So did the authors of the books channel the dogs? Or are they fiction?

DAD: Good question. I don't know.

BUSTER: Tell me about them. Maybe we can put our heads together and figure it out.

DAD: Okay, one of them is called *A Dog's Purpose*. The other is *The Art of Racing in the Rain*.

BUSTER: Racing in the rain—that must be about a greyhound in Seattle.

DAD: It's not about a racing dog. The narrator's human dad, Denny, is a race car driver. He excels at racing in the rain.

BUSTER: Even when the track is slick?

DAD: Especially when the track is slick. Enzo—that's the dog—and Denny watch videos of car races together.

BUSTER: Cool. What else do they do?

DAD: Well, there's a lot of sadness in the book. Denny falls in love and gets married, and he and his wife have a baby girl named Zoë. But then Denny's wife gets sick, and she goes to stay with her parents. They're rich and retired and can take care of her, and Zoë goes to stay with them too. After Denny's wife dies, her parents refuse to let Zoë go back to live with Enzo and Denny.

BUSTER: The scoundrels.

DAD: Enzo doesn't care for them, that's for sure. But they think they're doing what's best for Zoë. Anyway, they wind up fighting it out with lawyers.

BUSTER: Uh-oh. Nothing personal, Dad, but when lawyers get involved, you know two things for sure. It's going to be a mess, and the only people guaranteed to come out ahead are the lawyers.

DAD: That's what happens in the book. It's a huge mess, lasts a long time, and uses up all of Denny's money. He gets depressed and is about to give up.

BUSTER: But let me guess—Enzo comes to the rescue.

DAD: He sure does. Just when Denny's about to sign the papers and relinquish custody of Zoë to his in-laws, Enzo snatches the papers away from him.

BUSTER: Does he chew them up?

DAD: Better. He takes them out in the yard, hikes his leg, and fires away.

BUSTER: Sweet! I love it when a dog's the hero. Then what happens?

DAD: Denny decides not to give up and refuses to sign the

papers. He keeps fighting and gets custody, and in the end he and Zoë move to Italy so he can be a driver for Ferrari.

BUSTER: Ferrari—sweet again! But what about Enzo? Does he go to Italy?

DAD: No. By then Enzo is old. He is satisfied that he's done his job and served his purpose, and he dies peacefully before Denny and Zoë move to Italy.

BUSTER: Once again, we see the tragic unfairness of a dog's short life span.

DAD: But the book has a very happy ending. Enzo believes in reincarnation and thinks he will come back as a person.

BUSTER: Reincarnation? What's that?

DAD: That means, after you die, you come back to life as another animal or a person.

BUSTER: Cool. Is that possible?

DAD: Put that on your list of questions for God. In the book, after Denny gets to be famous for winning races, he meets a young boy who's his biggest fan. And guess what the boy's name is.

BUSTER: I guess Enzo.

DAD: You got it.

BUSTER: So was Enzo the dog reincarnated as Enzo the boy?

DAD: I don't know. But maybe. The book leaves that question unanswered.

BUSTER: That sounds like a good book.

DAD: I enjoyed it. I love dogs and books, you know.

BUSTER: I love dogs and dog stories. I want to hear about the other book too, but first let me try to get a straight answer from you. What's this got to do with a project you're working on?

DAD: Well, to do a good job on the project, I need to learn to think the way a dog thinks.

BUSTER: Sounds like a weird project for a lawyer but, then again, you're a weird lawyer. Plus I don't know why you need to read a book, much less two, to know how a dog thinks. You channel dogs, remember? You know exactly how they think, or at least how I think. But trying to get a straight answer from you is like tilting at windmills, so forget the project and tell me about the other book. What did you call it?

DAD: *A Dog's Purpose.*

BUSTER: Was it good too? What was the dog's purpose in A Dog's Purpose*?*

DAD: It was really good too. It also has a dog as the narrator, and it also involves reincarnation.

BUSTER: What are the odds? Tell me about it.

DAD: The dog in *A Dog's Purpose* is actually four dogs because he keeps dying and getting reincarnated as a different dog.

BUSTER: That's crazy. Is he always the same breed? Does he always have the same name?

DAD: Nope. He isn't even always a he.

BUSTER: So he has to learn to go from hiking to squatting?

DAD: I suppose, but I don't remember any mention of it.

BUSTER: What do you remember?

DAD: He starts out as a mutt named Toby.

BUSTER: Mutt? I thought I had made it clear that you're never to use that pejorative word in my presence.

DAD: There's nothing wrong with that word. It's affectionate, not pejorative.

BUSTER: To you, maybe, but not to me. I prefer mixed-breed.

DAD: Okay then, he starts out as a mixed-breed dog named Toby. Toby comes to a bad end, but then he comes back as a golden retriever named Bailey. He has a wonderful life with a boy named Ethan and Ethan's girlfriend Hannah, but then Ethan is badly injured in a fire. He's damaged emotionally as well as physically, and he and Hannah break up.

BUSTER: This one sounds as sad as the racing book.

DAD: There are sad parts, but it's not all sad by any means. After Bailey passes away after a long life, he comes back as a female German shepherd named Ellie. She works for the police as a search-and-rescue dog and saves people's lives. She's quite a heroine.

BUSTER: Enzo is a hero, and Ellie is a heroine. No surprise there. Saving people's lives sounds like something I would do.

DAD: You've never saved anybody, Buster.

BUSTER: You don't know that, Dad. Maybe I've been reincarnated and I saved people in a previous life. And I could've saved lots of people in this life before you and Mom adopted me.

DAD: Really? You saved people before you came to live with us?

BUSTER: Maybe. I don't remember.

DAD: If you had saved somebody, and especially if you'd saved lots of people, I think you'd remember.

BUSTER: You don't know that. That was a long time ago. Y'all have had me nearly seven years. How many dog years is that?

DAD: Forty-nine.

BUSTER: Don't tell me you remember everything that happened half a century ago. You don't remember where you left your iPhone five minutes ago.

DAD: Apples and oranges.

BUSTER: Apples and oranges? We're talking dogs, not fruit.

DAD: It's an expression. Apples and oranges means it's not a fair comparison. Like comparing whether you would remember saving somebody and I would remember where I put my iPhone.

BUSTER: But apples and oranges are both round and both fruit. You can make juice from both of them. They're very comparable. A better expression would be apples and water buffaloes.

DAD: Never mind. Anyway, in his last incarnation, the dog that started out as Toby is Buddy, a Labrador retriever. And here's the sweet part. His new dad is Ethan, the same person Buddy lived with decades earlier when his name was Bailey and Ethan was a boy.

BUSTER: What a coincidence!

DAD: Writers get to do that. Anyway, Ethan's now an old man. He's never gotten married and is sad and alone.

BUSTER: I thought this was the sweet part.

DAD: It is. Although Ethan and Hannah were high school sweethearts, they haven't seen each other in decades, but Buddy figures out a way to get them back together. When they see each other again, they realize they're still in love. They get married, and Ethan lives out the rest of his life happy and content. At the end, as Ethan is dying, he realizes that Bailey has come back to life as Buddy.

BUSTER: Sweet.

DAD: Very sweet. Anyway, after Ethan realizes that Buddy is Bailey, Buddy realizes that the purpose of his life has been to serve Ethan. And he pledges to serve Hannah as she goes through the grief of having lost her one true love. And that's how the book ends.

BUSTER: Sounds like a real tearjerker, but the author wasn't channeling any dog, I promise you that.

DAD: How can you be so sure?

BUSTER: Because no dog, or at least no honest dog, believes what the author claimed that Buddy believes.

DAD: What do you mean?

BUSTER: And come to think of it, the author of the racing book wasn't channeling Enzo either.

DAD: How do you know that? How could you possibly know?

BUSTER: Think about it, Dad. In both books, the dogs claim that their purpose has been to serve their human parents.

DAD: So?

BUSTER: That's not a dog's purpose, Dad. People are so gullible. They'll talk themselves into believing anything, even that a dog's purpose is to serve them.

DAD: It's not?

BUSTER: Are you that gullible too? Think about it, Dad. Who gets up and goes to work, you and Mom or me and Mollie?

DAD: Mom and I do. So?

BUSTER: And who makes the money and buys the food for all four of us?

DAD: We do.

BUSTER: And who makes the grooming appointments for Mollie and the vet appointments for both of us? And fills up our bowls with food? And throws the tennis ball for us? And takes us for walks? And pays the mortgage and utilities for the nice house we live in?

DAD: Mom and I do all of that. You know that.

BUSTER: Are you starting to get the picture here, Dad? Have I ever rubbed your belly or scratched you behind the ears? Patted you on the head? Given you a treat? Cooked you scrambled eggs with shredded cheddar cheese?

DAD: Of course not. You're a dog. You can't cook.

BUSTER: Whether or not I can *do any of those things is not the point. The point is that I* don't *do any of those things.*

DAD: Why is that the point? What are you saying?

BUSTER: I'll answer your question with one of my own: How exactly do Mollie and I serve you and Mom? Be specific.

DAD: Well, you greet us enthusiastically when we get home. There's that.

BUSTER: Because we're bored and we want some Pup-Peroni. What else?

DAD: I don't know. Y'all let us love on you.

BUSTER: So we serve you by letting you serve us—is that what you're saying?

DAD: Maybe.

BUSTER: Face the facts, Dad. Dogs don't exist to serve people. Dogs exist to be served by people. And any self-respecting dog should be honest enough to admit it.

DAD: I appreciate your candor.

BUSTER: And so one of two things is true: Either the authors of your two dog books aren't channelers, or the dogs are liars.

DAD: That's harsh. And I don't accept your premise. Just because you've got the cushiest life ever doesn't mean all dogs have it so good. And just because you think you exist to be served by us doesn't mean there aren't dogs who actually serve people. Look at Ellie in *A Dog's Purpose*. She was a search-and-rescue dog. She saved people's lives. Her whole life was about serving people.

BUSTER: There are exceptions to every rule, Dad. And Ellie's an exception.

DAD: I'm not so sure. There's an entire class of dogs called working dogs. They herd sheep and cattle, they serve as guard dogs, they do all sorts of things to serve people.

BUSTER: Bully for them. But as you well know, they are the exception. Maybe it was different in the olden days, but working dog has practically become an oxymoron in the 21st century. People may have gotten soft, but dogs have gotten even softer. For each dog who performs some actual service, how many dogs are there like Mollie and me who spend their days lying around waiting to have their food served and their ears scratched? Got to be at least ten. Maybe 20.

DAD: That seems like a lot to me. And I can't believe I'm the one taking the dogs' side in the debate and you're the one arguing that dogs are lazy.

BUSTER: I may live a life of leisure, but at least I'm honest about it. And, as an honest dog, I must admit that you and Mom serve Mollie and me a hundred times more than we serve you. You know that. And I'm not saying that we're lazy. If you hooked me to a plow and asked me to till the back 40, I'd give it a go.

DAD: But we don't have a back 40. A front 40 either.

BUSTER: Exactly my point. We live in a gated community with no work for dogs to do.

DAD: But you're forgetting your duties as watchdogs. You're on duty 24/7/365, or so you say.

BUSTER: You are some kind of gullible, Dad. In case you haven't noticed, Mollie barks at squirrels. If an actual thief ever broke in, she'd lick his hand. And if he gave her Pup-Peroni, she'd lead him straight to Mom's jewelry and her shoe collection.

DAD: That's a harsh assessment.

BUSTER: The barking is all for show, Dad. Surely you know that. And you also know that you and Mom live to serve Mollie and me, not the other way around.

DAD: I suppose we do. Especially Mom.

BUSTER: No kidding. Mom's the bomb. I like the sound of that. It's true, and it rhymes. When Mom calls me Bluth, I'll call her Mean Moe, but when she calls me Busteronious, she'll be Mom the Bomb.

DAD: You're a strange dog, Buster.

BUSTER: So says the dog channeler who asked a woman to spend the duration with him right after reading her a children's book about a dancing bear.

DAD: Enough already. It's past your bedtime.

BUSTER: Okay. Let me stretch and yawn a little and then I'll curl up in one of the beds you and Mom bought us. But before I do, could you do one more little thing for me? You know, one more act of service?

DAD: What now, Buster?

BUSTER: Could you flip my pillow over so the cool side is up?

DAD: Geez.

BUSTER: And while you're at it, could you plump it up a little?
DAD: Unbelievable. Go to sleep, Buster.

In All His Glory

Several years ago, my childhood friend Denise Monts Flint put a portrait of a dog she had painted on Facebook. It was excellent, and I asked if she would paint Buster and Mollie. She agreed, devoted countless hours to the project, and charged me far too little. I was planning to give it to Carrie for Christmas, but when it arrived and I saw it, I was too excited to wait. I videoed Carrie when she saw it for the first time. She cried. A photo of the portrait follows the table of contents at the beginning of the book.

BUSTER: Dad?

DAD: What, Buster?

BUSTER: I wish I could paint.

DAD: Paint what? Houses or pictures?

BUSTER: Pictures, of course. Landscapes, still lifes, portraits. I want to be the Delacroix of dogs, the Picasso of pooches, the Michelangelo of mutts.

DAD: I thought you regarded mutt as an offensive term.

BUSTER: When you use it, but not when I do.

DAD: I see. Well, I wish you could be an artist, but that would be tough to pull off without thumbs, I'm afraid.

BUSTER: Enough about the thumblessness. I know I'll never be an artist, but that doesn't keep a dog from dreaming.

DAD: So what got you dreaming that you'd like to be an artist?

BUSTER: Just gazing up at the portrait of Mollie and me.

DAD: Beautiful, isn't it?

BUSTER: I guess so, but I've got a bone to pick.

DAD: You excel at picking bones. As Roseann Roseannadanna used to say, if it's not one thing, it's another. What is it this time?

BUSTER: I love those early SNLs. And don't get me wrong. It's quite an honor to be immortalized in an oil portrait. By the way, has anybody ever painted a portrait of you?

DAD: Once. You know my friend Tommy Louis?

BUSTER: Is he the short guy who looks like Al Pacino when he grows a goatee?

DAD: That's the one. His wife Addie is a terrific artist. She painted a small watercolor of me a couple of years ago, and they gave it to me for Christmas. That's it right there.

BUSTER: That's you?

DAD: It is. I'm hiking in the mountains in Colorado.

BUSTER: Why'd she paint you from the back? In most portraits, you can see the subject's face.

DAD: I don't know. I think she went by a photo, and I guess she wanted to include both me and the mountains.

BUSTER: Maybe, but I have a better explanation.

DAD: What's that?

BUSTER: She wanted to paint your best side. BAM!

DAD: You're pleased with that one, aren't you?

BUSTER: Sometimes I slay myself. But back to the portrait of Mollie and me. It's an honor and all, and the portraitist got Mollie just right, even her Rod Stewart hair, and I guess the other dog in the painting looks like me.

DAD: You guess? The other dog in the painting looks exactly like you. The other dog in the painting *is* you.

BUSTER: It's a good likeness, I'll grant you that, but something's missing.

DAD: It's an exact likeness. What on earth could be missing?

BUSTER: I don't think she captured my regal bearing quite as I had hoped.

DAD: Your regal bearing? Really?

BUSTER: Sure. You know, the way I carry myself as an aristocrat, a member of the upper crust, the elite. As Busteronious, a Roman patrician.

DAD: An aristocrat? You're a mixed-breed hound from a shelter in Belzoni, Mississippi. Belzoni is the home of the World Catfish Festival, not aristocratic dogs.

BUSTER: That was then; this is now. And now I live in a gated community, do I not?

DAD: In a house Mom and I bought.

BUSTER: Don't hog the credit, Dad. You should be proud of me for overcoming a difficult puppyhood and being a self-made dog.

DAD: Buster, you are truly insufferable.

BUSTER: That's what peasants always say about aristocrats. It's a baseless accusation and a product of envy.

DAD: Wait a minute. You get to live in a nice house that Mom and I bought in a gated community, and I'm the peasant? And you're a shelter dog from the Mississippi Delta, and you're the aristocrat?

BUSTER: If the shoe fits. In this case, shoes. The peasant shoe fits you. The aristocrat shoe fits me.

DAD: How so?

BUSTER: Think about it, Dad. Who does all the yard work around here? You, a sweaty mower and edger of lawns. And who lies in the sun and eats Pup-Peroni? Me, a member of the idle rich. By the way, I'm thinking of taking up croquet and polo.

DAD: Try gripping a mallet without thumbs. Or holding the reins. You think you're an aristocrat? A snob, more like it.

BUSTER: I'm just teasing, Dad. I may not be an aristocrat, but I sure know how to get your goat. This is an aside, but how can I get your goat when you don't even have a goat? It's yet another weird expression. Anyway, you really need to lighten up. You don't want to go into cardiac arrest because you got upset while channeling a dog. Stop and ponder that one for a minute. When you tell the ER doc what happened, they'll unhook the defibrillator and send you straight to the psych ward.

DAD: I don't think I would mention the channeling.

BUSTER: Probably for the best. Listen, I really am just teasing, and I really do appreciate the portrait. Who painted it anyway? Mollie and I didn't have a sitting in a studio or anything.

DAD: Her name is Denise Flint. She painted the portrait from photos.

BUSTER: Why didn't she get us to sit for it? Given what was at stake—perhaps the only portrait of me there will ever be—I would have stood as still as a deer for as long as it took.

DAD: Not practical. She lives outside Philadelphia. That's more than 1,000 miles from here. And I have a feeling there may be other portraits.

BUSTER: But this was the first one, and you should have flown her down here. If she had spent time with me, she would have seen how distinguished I am and, because she's such a gifted artist, I'm sure that would have been reflected in the portrait. By the way, how did you come to get a woman 1,000 miles away to paint Mollie and me? I'm glad you did, but surely there are artists in Mississippi who paint dogs.

DAD: Denise and I grew up together in Tupelo. We're friends on Facebook. She posted a portrait of a dog she painted, and it was great. I asked if she would paint y'all, and she agreed.

BUSTER: Cool. I guess Facebook has value after all. All I hear about are the stupid cat videos and angry political rants.

DAD: There are plenty of those, for sure. Anyway, I started taking pictures of you and Mollie to send her. Lots of pictures.

BUSTER: Mollie and I wondered about that. It was sort of creepy when you were always stalking us and whistling and trying to get us to look at you.

DAD: There was nothing creepy about it. What could be more natural than photographing my fur children? And I took so many because of how hard it was to get y'all to pose and look at me.

BUSTER: We're dogs, Dad, and one of us is Mollie. What did you expect? Maybe taking some photos was normal, but you went overboard. Every time I started to scratch or lick and looked around, there you were, aiming your iPhone, invading my privacy.

DAD: But look how it turned out. I took a ton of pictures, Denise picked out the best ones, and now we have a portrait of our fur children.

BUSTER: It does look a lot like me, though not quite as handsome.

DAD: It looks exactly like you and exactly as handsome.

BUSTER: I'm kidding again, Dad. I tease you a lot but, in all seriousness, I must say that getting Denise to paint Mollie and me is the best thing you've ever done.

DAD: That's nice of you to say, but I just asked a friend to paint our dogs.

BUSTER: Maybe so, but it was a generous gesture to Mollie and me and, more than that, it was a wonderful gift for Mom. Sometimes Mollie and I will tiptoe into the bedroom, and there Mom will be, staring at our portrait and smiling. It's the sweetest thing.

DAD: She seems to like it, doesn't she?

BUSTER: Seems? Mom doesn't seem anything. And she doesn't like the portrait. She loves it.

DAD: She definitely loves you and Mollie.

BUSTER: You'll get no argument from me on that score. When she makes us bacon and eggs, she breaks up the bacon into small pieces so we can savor it instead of just scarfing it down. What a woman! And she puts cheese in our scrambled eggs. Being Mom's son is a sweet gig.

DAD: She spoils you; there's no doubt about that.

BUSTER: I've come a long way from Belzoni; there's no doubt about that either.

DAD: Light years, I'd say.

BUSTER: Light years? What's a light year?

DAD: A light year is an enormous distance. Light travels at 186,000 miles a second, so just think how far it goes in a year.

BUSTER: Farther than from here to Belzoni?

DAD: Much farther.

BUSTER: So why did you say I've come light years from Belzoni?

DAD: A light year is just an expression for a very long way.

BUSTER: How fast is the speed of smell? How many miles are in a smell year?

DAD: Beats me. I've never heard of a smell year. I don't even know if there is such a thing.

BUSTER: You can understand my curiosity, what with my interest in sniffing and all. The smell of bacon gets to me in a New York second.

DAD: And you get to the bacon in less than that.

BUSTER: Back to the portrait. Since you gave it to Mom, I'm betting she's been especially affectionate, if you know what I mean.

DAD: Mom's always affectionate.

BUSTER: But the portrait has resulted in an uptick. Admit it.

DAD: Maybe a little.

BUSTER: I knew it. Commissioning that portrait was not just the best thing you've ever done, it was the smartest thing too. It was a gift for all four of us and, like the Jelly of the Month Club in Christmas Vacation, *it's the gift keeps on giving.*

DAD: You really think it's the very best thing I've ever done?

BUSTER: Sure. What could possibly be better?

DAD: Adopting you.

BUSTER: I hadn't thought of that, but the portrait's definitely second.

DAD: What about adopting Mollie?

BUSTER: Okay then, third, but no lower than that.

DAD: What about signing up for eHarmony? Marrying Mom? Learning to channel you?

BUSTER: Alright already. Perhaps I engaged in a bit of harmless hyperbole. But wherever you rank it, it was a great thing you did when you asked Denise to paint our portrait.

DAD: Thank you. I'm glad I did it.

BUSTER: I'm going to drift off to sleep tonight gazing at the image of me staring back at me. What could possibly be better than that?

DAD: In your mind, I'm sure nothing.

BUSTER: Thank you for immortalizing me, Dad. Now I know I'll never be forgotten.

DAD: I don't think there was any risk of that even without the portrait. Goodnight, Buster.

BUSTER: Goodnight, Dad. (Then, after rolling over to stare at the portrait): *Goodnight, fair Busteronious.*

Spilling The Beans

People who know their conversations are being recorded are cautious about what they say. They want to be seen in a favorable light, so they don't let their guard down. They're less candid and more careful than they otherwise would be. They're reluctant to speak their minds. I don't know if dogs have the same tendency, but I wasn't taking any chances, at least not until the end.

BUSTER: Dad?

DAD: What, Buster?

BUSTER: Read me a book.

DAD: Where on earth did you get that idea?

BUSTER: You read that children's book to Mom the night you proposed to her. And I've heard you reading books to the little people. Now it's my turn.

DAD: Buster, I'm not going to read a book to a dog. That's crazy.

BUSTER: No crazier than talking to a dog.

DAD: I disagree. Everybody talks to dogs.

BUSTER: But not everybody channels dogs.

DAD: Not everybody, but some people do. I've asked around. But nobody reads to dogs.

BUSTER: Have you asked around about reading to dogs?

DAD: No, and I don't have to. Nobody reads to dogs.

BUSTER: Let me remind you of something, Dad. On more than one occasion, you've declared something to be the case when you couldn't possibly know, and you've turned out to be wrong. Mixed-breed dog shows come to mind as one example.

DAD: I'm not wrong this time. Nobody reads to dogs.

BUSTER: You don't know that. Right this minute, an heiress on 72nd and Park Avenue could be reading A Farewell to Arms *to her Maltipoo, and there's no way you'd know it.*

DAD: A crazy heiress maybe.

BUSTER: Pot kettle, dog channeler. Consider, just for a moment, that you told a dog you thought a hypothetical woman was crazy.

DAD: Channeling and reading are apples and oranges, Buster, and people don't read to dogs.

BUSTER: Man, you're stubborn. You couldn't possibly know, but let's assume you're right. Let's assume you would be the first person in the history of the world to read to a dog. You know what that would make you?

DAD: Yes. A lunatic.

BUSTER: No. It would make you a pioneer, a visionary, a thought leader.

DAD: It would make me a nut. What would somebody think who walked in the door and saw me reading to you?

BUSTER: Probably the same thing somebody would think who walked in and saw you channeling me. No, I take that back. Seeing you channeling me would make you seem even nuttier. You say something as you, then you say something in a higher voice as me. A sane person might think you've gone off your rocker. He might call 911 and say bring a straitjacket on the double.

DAD: Lots of people talk for their dogs, Buster. I think I'd be okay.

BUSTER: I wouldn't be so sure. At the commitment hearing, when the judge asks how you're able to channel my thoughts, what would you say?

DAD: I'd have to think about that one. Maybe I'd say that a dog is man's best friend, that you and I have a very close relationship, and that I understand you and know what you're thinking. Or maybe I'd just say I make it all up to amuse myself and, hopefully, others.

BUSTER: Neither story would fly. If you claim you know what a dog is thinking, the judge will think you're looney tunes. And if you claim you make it up to amuse yourself, you'll wind up amusing yourself playing Chinese checkers in the break room at the asylum.

DAD: Maybe they wouldn't fly, but they both sound better than anything I could say if somebody caught me reading to you.

BUSTER: Au, contraire. You could say I'm high strung and reading soothes me and helps me fall asleep.

DAD: But you never need help falling asleep.

BUSTER: We're not talking about the truth, Dad, we're talking about a cover story.

DAD: Honesty's the best policy, Buster.

BUSTER: Staying out of the loony bin's an even better policy. If you don't think the Buster-needs-soothing story would fly, you could say you're thinking about auditioning for a play and you're practicing reading with inflection.

DAD: You really think I could pull it off?

BUSTER: Why not? Reading aloud to a dog might be viewed as a bit eccentric, but it won't get you locked up in a padded cell. I can make no such promises if somebody catches you channeling.

DAD: If channeling can get you locked up, I'm gonna be in a world of hurt when people read this.

BUSTER: Read what?

DAD: Nothing. Never mind. Let's assume that I might be willing to read to you. What sorts of books do you have in mind?

BUSTER: All sorts. I'm thinking maybe an outdoor adventure book. It will be about my becoming the first dog to climb Everest.

DAD: But you haven't climbed Everest. In fact, you've never been more than 500 feet above sea level, and you'd get a nosebleed if you did. Plus here's an even bigger problem: There's no such book.

BUSTER: But there can be such a book, and the reader won't have to know that I suffer from acrophobia and have never left Mississippi. I'm thinking Buster Conquers Everest *for the title.*

DAD: Sounds good, but there have been lots of books about people climbing Everest. I'm not sure a dog has ever climbed Everest. I think it would be important to convey to the reader that you're a dog.

BUSTER: I agree, and I've thought about that. There would be a picture of me with my climbing gear on the front cover. The reader would know I'm a dog and a handsome dog at that.

DAD: If the reader saw the book, sure. But for people who don't see it, I think you'd need a title that would grab their attention and reveal that you're a dog.

BUSTER: Then we'll handle it with a subtitle. What about Champion Hound Summits World's Highest Peak*?*

DAD: But you're not a champion.

BUSTER: That's the subject of another book. We'll need to think about the best order for rolling them out.

DAD: Tell me about the champion book.

BUSTER: Not so fast. Don't you want to hear about the Everest ascent and how I use my keen sense of sniff to find and rescue climbers buried in an avalanche?

DAD: Not now, though I have no doubt that you're heroic. Tell me about the champion book, then I'll ask you the $64,000 question.

BUSTER: The $64,000 question?

DAD: Just an expression from an old TV show. It means the crucial question.

BUSTER: So what's the crucial question?

DAD: I'll ask you later. Tell me how you become a champion.

BUSTER: Well, I haven't worked out all the details, but the basic storyline is that I come from behind in the last event and defeat a heavily favored Labradoodle in the mixed-breed world championship.

DAD: Impressive.

BUSTER: There's more. My victory is so amazing that the Board of Directors of the American Kennel Club votes unanimously to allow me to compete against all the winners of Best in Breed at Westminster, the dog show of dog shows.

DAD: Let me guess. I bet you win that one too.

BUSTER: How'd you know? Anyway, the crowd goes wild when I vanquish all the purebreds with their pretentious names, their pampered lives, and their prissy hairstyles.

DAD: Everybody loves an underdog.

BUSTER: My win is celebrated as a victory for the common dog, the shelter dog, the dog who was neutered against his will, the dog who works as a watchdog to earn his keep.

DAD: Works as a watchdog?

BUSTER: Literary license, Dad.

DAD: It's got potential. You have a title?

BUSTER: Buster Conquers Westminster.

DAD: Sounds like you're planning a whole *Buster Conquers* series. You've really thought this out.

BUSTER: Series sell, Dad. Think about it. The Hardy Boys, Nancy Drew, National Lampoon vacation movies. Cousin Eddie was the best.

DAD: You've got two books so far. Any more?

BUSTER: I've got several on the drawing board. I know one will focus on my rags-to-riches story. It will trace my life from my difficult puppyhood in a poor town in the Mississippi Delta and how things went from bad to worse and I wound up in a shelter for the unwanted and unloved.

DAD: Sounds like a tragedy.

BUSTER: But it will have a happy ending. It will reveal how I pulled myself up by my bootstraps with grit and fortitude and made a better life for myself.

DAD: You don't wear boots, Buster.

BUSTER: Or shoes. I think you know an expression when you hear one, Dad.

DAD: Fair enough, but tell me just how you pulled yourself up by your bootstraps, figuratively speaking.

BUSTER: Do you realize how hard it was for me to stay calm when you and Mom walked in that day at PETCO? You know how excitable I am. And I could see that y'all were easy marks.

DAD: Easy marks?

BUSTER: I mean I could see that y'all would be loving parents. The pressure was on. And yet I somehow was able to pull myself up by my bootstraps and remain calm.

DAD: So it was all an act.

BUSTER: I'm an accomplished actor, Dad, in case you haven't noticed. I put on the wild-and-crazy show when Mom comes home, and I acted downright placid when y'all walked into PETCO.

DAD: But why did you feel the need to put on an act, Buster? Why not just be yourself?

BUSTER: Well, I could see that y'all were of a certain age, to use another expression, and I knew you'd want a calm dog, one that wouldn't be dodging here and darting there and tripping you and breaking your hip.

DAD: I go hiking in the mountains, Buster. I'm not about to fall and break my hip.

BUSTER: No one can escape the ravages of age, Dad. No man and no dog.

DAD: True enough. So your heroic efforts to go from rags to riches consist entirely of acting calm at PETCO?

BUSTER: It was a struggle, Dad. But there's more to the story. The book about my life will tie to the previous one. It will come to a poignant conclusion when I'm honored for using my winnings from Westminster to help the dogs I left behind at BARK.

DAD: Very generous.

BUSTER: I'll never forget my roots, Dad. I've been fortunate, and I want to give back.

DAD: Good for you.

BUSTER: I love that Buffet song, "Death of an Unpopular Poet." You know that one?

DAD: I know it well.

BUSTER: The best part is when the poet gets famous after he dies, and his dog Spooner gets all the royalties and grows old on steak and bacon.

DAD: In a doghouse ten feet round. It's a sweet song.

BUSTER: As a dog who loves steak and bacon, I say it's both sweet and savory. Anyway, thanks to my generosity, the dogs at BARK grow old on steak and bacon.

DAD: What about the cats at BARK?

BUSTER: They're on their own.

DAD: Of course they are. So what's the name of this one?

BUSTER: Buster Conquers Adversity.

DAD: Of course again. Any more books in the *Buster Conquers* series?

BUSTER: I've got a few ideas rolling around in my head. The one I think has the most potential involves my sniffing out a bomb planted by terrorists and saving thousands of my fellow Americans.

DAD: I don't think it's likely that terrorists will attack a suburb of Jackson, Mississippi, Buster. Not exactly a target-rich environment.

BUSTER: It doesn't happen here. It happens when we're on vacation seeing the sights in Washington, D.C., our nation's capital.

DAD: A more credible storyline.

BUSTER: I strive for verisimilitude. So the bomb is hidden in the base of the Washington Monument. The blast, had I not intervened, would have levelled everything within a two-mile radius, including the Capitol and the White House.

DAD: I bet you get a ticker tape parade for stopping it.

BUSTER: Well, at first nobody knows I'm the one who saved the day. Let's just say the intelligence community doesn't want the world to know they were outsmarted by a mixed-breed hound. But it's hard to hide a story as big as this one and, when word gets out, man oh man.

DAD: I bet it makes the reaction to your Everest ascent seem like nothing.

BUSTER: Less than nothing. I get the ticker tape parade you mentioned and, believe it or not, the Congressional Medal of Honor. I'm the first dog ever to receive it, the first animal in fact. I'm also given a gold collar and a personal chef and masseuse for life.

DAD: *Buster Conquers Terrorism.*

BUSTER: I like it.

DAD: If it were true, it would be amazing, but unfortunately it's not. And just as unfortunately, there are no *Buster Conquers* books. So here's the $64,000 question: Before I can read one of these books to you, somebody's got to write it. Who, I ask, is going to write the *Buster Conquers* books?

BUSTER: Look in the mirror, big guy.

DAD: I don't know why I even asked.

BUSTER: You know you love to write, Dad. And it's obvious that you also love making stuff up. I'll help you construct the plots, you'll read the drafts to me, and I'll give you constructive criticism, like you were going to give me about my gait. We'll be a father-son team or, to be more precise, son-father. I'll be the creative genius, and you'll be the scrivener. It'll be like channeling.

DAD: Except far more work.

BUSTER: Work is good, Dad. Work is honorable.

DAD: So says a member of the idle rich. Plus I already have a job. I already work.

BUSTER: You can write at night and on weekends.

DAD: So no more leisure time for me.

BUSTER: But just think of the money we'll make when the royalties come rolling in.

DAD: We?

BUSTER: Sure. I'll need to decide on an equitable arrangement. The books are my brainchild, but you should get a decent wage for typing them.

DAD: How generous. But at least for now, I don't have time. I'm in the middle of another project.

BUSTER: Put it aside. Nothing could be more important than the Buster Conquers *series. Just what is this other project?*

DAD: I guess there's no harm in telling you at this point. I've been writing a book consisting entirely of our bedtime conversations.

BUSTER: What? I should have known something was up when you slipped up and said something about people reading this. You've done it more than once.

DAD: I guess I should have told you sooner, but I was afraid you would be less candid when we talked.

BUSTER: Did you ever bother to ask my permission for this project of yours?

DAD: I did not.

BUSTER: Do you have a signed release?

DAD: You can't write, Buster, and you can't sign your name.

BUSTER: So that's a no. Have we agreed on a split of the royalties?

DAD: There will be no split. If there are any royalties, I'll get them.

BUSTER: That's outrageous. You need to put the brakes on this project until we get some fundamentals ironed out. In addition to an equitable royalty split, we'll need to agree on an appropriate fee for the use of my likeness. I'll also need control over the manuscript so I can delete anything that depicts me in an unflattering light. And we'll have to decide how to choose the title of the book as well as the illustrator and publisher.

DAD: Is that right? Well, here are some fundamentals that have already been ironed out. Number 1—you're a dog. Number 2—dogs have no legal rights. No right to share in the royalties, no right to edit the manuscript, no right to name the book.

BUSTER: We'll see about that. I'll get a lawyer.

DAD: And just how will you pay a lawyer, Buster?

BUSTER: Contingency fee. The same arrangement you refused when I wanted to sue Elvis's estate.

DAD: And how will you make an appointment? How will you get to the lawyer's office?

BUSTER: Where there's a will, there's a way.

DAD: And how will the lawyer know what you want? You can't talk, remember?

BUSTER: I'll find a lawyer who channels dogs. Lots of people channel dogs, at least that's what you say.

DAD: But how will you find one? It's not like lawyers put dog channeling on their websites.

BUSTER: Trial and error, I guess. If the lawyer says something to me and doesn't respond as me, I'll know to keep looking.

DAD: Good luck with that. And even if you do find a lawyer/channeler, he's going to tell you that you have no legal rights.

BUSTER: Let's say you're right, Dad. Do you really think it's fair for you to get all the money from a book of conversations between you and me?

DAD: Buster plays the fairness card once again. Actually I think it's very fair. I'm the one doing the writing. I even do all the talking. Speaking as me and channeling you.

BUSTER: But I'm the one being channeled. Surely I have intellectual property rights in my own thoughts.

DAD: Surely you don't. But I'll tell you what I'll do. I'll give five percent of the profits to dog shelters. You say you want to give back. That would be a real gift, not the faux gift in *Buster Conquers Adversity.*

BUSTER: Twenty percent.

DAD: No way. Seven percent and Pup-Peroni for life.

BUSTER: Pup-Peroni for life gives me nothing I don't already have. As long as Mom's around, I'm already guaranteed that. Fifteen percent.

DAD: Eight.

BUSTER: Twelve.

DAD: Ten, and if it's a bestseller I'll take all four of us—you and Mollie, Mom and me—to the Westminster Dog Show. It's in Madison Square Garden in New York City.

BUSTER: New York, New York—the place so nice they named it twice. If it's a bestseller, will I be a celebrity?

DAD: I don't know, Buster. We can continue this talk later. It's past your bedtime, and I'm tired of writing.

BUSTER: Writing? I can't believe you've been writing down everything I think without my permission. A trip to the Big Apple sounds fun, but ten percent is grossly inadequate. You're appropriating my thoughts and words without my consent and without just compensation. It's cultural appropriation. You've heard of that, I'm guessing. And you're appropriating my canine culture. For the record, I object.

DAD: Too bad, so sad.

BUSTER: I'll see you in court.

DAD: Good luck getting there.

BUSTER: Don't underestimate me, Dad.

DAD: Don't overestimate your legal rights, Buster.

BUSTER: This is a travesty.

DAD: Nighty night.

Best Dog In A Leading Role

Books that are made into movies are as rare as hen's teeth. They're almost as rare as talking dogs.

Just two days before I typed this, my publisher posted some discouraging statistics on Facebook. Major publishers in the country released more than 300,000 new books in 2019. Counting small presses and self-published books, the number topped 1,200,000. In contrast, only 786 movies were released during the year. Unlike Buster, I do math. Even if every one of the 786 movies was based on a book, the odds against a book's being made into a movie were more than 1500 to one.

I try to be a realist in my conversations with Buster, to point out the flaws in his schemes to get rich and famous, to bring him back down to earth. But this time, though I stressed that time was of the essence, I decided to let him dream his dream. I chose not to tell him it was a pipedream.

BUSTER: Dad?

DAD: What, Buster?

BUSTER: I'm thinking about Jennifer Aniston.

DAD: That's strange.

BUSTER: And Meg Ryan.

DAD: Once again, Buster has forgotten he's a dog.

BUSTER: I'm not thinking of them like that, Dad. I'm thinking of them for Mom.

DAD: Even stranger. I'm pretty sure Mom prefers men.

BUSTER: I'm not thinking of them for her like that. I'm thinking of them to play her.

DAD: Play her?

BUSTER: In the movie.

DAD: What movie?

BUSTER: The movie based on the book you're writing. Duh.

DAD: Wait a minute. Last time I checked, which was just last night, you were adamantly opposed to the book. Now you're not only in favor of it, you're also thinking about a movie based on it?

BUSTER: It's an unwise dog who won't revisit an unwise decision.

DAD: I agree, but what caused the change of heart?

BUSTER: Several things. First of all, even if you hoard all the royalties and won't agree to an equitable split, you're still my dad. And if you get rich, I'm bound to benefit. Trickle down economics may be a controversial theory for people, but it works great for dogs.

DAD: Good thinking.

BUSTER: I'll be like Spooner, growing old on steak and bacon.

DAD: Not many dogs get to do that, especially BARK alums.

BUSTER: Exactly. But fortune's not the main thing. Fame is. I'm quite concerned about my legacy, as I may have mentioned.

DAD: About a hundred times.

BUSTER: My other plans to become famous haven't panned out yet. It's possible they still could, but I can't just wait around and hope. Every day that goes by, the sands of time slip through the hourglass.

DAD: It's wise to be a realist.

BUSTER: I could still get famous by winning a major dog show, but last time we checked, no shows for mixed-breed dogs were even scheduled.

DAD: And who knows when one will be.

BUSTER: Plus if one does get scheduled, I might not win because I might not be in peak condition. It's not like I'm going to give up Pup-Peroni for a show that may never take place. I'm not sacrificing one of life's great pleasures for what may be nothing but a pipedream.

DAD: Who could blame you?

BUSTER: We've discussed the difficulties with my getting famous by proving I can read.

DAD: They're substantial.

BUSTER: Or becoming a spy.

DAD: The longest long shot of all.

BUSTER: It's a shame, but I have to agree. And, as you just said, it's wise to be a realist, and I'm nothing if not wise. But I figure the book, followed by a movie, then a prequel about my puppyhood, will be my ticket to fame.

DAD: Already planning a prequel?

BUSTER: Prequels are big, Dad, but back to the first movie. We don't want to get ahead of ourselves.

DAD: We wouldn't want to do that.

BUSTER: So Jennifer Aniston or Meg Ryan—who should play Mom?

DAD: Not to get ahead of ourselves, but I think either one would be great. Both are beautiful, vivacious, and funny, just like Mom.

BUSTER: Contact their agents. Let's keep our options open.

DAD: Buster, I don't even have a finished manuscript yet, much less a book, much less a screenplay or a movie deal. It's way too early to be contacting agents.

BUSTER: It's never too early to plant a seed, Dad.

DAD: Whatever. Have you given any thought to who should play me? What about Brad Pitt? Or maybe Hugh Jackman.

BUSTER: That's not exactly what I had in mind. I was thinking Ned Beatty or Drew Carey. Or maybe that guy who played Norm on Cheers.

DAD: So you think an old fat guy should play me.

BUSTER: As someone once told me not so very long ago, it's wise to be a realist. And we want the movie to be real. We want it to be true. It's all about verisimilitude. That word breaks my four-syllable limit by two, but it's a cool word.

DAD: And to be real and true, you're saying the actor who plays me needs to be old and fat.

BUSTER: Don't get your feelings hurt, Dad. He doesn't have to be real old and real fat. But Hugh Jackman? Really? Look at him, then look in the mirror. You're in your seventh decade, he's got a six-pack, and you've got a keg.

DAD: So for Mom you're thinking Jennifer Aniston, and for me you're thinking an old fat man. That's really how you see us.

BUSTER: We've discussed this topic before, Dad. You and I both know you outkicked your coverage. I think you should regard it as a great achievement that a man who looks like you scored a woman who looks like Mom.

DAD: I didn't think I'd outkicked it by that much.

BUSTER: You should be proud of how far you outkicked it. Look at photos of the two of you and pat yourself on the back.

DAD: She was very excited to marry me, I'll have you know.

BUSTER: Overdue to get her eyes checked, I'm guessing. Though it's a mystery to me, I'm happy for you. You should be proud. And relieved too. You wouldn't want to crawl under the covers at night with a woman who looks like Ned Beatty.

DAD: I look nothing like Ned Beatty.

BUSTER: You look more like Ned than Hugh, I promise you that.

DAD: You are truly man's best friend, Buster.

BUSTER: Don't pout. A man's best friend should be a realist, not a sycophant. And having some male hunk eye candy play you in my movie wouldn't be realistic.

DAD: So now it's your movie, is it?

BUSTER: It's my story, isn't it? But call it our movie. You can even call it your movie if it'll keep you from pouting. I just want it to be a great movie. I can't wait to go on the stage at the Oscars.

DAD: So says the dog who doesn't want us to get ahead of ourselves.

BUSTER: I'm a dreamer, Dad. Always have been. A dog's reach should exceed his grasp, or what's a heaven for?

DAD: So we've got a gorgeous blonde for Mom and an old fat guy for me. What about for you and Mollie? Who will play y'all?

BUSTER: One of those roles is easy to fill, the other one, not so much.

DAD: Let's deal with the hard one first.

BUSTER: Mollie's an undersized cocker spaniel, so that's what we'll want.

DAD: For verisimilitude.

BUSTER: Exactly. Plus we'll need a female.

DAD: Agreed. No male dog could play sweet Mollie.

BUSTER: Male dogs can be sweet too, Dad. Me, for example. But I agree a female would be better. If we had a male dog, eagle-eyed members of the audience might notice. And finding an undersized female cocker spaniel who also happens to be a trained professional actress might be a challenge.

DAD: You don't think Mollie could play herself? What could be more true and real than that?

BUSTER: C'mon, Dad. You know I love that sweet girl with all my heart, but she's not exactly a rocket scientist.

DAD: But she won't be playing a rocket scientist.

BUSTER: Think about this: You know when you and Mom ask her to do something and she just stands there looking confused?

DAD: I know the look.

BUSTER: So consider what she would be like on a movie set. The director would tell her what to do. Her response: the look.

DAD: It would be a challenge.

BUSTER: Think of how much time would get wasted. Production costs would soar. Jennifer Aniston doesn't come cheap, you know.

DAD: Fair enough. An actress for Mollie. What about for you?

BUSTER: I'll play me, obviously.

DAD: I saw that coming.

BUSTER: Buster plays Buster. What could be more real and true than that?

DAD: So we need professional actors for everyone in the family but you.

BUSTER: We just discussed Mollie, and we need accomplished actors for you and Mom. Y'all have never acted.

DAD: Neither have you.

BUSTER: Not true. I'm an accomplished actor, as I told you last night. I can fake being excited, fake being calm, and convince people I'm both. Whatever the scene calls for, I'm your dog. And I'll promise you this: You'll never find another dog who's as handsome as I am, who carries himself like I do, and who exudes both pride and sensitivity.

DAD: I can't argue with the pride.

BUSTER: I'm just being a realist, Dad. Let's face it. The dog who could accurately portray all of my traits and also happens to be a professional actor and a mixed-breed hound simply does not exist. No other dog could possibly capture my elan or my joie de vivre. You know it, and I know it. There's but one option: Buster plays Buster.

DAD: So I write the book, I write the movie, you get to star in it, and some old fat guy plays me.

BUSTER: As my dear friend, a realist, once told me, life's not fair.

DAD: Not the way you've scripted it, that's for sure.

BUSTER: Don't be a crybaby. You get the fortune, I get the fame. Win, win.

DAD: So I do the work, and you get the steak and bacon.

BUSTER: Cry me a river. Like you don't have a good life. You're married to a gorgeous woman who's a gourmet chef. You have a love live, and you have thumbs. I have neither. Cut me some slack if I want to play me in the movie based on the book you've written without my permission.

DAD: But even if I agreed to let you play you, it might not be possible.

BUSTER: And why on earth would that be?

DAD: Well, as I explained earlier, first I've got to finish the manuscript, then I have to get it published, then somebody who makes movies has to be convinced that it's worthwhile, then comes a screenplay, followed by casting. All of that must take place before the first scene is filmed.

BUSTER: So?

DAD: So all of that could take years. And, as you often remind me, years are what you're getting on up in. Sands through the hourglass and all.

BUSTER: Are you saying what I think you're saying? That I might not be around for the filming of the book about my own life? That I might be ... I can't even say the word.

DAD: That's what I'm saying. You might not be around, or you might be too old and feeble to do the role justice.

BUSTER: Too old and feeble? I'm a long way from needing a cane or a walker.

DAD: Maybe so, but time stops for no dog, and the dog who plays you should be robust and vibrant, a handsome dog in the prime of his life. Not a dog who's been victimized by the ravages of age.

BUSTER: I can't argue with that. But the prospect that I won't be able to play myself in the movie about me is the worst thing I've ever heard. It's my dream. I have my heart set on it.

DAD: You're always hearing the worst thing you've ever heard, and you're always claiming that something is your dream. How could this possibly be your dream? You didn't even know I was writing the book until last night.

BUSTER: You know how dog years go by seven times faster than human years?

DAD: So?

BUSTER: So this has been my dream for a full dog week.

DAD: Maybe so, but to get from a rough draft of a manuscript to a movie takes time. There's no way around it.

BUSTER: There's got to be a way. Posthumous fame is nice, but it's, well, posthumous.

DAD: I thought your primary concern was your legacy.

BUSTER: But I want to bask in the fame and glory while I'm still here. Preferably while I'm still robust and vibrant. We need to put this project on a fast track. You need to quit your day job and devote every waking hour to it.

DAD: Quitting my day job would mean no more Pup-Peroni.

BUSTER: The glass is always half empty with you, isn't it? There's got to be a way to speed this along. You could finish the manuscript immediately; that would be a start.

DAD: So this would be the last conversation I write, I guess.

BUSTER: You're writing this?

DAD: Sure. I told you that.

BUSTER: Again without my consent.

DAD: Again without needing it.

BUSTER: Okay then, write it. But no more. This has got to be the last one. And to expedite the process, I'll even relinquish my right to review and revise.

DAD: A right you don't have.

BUSTER: Okay, so I'm relinquishing a right I don't have. You need to quit running your mouth so you can work on the manuscript.

DAD: Thus sayeth the dog of few words.

BUSTER: I'm going to be the dog of no words until you finish.

DAD: How refreshing.

BUSTER: Always the comedian. We need to decide on a name. Have you given any thought to what the name should be? It should be something that reflects my personality, my zest for life.

DAD: Thus continueth the dog of few words. I've thought of several names: *Channeling Buster* or *Conversations with a Hound*, but I'm leaning toward *Bedtime with Buster*.

BUSTER: Bedtime with Buster*? Why that? People might get the wrong idea.*

DAD: Because we have all our meaningful conversations, or at least all the ones I write, when I put you to bed.

BUSTER: I've got some other ideas. Better ideas.

DAD: Shocking.

BUSTER: I first thought of Buster the Super Dog. *But now I'm leaning toward* The Wisdom of Buster.

DAD: And you're such a wise dog. I'll tell you what we'll do. We'll add a subtitle: *Conversations with a Handsome Hound*.

BUSTER: I like the sound of that. I am, after all, quite handsome.

DAD: You're handsome and precocious and many other things. Many, many other things. And so, for the last time in *Bedtime with Buster*, go to sleep, Buster.

BUSTER: Before I nod off, one more thing.

DAD: Precocious but predictable.

BUSTER: Can we be serious for a second? If this is really going to be the end of the book, I want to thank you from the bottom of my heart. Make sure you write that down so the readers and the audience will know how grateful I am.

DAD: Got it. But you don't need to thank me. I enjoy our conversations.

BUSTER: I'm not thanking you for channeling me. I'm thanking you for making me famous.

DAD: Don't count your chickens before they hatch, Buster.

BUSTER: Why are you bringing up chickens again? We're talking about a dog and a book, about a movie and fame and glory. There's been no mention of chickens. You're a strange man, Dad.

DAD: True enough, but not for the reason you think. Go to sleep, Buster.

Epilogue

Buster here. Dad wrote the prologue, so he's letting me wqrite the epilogue. It's the least he should do after transcribing our conversations without telling me, much less requesting my permission. Having said that, I apprecxiate this opportunity to address you directly.

Please pardon the typios. My spelling, punctuation, and gramm,ar are just fine—you grammar nerds out there, note that Oxford comma—but hitting just one key at a time with my right forepaw is a constant challengfe. (Just as most people are right-handed, most dogs are right-pawed. I bet you didn't know that.)

Anyway, it would be the easiest thing in the worlkd for me to deny it all and take the position that Dad made up every word of the conversations you just read. After all, he has no corroborating evidence, no documents, no witnesases. And even if he could produce a witness who heard our talks, who's to say Dad didn't invbent the thoughts he claims he channeled from me? And even if he doesn't think he invbented them, who's to say he's not just some dotty old man who's lost it?

And, to be frank, I was tem,pted to deny it all because my conversations with Dad don't always portray me in a flattering light. When Dad let me read the manuyscript, I winced at how arrogant I sounded about my appearance or, rather, how arrogant Dad sounded when he was speaking for me. At times I came off as a narcissist and a whiner, wallowqing in victimhood. It was not a good look, though in all fairness—and I certainly want to be fair to me—I often acknowledged in our talks what a weonderful life I've been given, especially by Mom. Mom the Bomb.

But as I pondered what to share with you in this epiloghue, I thought about the story of George Washington and the cherry tree. Even if the story is apocryuphal, it serves as an excellent life lesson. Honesty really is the best policy. And I thought about Big Paul, the granmdfather I never knew. What would Big Paul do? We all know the answer to that. He would tell the truth; that's what he would do. And so I made a vow to tell the trtuth and let the chips fall where they may.

And so, painful though it is to admit it, I must confess that every word of the manuscript is the unvarnishjed truth. Dad's transcriptions of our chats are not just accurate, they're verbatim,. You may wonder how I could possibly know that, how I could rem,ember 80,496 words. Well, consider this: I may not be able to talk, but I can sure listen. And I listenmed to every word of my talks with Dad, both his and mine. (If you're wondering where the 80,496 came from, it's the word count for the manuscrip[t on Mom's laptop. Turns out that Dad was always mooching her lap[top to type our talks.)

As for the arrogance about my appearance, I offer two poinmts in my defense. First, I would have tried to appear humbler if I had known my talks with Dad would evber see the light of day. He was able to gauge his words, but I wasn't afforded the same opportunityu. People recoil when they learn a trusted confidante has secretly recorded their conversations. They realizxe the unfairness of it all. Please take that into account. Second, I have been told over and over, constantly by Mom, occasionally by Dad, and often by strangers, that I am one handfsome hound. Who am I to question the wisdom, of my elders?

Regarding the whining and the victimhood, I stand by my complaintys. I admit that there are many good things about life as a dog, especially my life as a dog, but let me ask you a few qwuestions to help you understand my perspective: How would you feel if you couldn'ty talk, if you had to go your entire life without saying a single word? And you had an abbreviatedf life span, a life so short you probably wouldn't be around to read this if you were a dog? What ifg you had to eat the same boring food every day, and you had to eat it from a bowl on the floor? And had to wear a leash every time you went for a walk? And you got left behind when the rest of your family went on vacation? And last, but far from least, what if you had to go through life without thuimbs? I challenge you to spend an entire day with your thumbs folded into the palms of your hands and see how much you ghet done.

So I ask you to ask yourself: How would you feel if all of this described your life? If you had a short, thumbless life of suffering in silence and eating from a bowl on the floor? I can't speakl for you, but I'm guessing you'd feel pretty lousy. So, if you have dogs in your family, consider the burdens they bear. Be kind to them. Give them lots of love and lots of treats. Hold them close to your heart.

Most of the talks Dad transcribed happened a good while back, more than two yuears ago. Consistent with my status as a seconmd-class citizen and his warped sense of priorities, Dad set aside this book about me, his adopted son, to write some other book about him and his own adop[tion. The day this book surpasses that one in sales will be a sweet day indeed.

You read in our last talk about the need to put this project on a fast track. The passage of time has of course only added to the urgency of the situastion.. I'm getting gray around the muzzle, my joints ache in the morning, and Google says Ned Beatty, who for my money is the best choice to play Dadf, is now 83. He probably won't be like Clint Eastwood, still making movies as a nonagenarian. So we've got to get this manuscript to the publishjer pronto so we can bring my story to the big screen, or at least Netflix, as fast as caninely possible. I thus won't keep you much longer, but before saying sayuonara, I thought I'd give you a quick update on the significant changes in our lives since my last talk with Dad.

First of all, we've moved to a new house in a new neighborthood. The best thing about it is all the dogs here. It's a sniffing and leg-hiking paradise. On my walks with Dad, I've had to become very disciplined to ensure that my tank doesn't run dry when there's still terrtitory to mark.

Second, Dad is now semi-retired. I'm sure he gets on Mom's last nervbe, sitting around typing conversations with a dog while she's still holding down a full-time job and doing all the cookling. But it's been a great development for me, a walking bonanza. Dad and I now walk three or four miles every morning. He's actually lost a few pounds, believe it or not. Now, for the first time in years, he might even be able to see his toes when he looks dowen.

Third, we've had two additions to the family, neither good. First, sweet Mom decided she and Dad should give a senior dog approaching the on ramp to the Rainmbow Bridge a good dotage. Dad denies Mom nothing, so they adopted Maddie, and she's now an Eason too. But Mom didn't take into account what giving Maddie a good life would do to my life. Maddie's sweert, I'll grant her that, and she's cute too. She has no front teeth, and her tongue often sticks out and she doesn't even know it. Absurd but adorabnle.

But cute and sweet are as far as it goes. To call Maddie as dumb as a stump is an insult to stumps. I mean, she doesn't even know how she lost her teeth. It was her only teeth. How could sshe not know? Mom says it's mean to say that Maddie's not playing with a full deck, but I told her the same thing I told you: Honesty is the best policy. Maddie also has several annoying habits. She follows me around the house licking my head and ears, like she thinks being coated in dog spittle is my life's dream or something. She also licks herself all the time. Slurp, slurp, slurp – disgusting. Worst of all is the incessant barking. The dog won't shut up. She barks at people, at other dogs, at shadfows, at the wind. At my age, I just long for peace and quiet, and fame of course, but there's no peace and quiert with her around.

The second addition to the family is even worse. It is, believe it or not, a cat. Mom found the littyle demon under a shruib beside a busy street when he was just a wee lad. Left to his own devices, he had a life expectancy of 45 minutes. But instead of letting nmature take its course, Mom, being Mom, brought him home. You know that great Amor Towles book A Gentleman in Moscow*? Well, our ridiculouis cat is named for the principal character. Who names a lowly feline for a member of the Russian aristocracy? Ada Brooks, that's who. Mom and Dad let her name the kitten. Ada's a total bookworm and named him for her favorite character in one of her favorite books. Mom and Dad call him the CVount or just plain Count. The little people call him Rosty.*

You remember when I said cats were aloof? Well, if only the Count were aloof. Unfortunmately he's anything but. The terrorist, who is now grown, hides behind furniture and in the bushes. Then, when I walk by, minding my own business, he pounces on me. I should be used to it by nowe, but it nearly gives me a heart attack every time. Speaking of heart attacks, here's another one the Count nearly gave me. He is, it's fair to say, an assassin as well as a terrorist. He catches and kill;s wild animals and brings them in through the pet door. Gross. You know what it's like to awaken from a deep slumber to a huge dead rat at eye level not two feet away? You probably don't, so let me tell you. I had heart palpitations and nightm,ares for a week.

I've saved the worst news for last. We lost Mollie last year. She had terminal cancer and had to be put to sleep. I takle back what I said about the vet. To spare that sweet little dog a final trauma at the end of her life, he made a houise call. She died in Mom's arms with Mom's tears dripping on her head. Dad buried her in the azalea bed in the front yard.

You may recall when Dad and I talked about that Jonmi Mitchell song "Yellow Taxi." Well, I didn't really know what a treasure I had in Mollie until she was gone. When Mom and Dad adop[ted me, Mollie welcomed me with open paws. Most dogs would not have been so gracious, especially to a handsome alpha dohg like me. For many years, she was my soulmate and constant companion. She was always cheerful and kind and deferred to me in all things. Moll;ie was never going to be college material, it's true, but what she may have lacked in IQ, she more than made up for in EQ. She made us all feel better all the time. She enricvhed my life. I'm sure Mom and Dad would say she enriched theirs too.

So my last words to you will be these. Dad told me he was planning to dediocate the book to all the dogs of his life. Well, the book is about conversations with me—my name's even in the title—and the way I look at it, I shoul;d be the one to get to dedicate it, and Dad agreed. And so I dedicate it to Mollie, my kind sister, the sweetest dog there ever was. I miss her ecvery day.

Acknowledgements

Buster and I owe a debt of gratitude to our friend Michael de Leeuw of Glen Ridge, New Jersey. Michael has read the manuscripts of all three of my books and offered excellent suggestions each time.

We also thank Robert Fugate for his wonderful illustrations. He emailed them to me one at a time as he completed them. Opening the emails was like opening presents on Christmas morning.

Buster and I want to express our appreciation for the staff and volunteers who work at animal shelters, including BARK (Belzoni Animal Rescue Kennel), from which Carrie and I adopted Buster, and CARA (Community Animal Rescue and Adoption) from which we adopted Mollie. A portion of the proceeds from the sale of each copy of *Bedtime with Buster* will be donated to BARK and CARA.

Finally, I want to thank Buster and all the dogs of my life who came before him. They have enriched my life beyond measure. There is very little in all the world better than a good dog. I am grateful that Carrie loves dogs as much as I do.

About the Author

Brooks Eason, his wife Carrie, and Buster live in Madison, Mississippi, with a toothless old dog named Maddie and a wild young cat named Count Rostov. Eason is also the author of *Travels with Bobby*, about hiking trips with his best friend, and *Fortunate Son*, a memoir about his adoption and discovery of his birth mother's identity. In 2020 the memoir was nominated for best nonfiction book by a Mississippi author. Eason believes that he's normal but, as Buster has told him, self-diagnosis is fraught with peril.

Visit Eason on Facebook and at:

www.brookseason.com

About the Illustrator

Robert Fugate is a finance executive and has worked in the communications business for most of his career. A self-taught artist, he specializes in watercolor landscapes. These are his first book illustrations.

He and his wife Lucy live in Atlanta, Georgia, with Flora, a cairn terrier, and Felix, a rescue Lab.

Visit his art website at:

www.robert-fugate.pixels.com

Also Available From
WordCrafts Press

Fortunate Son: The Story of Baby Boy Francis
by Brooks Eason

In the Company of Dogs
by Jeannette Barnes, DVM

What the Dog Said
by Joanne Brokaw

White Squirrels and other Monsters
by Gerry Harlan Brown

www.wordcrafts.net